I0091737

Volume 12

EIGHTY THOUSAND ADOLESCENTS

EIGHTY THOUSAND ADOLESCENTS

A Study of Young People in the City of
Birmingham by the Staff and Students of
Westhill Training College

BRYAN H. REED

R Routledge
Taylor & Francis Group

LONDON AND NEW YORK

First published in 1950 by George Allen & Unwin Ltd

This edition first published in 2023
by Routledge
4 Park Square, Milton Park, Abingdon, Oxon OX14 4RN

and by Routledge
605 Third Avenue, New York, NY 10158

Routledge is an imprint of the Taylor & Francis Group, an informa business

© 1950

ISBN: 978-1-032-37655-4 (Set)
ISBN: 978-1-032-39813-6 (Volume 12) (hbk)
ISBN: 978-1-032-39820-4 (Volume 12) (pbk)
ISBN: 978-1-003-35152-8 (Volume 12) (ebk)

DOI: 10.4324/9781003351528

Publisher's Note
The publisher has gone to great lengths to ensure the quality of this reprint but points out that some imperfections in the original copies may be apparent.

Disclaimer
The publisher has made every effort to trace copyright holders and would welcome correspondence from those they have been unable to trace.

EIGHTY THOUSAND ADOLESCENTS

WHERE BIRMINGHAM'S ADOLESCENTS LIVE

Birmingham is divided into three main areas. (Top) The Central Wards, with houses—many built back-to-back—a century or more old, long overdue for demolition; (centre) the Middle Ring, with depressing miles of streets of 'tunnel-backs', mostly built about 50 years ago; and (bottom) the Outer Suburbs, where are situated the great municipal estates built between 1919 and 1939. (see Chapter II).

EIGHTY THOUSAND ADOLESCENTS

A STUDY OF YOUNG PEOPLE IN
THE CITY OF BIRMINGHAM
BY THE STAFF AND STUDENTS
OF WESTHILL TRAINING COLLEGE
for the
Edward Cadbury Charitable Trust

DIRECTED AND DESCRIBED BY
BRYAN H. REED, B.D.
Youth Tutor

LONDON
GEORGE ALLEN & UNWIN LTD

First Published 1950

PRINTED BY
BALDING AND MANSELL
PARK WORKS
WISBECH
CAMBS

ACKNOWLEDGEMENTS

WHEN THE TRUSTEES of the Edward Cadbury Charitable Trust suggested to Westhill Training College that it should make this survey of Birmingham Youth, the work was gladly undertaken by the Principal, the Rev. H. A. Hamilton, B.A., and by the Staff and Students of the College. To them the Trustees express their thanks, and are particularly grateful to the Rev. Bryan H. Reed, B.D., the Youth Tutor, who directed the Survey and who has described it in this book. He in his turn would especially thank Miss Doris Hite, Assistant Youth Tutor, and Miss Winifred Hudson, his secretary.

No work of this kind, however, could have been carried through without the co-operation of a large number of organizations and private individuals. The Trustees and the author are grateful, therefore, to all those upon whose time they made so many and such prolonged demands. In this connexion they are deeply indebted to the Chief Education Officer of Birmingham (Mr. E. L. Russell, M.A.) and to members of his staff, particularly to Miss M. Stuart Miller, M.B.E. (Youth Employment and Welfare Department), to Probation Officers, to local officials of various youth organizations, to Heads of Schools and Evening Institutes, to industrialists and members of factory and office management staffs, and, last, but not least, to many busy Youth Leaders who answered with courtesy a great many inquisitive questions, the point of which could not always have been immediately apparent.

Again, thanks are due to Messrs. Cadbury Brothers Ltd. for placing at the disposal of the Trustees the resources of their Publications Department and Advertising Studio. Mr. W. E. Cossons, of the former, and Mr. F. T. Lockwood, of the latter, have taken a personal interest in the production of the book. Mr. Cossons carried out the editorial work, read the proofs, and saw the book through the press. Mr. Lockwood supervised the preparation of the diagrams and other illustrations and designed the general lay-out.

ILLUSTRATIONS

Permission to use photographs was readily given by the organizations illustrated and by newspaper editors and others; many of them lent prints or actual blocks. Below is a list of bodies and individuals to whom the Trustees are thus indebted. Where known to the author the name of the photographer is also given; every endeavour has been made to trace the appropriate information, but for any unavoidable omissions apologies are made in advance.

The Birmingham Education Authority lent both the blocks used on page 22, and provided the County Colleges map (page 144); Mr. G. E. F. Ross, General Manager, Parks Department, gave invaluable assistance in supplying and checking the information used in the diagram on page 106, showing the city's public facilities for open-air recreation; Mr. H. J. Manzoni, C.B.E., City Engineer and Surveyor, gave permission for the use of the Duddeston and Nechells Re-development Plan (page 16); the Chief Constable (Mr. E. J. Dodd) allowed the use of the information on which the diagram relating to Juvenile Delinquency (page 132) is based.

The photographs of Birmingham houses used as a frontispiece and on pages 13, 14 (upper) and 16 were taken by Mr. P. B. Redmayne, M.A., and the lower picture on page 14 by Mr. J. H. L. Adams, A.R.P.S., and are reproduced from *When We Build Again* (Allen & Unwin) by permission of the Bournville Village Trust. The diagram (Density of Population) on page 17 is based on a similar one appearing in the same book.

The pictures on page 27 were provided by the Hall Green Youth Fellowship (the Rev. P. L. D. Chatterton); on pages 48, 169, and 182 (lower) by Weoley Castle Boys' and Girls' Club (photographs by Mr. A. Sewell); on pages 60, 110 (lower), and 160 (lower) by Bournville Youths' Club; the lower photograph on page 9 is by Morland Braithwaite Ltd., and was lent by the Birmingham 'Youth for Christ' Movement; the upper picture on page 74 was lent by Wing Commander W. B. Henson, of the Warwickshire and Birmingham Wing of the Air Training Corps, and the lower one is by the *Birmingham Gazette*; the Birmingham Girl Guides' Association lent both blocks on page 80; and the Birmingham County Boy Scouts' Association the photographs on page 84, the upper one being by the *Birmingham Post and Mail*, and the lower by Mr. F. C. Barrington; the upper photograph on page 92 was lent by the Birmingham Battalion of the Boys' Brigade and is by Morland Braithwaite Ltd., while the lower picture is by Photo Press Ltd., London, and was supplied by the Birmingham Division of the Girls' Life Brigade; that of the Sword Dance on page 110 is by Citizen Photos. (London) and was lent by the Birmingham Y.W.C.A.; those on page 120 were lent by the Birmingham Youth and Sunday School Union, the Birmingham Association of Girls' and Mixed Clubs, and the Selly Oak Colleges respectively; that on page 150 is by Adcraft Ltd., and was lent by the Birmingham Region of the Youth Hostels Association; the upper picture on page 155 was lent by the Birmingham County Centre of the St. John Ambulance Brigade, and the lower (by Mr. J. R. Such) was lent by the Birmingham County Branch of the British Red Cross Society; the upper left picture on page 160 was lent by Mr. H. H. Webb, of the Stonehouse Gang, and the upper right is by the *Birmingham Post and Mail*, and lent by the Bishop Lightfoot Youth Club, Yardley. The *Birmingham Post and Mail* kindly gave permission also for the use of the pictures on pages 138 and 188.

Those on pages 9 (upper), 133, and 182 (upper) are from *Picture Post* Library.

CONTENTS

VARIED OPINIONS

Men and women who have not previously acted as youth leaders will, it is hoped, feel a call to assist in this most important work.

THE LORD MAYOR OF BIRMINGHAM, appealing in the Press for voluntary youth leaders, November, 1947.

Youth and Community Centres have become meeting places for potential criminals.

MR. LINTON T. THORP, K.C., Recorder of Saffron Walden, speaking on 25th February, 1949.

The suggestion that the Birmingham Education Department should teach boys how best to use their leisure time was made by the Chairman (Mr. David Thirsk) at the Birmingham Juvenile Court today when he spoke of his experience in dealing with numbers of boys who aimlessly drift around completely at a loose end for something to do after they come out of school.

A Birmingham paper, January, 1948.

Are youth clubs rapidly becoming a home-destroying nuisance? If young people are encouraged to spend their evenings out of their homes, what will their own homes be like later on?

Question in correspondence column of a religious weekly, February, 1949.

The young are blamed for not putting their leisure to good use, and sometimes falling into bad ways as a consequence—preferring to watch other people playing games rather than play themselves; reading no books; letting their school education fall into disrepair; the great majority joining no clubs or movements; finding their amusements in 'Fun Fairs', football pools, murder stories and gangster films. But consider, before you pass a general condemnation, what little chance many of them have for anything better. Games: Is there a playing-field within reach? Reading: Where can they read with four or five people in a home of two or three rooms? Interesting hobbies: Where to practise them? Clubs: Are there club leaders enough to provide them for more than a fraction of all the millions needing them? Murder stories and gangster films: What better ones are offered?
VISCOUNT SAMUEL, addressing the National Book League, November, 1948.

I would like to see all open boys' clubs and girls' clubs 'nationalized' or brought under a centralized control. I think this would be an improvement on Youth Service which at present is somewhat disjointed, and which, in my opinion, does not produce results commensurate with the very large amount of money spent on it.

FIELD MARSHAL LORD MONTGOMERY, April, 1948.

When I came to this school I found a Youth Club which was little more than an organized petting party. I closed it down and established pre-Service units.
A Birmingham Headmaster, 1948.

I am one of those who believe that the sight of a boy of fourteen in battle-dress puts all Heaven in a rage.

Writer in a religious weekly, April, 1948.

The tendency today is to sap the virility of the nation by encouraging a boy to join a mixed club.

MR. BASIL L. Q. HENRIQUES, in 'The Times', 31st March, 1947.

There are socially ill-adjusted adults today who would have been different if they had not taken refuge from the effort of adjustment in purely separate constituencies.

REV. DOUGLAS A. GRIFFITHS (Secretary, Methodist Association of Youth Clubs), in 'The Times',
21st April, 1947.

CHAPTER I

OPERATION YOUTH

THESE VERY VARIED OPINIONS serve to illustrate the confusion of thought which exists in this country at the present time concerning the place and the purpose of the Youth Service. While a number of voluntary organizations have been at work for many years, the Youth Service as we know it today is on the whole a recent growth. It has been remarked that the Youth Service, which is concerned with the welfare of adolescents, is passing through its own adolescence. Indeed, if one considers the broad sweep of English history as a whole, one is rather surprised to discover how comparatively recent is any provision for the welfare of the nation's youth.

Before the second World War there was comparatively little statutory provision for the leisure-time needs of young people. In 1937 the estimated population in the 14-18 age-group in England and Wales was 2,945,000,* of whom 386,000 were receiving full-time education. Six children out of seven left school at fourteen. Young people enrolling for part-time courses in Evening Institutes, Technical Colleges or Day Continuation Schools numbered rather less than half a million. In a few areas Juvenile Organizations Committees existed to co-ordinate the work of voluntary youth organizations and the statutory authorities which concerned young people, but, with a few striking exceptions, they accomplished very little. In only six cases were salaried officials employed by these committees. They are chiefly important as marking the first expenditure of public money on youth work undertaken by voluntary organizations. In 1937 a National Fitness Council was set up, only to be dissolved on the outbreak of war in 1939. Dr. Macalister Brew has said of the work of this Council that 'never was so much spent by so few with so little result'.†

To what extent were the leisure-time needs of young people being met by the voluntary organizations? There were, in England and Wales, in 1937, over two and a half million young people between the ages of 14 and 18 who were no longer receiving full-time education. It has often been asserted that at that time only forty per cent of the nation's youth was attached to any youth organization. It is more probable, however, that if we confined our inquiries to England and Wales and to the age-group 14-18 we should find that the total membership of all the voluntary organizations together was not more than half a million. This represents only approximately one-sixth of the total population in the age-group concerned; and, even if we assume (with no justification) that youth organizations catered only for young people not receiving full-time education, it cannot be claimed that they were in touch with more than twenty per cent of such young people. This must not be taken as a condemnation of the voluntary organizations. As the Youth Advisory Council said in 1943: 'For long they worked with little encouragement and with still less financial help. The remarkable thing is not that they have not done more, but that they have done so much'. A church which opened a Youth Club in, say, 1936, was liable to be assessed for increased rates, on the grounds that the premises were no longer being used only for religious purposes!

THE WAR AND AFTER

It is an interesting fact that years of war should so often be years of social progress. Certainly, during the second World War, the education, the health, the home-life, the working conditions

---

* The estimated population in the same age-group in June, 1948, was only 2,243,000.

† *In the Service of Youth*, page 22.

and the leisure of young people became the subject both of inquiry and of action. 'The social and physical development of boys and girls between the ages of 14 and 20, who have ceased full-time education, has for long been neglected in this country.' This was the opening sentence of the now famous Circular 1486: *The Service of Youth*, issued by the Board of Education to Local Education Authorities on the 27th November, 1939—a circular which takes its place as an important document in British social history. Youth Committees were set up in all areas, and it was to be their responsibility to see that there was adequate local provision for the leisure-time needs of young people. There was to be the fullest partnership between the L.E.A. and the Voluntary Organization, while expenditure on salaries of club leaders, on the rent or upkeep of premises, and on the provision of equipment would rank for grant on a fifty per cent basis.

Local Youth Committees soon came into existence, and although rumour has it that the average age of their members was occasionally something in the seventies, a good many organizations which might have become war casualties were kept alive.

In December, 1941, boys and girls of sixteen and seventeen were called upon to register for National Service, and it is significant that the responsibility for this registration rested with the Board of Education and not with the Ministry of Labour. Young people who registered were invited to interviews at which those found to be 'unattached'* were urged to join a youth organization of their own choice. Early interviews showed that in spite of the efforts of the previous two years, nearly half the boys and about three-quarters of the girls were still outside the Youth Service.

Mention should be made of the fact that during the war, existing pre-service organizations were expanded and new organizations were brought into being. Both girls and boys were glad to feel that the country needed them and that they too, like their older brothers and sisters, could appear in uniform. One saw the astonishing sight of the grocer's errand boy, ambitious to win a place in the R.A.F. air crew, spending night after night studying mathematics. At their highest peak of popularity, the three boys' organizations between them numbered something approaching half a million lads.

The National Association of Training Corps for Girls, which came into being in 1943 to co-ordinate the work of several girls' pre-service organizations, is unlike the boys' organizations in that it remains a purely voluntary body while they are sponsored and grant-aided by the various Service Ministries. The girls are required, for instance, to provide their own uniform and even (when this was necessary) to find the clothing coupons. During the first twelve months of their existence the organizations which now constitute the N.A.T.C.G. were joined by some 140,000 girls. All the voluntary organizations felt the benefit of the new interest in Youth Service, and under the ægis of the churches and the Local Education Authorities many new youth clubs, mainly mixed, came into existence. It became apparent that there was a great need of trained youth-leaders, and in July, 1942, the Ministry issued its Circular 1598: *Emergency Courses of Training for those Engaged in the Youth Service*, as a result of which a few Universities established a twelve months' course of training for youth leaders. Some 330 students have taken one or other of these University courses. Side by side with these Government-sponsored training courses the voluntary bodies continued to promote their own various training schemes.

The 1944 Education Act altered the whole pattern of education in this country. In spite of a great shortage of juvenile labour the school-leaving age was raised to fifteen years in April, 1948, and will eventually be raised to sixteen. The aim of the Ministry may be defined as 'opportunity according to ability for every boy and girl in the country'. In some areas at the moment 'Secondary Education' may mean little more than an extra year at school, but, with the provision of more buildings and more teachers during the next few years, every child will receive a Secondary Education designed to suit his particular abilities. Every L.E.A. will be required to provide County Colleges for all young persons from school-leaving age to 18 years, unless they are already receiving full-time education. Young people will be required to attend County

---

* By the 'Unattached' is meant those young people not engaged in full or in part-time education, and not in membership of any youth organization.

Colleges one whole day or two half-days per week, or one period of eight weeks or two periods of four weeks in a residential college. Milk and meals will be available, and medical inspection and treatment will be provided. The Act also makes it the responsibility of every L.E.A. to see that in its area there are adequate facilities for recreation and social and physical training, and for that purpose may establish or assist the establishment of camps, holiday classes, playing fields and play centres. It is explicitly laid down that, in making arrangements for the provision of these facilities, the Authority shall 'have regard to the expediency of co-operating with any voluntary societies or bodies whose objects include the provision of facilities or the organization of activities of a similar nature'.* The Ministry of Education itself implements this policy of partnership by making direct grants to the Headquarters of National Voluntary Organizations in aid of their expenditure upon administration and organization. The total amount of these direct grants paid in the year 1947-1948 was £164,552, this sum being distributed among nineteen organizations. In addition to this, in 1947-1948 the Ministry paid £110,560 to individual units as direct grants towards capital expenditure

There is at the present time little uniformity of pattern in the organization and administration of the Youth Service throughout the country. The Ministry of Education has repeatedly stressed the desirability of partnership between the Local Education Committee and the voluntary organizations, but this policy is being very variously implemented.

If there is a good deal of present confusion there is still more uncertainty as we contemplate the future. Is the Service of Youth a temporary therapeutic expedient designed to fill the gaps left in an inadequate national system of full-time education—a service which will no longer be necessary with the raising of the school-leaving age and the establishment of the County College? Is it, on the other hand, to be looked upon as a permanent part of our total education system? Do we need both Youth Organization and County College, club leader and teacher? Has the voluntary youth organization served its day, and, if so, what should take its place in the future? Is it possible to define the particular contribution which in an ideal society would be given to young people by home and school, by Industry and County College, by Voluntary Youth Organization and Youth Employment Service? During the last few years great efforts have been made to attract young people to various organizations, and large sums of public money are being spent both by the Ministry of Education and by Local Education Authorities on the Youth Service. The total annual expenditure of the Ministry and of Local Authorities on the Youth Service is approximately £1,710,000. In addition, the King George's Jubilee Trust distributes about £80,000 a year among youth organizations.† Is this money well spent, or is the Service of Youth an elaborate and costly piece of machinery for the provision of darts and dancing? Is there still a gap in our provision for the needs of young people, so that many of them when they leave school are thrown into the deep end, as it were, to sink or swim for themselves? Are we, on the other hand, in danger of 'doing too much for young people', thus sapping their vigour and independence? Must youth clubs share part of the responsibility for the alleged disintegration of home-life? Are secondary schoolchildren dancing or playing table-tennis at the youth club when they should be doing their homework? What are the aims of the various youth movements, and are these aims in fact being achieved? How many young people belong to youth organizations? How often do they attend? What do they do? Are youth clubs making a positive contribution to the development of their members? Are there too many organizations, or too few? Are they too large, or too small? Is it possible to compare the methods of one type of organization with those of another? Do we need still more youth organizations in order to meet the needs of those young people who are still outside the influence of any educational provision? Are there, on the other hand, too many agencies already at work—sometimes almost quarrelling with one another for the bodies of young people—young people whose needs may tend to be forgotten by organizations which are chiefly concerned that they themselves should retain a place in the sun?

* *Education Act*, 1944, Section 53 (2).
† King George's Jubilee Trust was founded in March, 1935, and has made grants to the National Youth Organizations of approximately £750,000 to date.

3

YOUTH SURVEY QUESTIONNAIRE

★

GENERAL

1. Name and address of Club or Unit.

2. Date of Foundation.

3. Names of any central organizations to which affiliated.

4. Name of any local organization or church to which attached.

5. Name and address of Leader and Secretary.

PREMISES

6. Brief description of premises used. How many rooms?

    Are they owned and used exclusively by your Club or Unit?

    Are they rented? If so, how much rent is paid?

    Do you share the premises with other organizations?

    Are you often inconvenienced because your premises are wanted for other purposes?

LEADERSHIP

7. Have you any professional leaders? (a) Full-time (b) Part-time?

    How many voluntary helpers? L.E.A. Instructors?

    Have you any method by which voluntary helpers are recruited from among your own senior members?

FINANCE

8. Do you receive financial assistance from the Local Education Authority?
    (a) For payment of leaders; (b) For maintenance of premises; (c) For equipment; (d) For any other special objects?

9. Is your Club financed by
    (a) Members' subscriptions? If so, how much weekly do members pay? (b) Regular outside subscriptions, large or small; (c) Grants; (d) Income from investments; (e) Special efforts; (f) Other sources.

10. Note any way in which your work is seriously handicapped by financial consideration.

MEMBERSHIP

11. How many members have you in each age-group for which you cater?
    (a) Boys; (b) Girls.

12. Have you any conditions of membership? If so, which of the following apply:
    (a) Membership of a religious body; (b) Residence in a particular area; (c) Employment of a particular kind; (d) Compulsory attendance at certain activities (please specify what); (e) Age limit; (f) any other conditions of membership.

13. How many of your members
    (a) Are still at school? (b) Are engaged in clerical occupations? (c) Are engaged in manual occupations?

14. How many of your members
    (a) Also belong to other youth organizations? (b) Attend evening classes or evening institutes?

15. Do you in general succeed in retaining your members until the age of 18, or do you tend to lose them before that age, and, if so, when?

16. Have you as many members as you can cater for efficiently, or would you welcome any considerable increase in membership?

17. Do you consider that the area from which your members are drawn
    (a) Is under-provided with youth organizations? (b) Or adequately served? (c) Or over-provided?

AIMS

18. What are the aims of your organization?

19. Are new members made acquainted with these aims?

20. Have they to accept them in any formal way?

21. Do would-be members spend some time on trial or on probation before being recognized as full members?

22. Have you any form of initiation ceremony for new members, or for their reception into membership?

23. Describe any form of graded membership you may have, e.g. associate and full.

ORGANIZATION

24. Is there a Committee of Management?

25. If so, are your members represented upon it?

26. Have you a Parents' Association?

27. Have you a Members' Committee? If so, has the Members' Committee any real responsibility for (a) Arranging the programme? (b) The control of finance? (c) The administration of discipline?

ACTIVITIES

28. What activities normally form a regular part of your programme:

    1. Physical and Recreational
    (a) Indoor Games, Gym or P.T., Boxing, Socials, Dances? (b) Outdoor Sports and Athletics? (c) Camping, Swimming, Cycling, Youth Hostelling, Foreign Travel? (d) Have you a Canteen?

    2. Cultural
    Music, Drama, Discussion Group, Library, Handcraft, First Aid, Art, Concert Party, etc.?

    3. Devotional
    Religious Services, Epilogues, Bible Classes, etc.

29. To what Sports Leagues do you belong?

30. Do you experience difficulty in securing the use of Sports Grounds or Playing Fields?

31. If a single-sex organization, how often do you promote mixed evenings?

32. Do you, from time to time, make any effective provision for
    (a) Sex education; (b) Film appreciation; (c) Education in Citizenship; (d) The appreciation of the countryside?

33. Is your organization usually open on Sundays, and, if so, for what kind of programme?

34. Is it one of your aims to encourage your members to render service
    (a) To the community; (b) To a Church; (c) Within your own organization; (d) In any other way?
    If so, can you mention any outstanding form of service so rendered by any of your members.

YOUR ORGANIZATION AND THE COMMUNITY

35. Is your organization directly associated with any adult body? (If so, please specify what).

36. When your members become too old for membership of your organization, have you any method of introducing them to the life of any adult organization?

37. Have you found any way of keeping in touch with members (a) Who leave the district; (b) Who join the Armed Forces; (c) Who leave you on attaining the upper age-limit?

38. Are any of your former members now playing any part in public life?

ONE WEEK'S PICTURE

DETAILED INVESTIGATION OF ONE WEEK'S ACTIVITIES

From Sunday.........until Saturday.................

39. Number of members present on each evening in week : Boys under 14; Boys 14 and over; Girls under 14; Girls 14 and over.

Number of Boys and Girls in the age-group 14-20 actively participating in particular activities of any kind
(See Question 28).

Please list each activity with number taking part on each evening:

(a) Boys; (b) Girls.
40. How many of your members, during this week attended:

Once; Twice; Three times; Four times; Five times; Six times; Seven times.?

Signature of Investigator...

There is surprisingly little information available on some of these questions, and for this reason the Edward Cadbury Charitable Trust invited Westhill Training College, Selly Oak (a college sponsored by the Free Churches of England and Wales for the training of leaders in Christian education) to undertake a Survey of the Youth Service in the City of Birmingham. The invitation was accepted, and now, after an investigation over a period of three years, this Report is offered in the hope that it may make some contribution to future thought and discussion.

METHOD OF INQUIRY

The Survey, which has been limited to the area within the Birmingham City Boundary, and which has been concerned in the main, but not exclusively, with young people in the 14-20 age-range, has been conducted as follows:

(a) In the first place statistical information was sought about the number of young people living in the city, and the extent to which they were engaged in whole or part-time education, or were members of any youth organization. A study was made of the number, size and location of these organizations and of the pattern of the Local Youth Service. A summary of the facts discovered will be found in Chapters IV and V.

(b) A study of the general social and industrial background of life in Birmingham, with particular attention to housing and to the distribution of young people in various types of employment, has furnished the material for Chapter II.

(c) Having discovered that there appear to be no less than 1,384 separate units catering for young people in the 14-20 age range, actual visits were planned to a quarter of this total number. In this visitation, which took place in the months of October and November, we were assisted by a few University Social Study students and by students from some of the other Selly Oak Colleges. Arrangements were made with the leaders concerned for visits to be paid to 350 units. These included organizations of every type and in all parts of the city (Figure 1). Visitors took with them a rather formidable eight-page questionnaire (reproduced on pages 4 and 5). Students had very varied experiences, being present at a wide diversity of activities ranging from a cabaret show to a prayer meeting. One student was given a trip in a 'plane. In a few cases difficulties were encountered through a variety of reasons, including a local transport strike. Several return visits were made to some units, and completed questionnaires were ultimately obtained in respect of 321 units. These were made up as follows:

TABLE I

ORGANIZATIONS VISITED

Uniformed Voluntary	143
Clubs	103
Political	7
Boys' Pre-Service	11
Co-operative Movement	22
Y.M.C.A., Y.W.C.A., Community Centres, Neighbourhood Centres, Citizens' Clubs	15
Others	20
TOTAL	321

We obtained in this way a complete account of a week's activities in nearly one in four of all the City's Youth units. At a later stage we circularized the leaders of these 321 units in an endeavour to obtain further information about the number of secondary school-children in membership, about the distribution of membership in different age groups, and about the length of time during which young people remain in membership. The information discovered in this way will be found, in the main, in Chapters V and VI.

(*d*) In an endeavour to assess the quality of the work done by a particular unit (a task, we realize, of the greatest difficulty: by what yard-stick does one measure the intangibles and the imponderables?) a few senior students were attached to a particular organization, in the life and activity of which they shared for a period of several months. At the end of that time, they were asked to attempt a qualitative estimate of the value of the work done by the particular unit to which they had been attached. The essays written by these students are not, of course, reproduced in this Report, but they have helped us in our own thinking. The results of this investigation are described in Chapter VII.

(*e*) In order to discover information about the leisure-time habits of young people, whether they are attached to youth organizations or not, we obtained answers to *Twenty Questions* from a

FIGURE 1
UNITS
VISITED

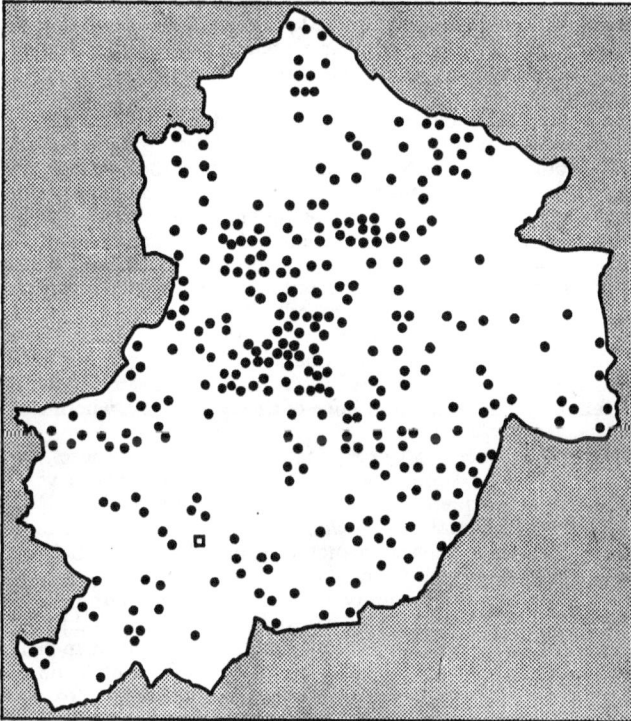

Each dot represents one of the 321 units visited, and the map shows the distribution of youth organizations throughout the city. A detailed analysis of the types of organizations is shown in the diagrams on pages 82 and 83.

representative sample of 1,000 adolescents. A complete report of the findings of this particular investigation would need a volume in itself, but a description of the inquiry and a summary of the results obtained is offered in Chapter III, in which also specimens of completed questionnaires are reproduced.

(*f*) In the autumn of 1948, twelve senior students addressed themselves to a special study on a subject related to the Survey as a whole. This piece of research included investigation into such facts as the housing of the Youth Service, its geographical distribution, the contribution of industry, of political organizations and of Community Centres to the Youth Service, the provision of playing-fields, the training of leaders and the approach to the 'unattached'.

(*g*) An attempt was made to compile a number of case histories of individual members in different types of youth organizations. The attempt was not as successful as we hoped, partly no doubt because any such history, to be of value, must be based upon a knowledge of the individual boy or girl over a longer period of time than circumstances allowed us.

(*h*) In order to compare the pattern of the Youth Service in Birmingham with that elsewhere, a number of visits were paid to other cities where conversations were held with representatives both of the Local Education Authority and of voluntary organizations. Visits were also paid to the Peckham Health Centre, and to the Day Continuation School at the Rugby College of Technology and Art. Members of the staff throughout the period have visited a great many youth organizations in the city. We have had many conversations with L.E.A. officials, youth organizers, club leaders, parents, teachers, probation officers, welfare officers, ministers and clergy, and, most important of all, with young people themselves. In order to check the accuracy of information obtained from other sources we have talked to young people, not only in youth organizations, but in dance halls, fun fairs, public houses, street corners, and in all the places where young people come together. Here, by way of illustration, is an actual extract from the diary of one member of staff for the last week-end of January, 1949:

> *Saturday:* Attended 'Birmingham Youth for Christ' Rally in the Town Hall. Building crowded to its utmost capacity, but should judge that only a quarter of those present were under the age of twenty. Later in the evening looked in each bar of about a dozen public houses, in none of which did we see any young people whom we judged to be under the age of twenty. This, on a Saturday night, is surely remarkable.
>
> *Sunday:* Spent a few minutes in a crowded amusement arcade full of young girls and coloured men. Why do coloured men congregate here? Has no one set out to cater for their leisure needs? Children here, too. Should it be possible for children to enter these places? Visited —— public house. This appears to provide an exception to the general rule that young people do not frequent licensed premises. Nearly all the people here are young; some of them, surely, under eighteen. Most of them are drinking shandy. Attended meeting of —— Young Communist League. Eight young people sitting round a gas-fire underneath an enormous photograph of Stalin. Four of them looked very bored and said nothing. One wondered how they came to be there and whether they would ever come again. The others were tremendously in earnest, and were making arrangements for an open-air meeting in the Bull Ring, the sale of literature, the organization of a petition on housing for submission to the City Council, and propaganda about British Imperialism in Malaya among the next batch of 'call-ups'. Back to the same public house, just before closing time. Still full of young people, but none of those, we think, whom we saw earlier in the evening.
>
> *Monday:* Visited —— Youth Service Corps meeting on school premises, where at a weekly discussion group, well led by an L.E.A. instructor, nine girls and five boys spent an excellent hour and a half discussing the question: 'Should there be class distinctions?' After agreement had been reached on a negative answer they admitted to us, not without amusement, that they had no desire for any closer association with another youth club which met in the same building the same night, 'because they are a different class'.
>
> *Tuesday:* 'Youth Night' at —— Community Centre. About two hundred young people here enjoying a weekly 'sixpenny hop' with billiards and snooker as an additional attraction. No weekly subscription: one pays sixpence when one comes. There appear to be no other activities. 'We aim to be keeping them out of the pubs, but they don't want to do anything else. We offered them a room in which to listen to the 'To Start you Talking' Broadcasts, but only two turned up.' One wonders whether, on balance, this weekly 'Youth Night' is doing good or harm. The young people present have certainly no awareness of belonging to a 'Community'.

(*j*) Finally, members both of the staff and of the student body have met together in regular seminar for the discussion of questions arising out of the Survey as a whole. On several occasions leaders of various organizations in the city have joined us in these discussions. On two occasions, also, we invited young people belonging to various organizations to meet with us for the consideration of particular questions. We offer in the later chapters of this Report some of the judgments and conclusions to which we have been led. For the titles of our chapters we are in part indebted to Mr. L. J. Barnes's study of the Youth Service in the City and County of Nottingham and Nottinghamshire, published in 1945 under the title of *Youth Service in an English County.*

THE FUN FAIR: *Games of chance, which are often only just 'within the law', attract crowds of young people and many 'undesirables'.*

'YOUTH FOR CHRIST': *An inter-denominational Rally in Birmingham Town Hall.*

FIGURE 2

BIRMINGHAM

The Municipal Wards, 1949

*This map is inserted as a guide to the position of some
of the youth organizations referred to in later chapters.*

CHAPTER II

MIDLAND CITY

THE YOUNG PEOPLE who are the subject of this study all live in Birmingham—the second city of the country, with a population of about 1,100,000 living in eighty square miles. Immediately to the north-west lie the West Midland towns of Wolverhampton, Walsall, Dudley, West Bromwich, Oldbury and Smethwick—which with the areas surrounding them constitute the vast industrial conurbation commonly known as the Black Country.

It would be quite outside the scope of this Survey for us to attempt to give any detailed account either of the history of the city or of the achievements of her citizens in many departments of the nation's life. It would be foolish, however, to enter upon a study of the youth organizations to which young people belong without first finding out what we can about the homes in which they live, the schools to which they go, the occupations in which they are employed, and the general social amenities of the area in which they spend their leisure.

We propose in this chapter—under the four headings of Work, Home, School, and Leisure—to make a few comments about the background against which young people in our city are growing up; and, in the following chapter, to summarize the results of our inquiries among a sample group of a thousand of Birmingham's young citizens.

WORK

There was a time, in the Middle Ages, when Birmingham was little more than a hamlet, a few buildings clustered round a village green; but as early as the sixteenth century it was noted for its industries. John Leland, when making investigations for Henry VII, passed through Birmingham and recorded that 'there were many smiths in the town that used to make knives and all manner of cutting tools and many lorimers that made bittes, and a great many naylors so that a great part of the town is maintained by smiths who have their sea cole out of Staffordshire.'

The industrial development of Birmingham has been attributed to the fact that Birmingham had no Charter until 1838. During the religious persecution of the seventeenth century many Protestant Dissenters found refuge in Birmingham. The Five Mile Act of 1665 prevented any Minister of the Church who had been ejected from his living to go within five miles of a corporate town unless he was willing to take an oath of non-resistance and to swear that he would not 'at any time endeavour any alteration in Government either in Church or State'. Birmingham was not a corporate town and at least twelve ejected clergy settled in the town with members of their congregations. George Fox, born on the borders of Warwickshire in 1624, did much to further and strengthen the cause of individual religious freedom and helped to make Birmingham a Nonconformist stronghold. Many later Nonconformists were in the forefront of industrial developments in the town. Craftsmen who were debarred from entering an incorporated town unless they were Freemen or members of a Guild found a home in Birmingham where such a qualification was not a term of settlement. This freedom enabled many foreign artisans to make their contribution to the growing industries of the seventeenth- and eighteenth-century town, and at the beginning of the Industrial Revolution, Birmingham was already famed for its button-makers, platers, buckle-makers, brassfounders, gun- and pistol-makers, jewellers and engravers, to mention only a few of the local crafts.

The development of canals in the eighteenth century connected the town with the Mersey, the Humber and the Bristol Channel ports, and this provision of cheap transport still further aided the development of its heavy industries.

Birmingham today is a city of 1,500 trades, and while on the one hand there are large enterprises employing 19,000 people there are on the other hand a large number of one-man workshops, particularly in the Jewellery Quarter of the city, where what was once a quiet residential area is now a network of craftsmen's shops.

The house-factory is still a characteristic industrial unit, and the general industrial background is that of a large number of comparatively small firms. There are 10,650 factories in which less than twenty people are employed. Some of the more obscure trades include the making of artificial eyes, handcuffs, hangman's ropes, sundials, jew's harps, sausage skins, and the stuffing of animals and birds; but the main industry of the city is the manufacture of metal goods. The metal industry employs over 37 per cent of the industrial working population of the city—the comparable figure for the country as a whole being 11 per cent.

The following table shows the distribution of young people under the age of twenty in various types of employment:

TABLE II

DISTRIBUTION OF YOUNG PEOPLE (AGE UNDER 20) AMONG THE MAIN BIRMINGHAM INDUSTRIES*

INDUSTRY	BOYS	GIRLS	TOTAL
Miscellaneous Metal Goods	7,033	12,490	19,523
Distributive Trades	3,731	8,588	12,319
Miscellaneous Trades and Services	2,289	6,761	9,050
Engineering, etc.	4,096	3,115	7,211
Construction and Repair of Vehicles ...	3,261	2,331	5,592
Building and Contracting	3,679	248	3,927
Food, Drink and Tobacco	1,040	2,727	3,767
Clothing	388	2,492	2,880
Other Manufacturing Industries	825	1,879	2,704
Paper, Printing, etc.	673	1,642	2,315
Metal Manufacturers	850	1,205	2,055
Transport and Communication	1,260	657	1,917
Woodworking	1,073	414	1,487
Other Industries ... ..._	1,352	2,630	3,982
TOTAL	31,550	47,179	78,729

* Included in these figures are many young people who work in Birmingham but live outside the city.

HOME

In later chapters we shall be discussing the extent to which young people in Birmingham do or do not spend their leisure at home, but at this point it would be useful to discover what we can about their homes. A house is not necessarily a home, but physical and material factors have a good deal to do with the quality of home life.

During the Industrial Revolution the town's reputation as a centre of trade attracted the poor labourer as well as the skilled craftsman, and houses of the cheapest kind were thrown up round the new factories by speculative builders. During the course of our Survey we discovered

HOUSES CONVERTED INTO FACTORIES *are characteristic of Birmingham's Jewellery Quarter.*

HOUSES AND FACTORIES *inextricably entangled are characteristic of Birmingham's unplanned Central Wards.*

THE 'BACK-TO-BACK'. *Birmingham's Central Wards still possess 29,000 back-to-back houses opening on to streets and courts.*

THE 'TUNNEL-BACK'. *These houses were an improvement on the 'back-to-backs', but were built in dreary rows, 20 or 30 to the acre. They are characteristic of the Middle Ring.*

more than 300 factories and workshops within an area of little more than one mile square with many back-to-back houses crowded among them. Houses on one side face a court while those on the other side face a similar court or a drab street. The entrance to the courtyard of these is often through narrow passageways. (See page 14). A stand pipe in the middle of the court is often the only supply of water for all the houses, and the lavatories in a row at one end of the court are each shared by two or more families. The houses are usually very small, consisting of one room downstairs and two small rooms upstairs. They are dark, damp, and ill-ventilated owing to the proximity of factories and workshops. We visited one such house in which ten people were living. Of the city's total of 283,611 houses, 29,182 are back-to-back*, though not all are as small as those described above. One-seventh of the city's houses are to be found in the small central wards, where people are living at a density of sixty-two people to the acre. Around the Central Wards there is a Middle Ring which contains miles of unimaginatively built 'tunnel-back' houses crowded together at a density of twenty to thirty per acre. In this area are two-sevenths of the city's houses, with little room for gardens or space for children's recreation.

TABLE III

DENSITY OF POPULATION IN BIRMINGHAM

Based on figures given by the Medical Officer of Health and the City Engineer and Surveyor.

Zone	Population (Estimated 1949)	Area in acres	Density in persons per acre
Central Wards	131,700	3,023	43
Middle Ring	279,900	8,944	31
Outer Ring	684,500	39,180	17
Entire City	1,096,100	51,147	21

NOTE:—While this book was in the press the 1949 figures became available; these are given in the above table. The density of population in the Central Wards has been reduced since 1938 from 62 to 43 persons per acre, which is still more than twice that of the entire city. In some areas, however, the density is several times that of the average for the Central Wards as a whole.

In the city's Outer Ring are to be found such diverse types of housing as miles of ribbon development, and vast City Council estates. If some of the first estates were unimaginatively planned, at least there were not more than twelve houses to the acre and each house had a garden both back and front.

Some development schemes are deserving of special mention. George Cadbury was very concerned about the problem of Birmingham slums, and in 1879 moved his factory from the centre of the city to open country then four miles out. It was here that the village of Bournville† gradually took shape, with well-planned open spaces and parks. At a time when houses were being built in long terraces, George Cadbury experimented with variety in design and layout. It was, as he said, a small contribution to the solution of the housing problem in large cities. Houses were not tied to workers in a particular factory. In 1900 the ownership and management of the estate was vested in the Bournville Village Trust, which has added many other housing or planning interests to its purely local activities. Another experiment was the founding of the Copec (Conference on Politics, Economics and Citizenship) House Improvement Society in 1925. Under this Society nineteen reconditioning schemes were prepared and many houses

* M. of H. Report on Housing Survey, 1946.

† Now an estate of nearly 1,200 acres embracing five or more centres of population, and constituting what may be called an area of 'Controlled Suburban Development'.

MUNICIPAL HOUSING. *Between the wars Birmingham built 104,000 houses of all types. During the period 1945-1949, more than 3,600 permanent-type municipal dwellings have been provided.*

REBUILDING BIRMINGHAM. *One of Birmingham's most populous areas has been re-planned on a basis of 'neighbourhood units', with ample provision for local social amenities, and with industrial buildings separated from the residential districts. Compare this with the lower illustration on page 13.*

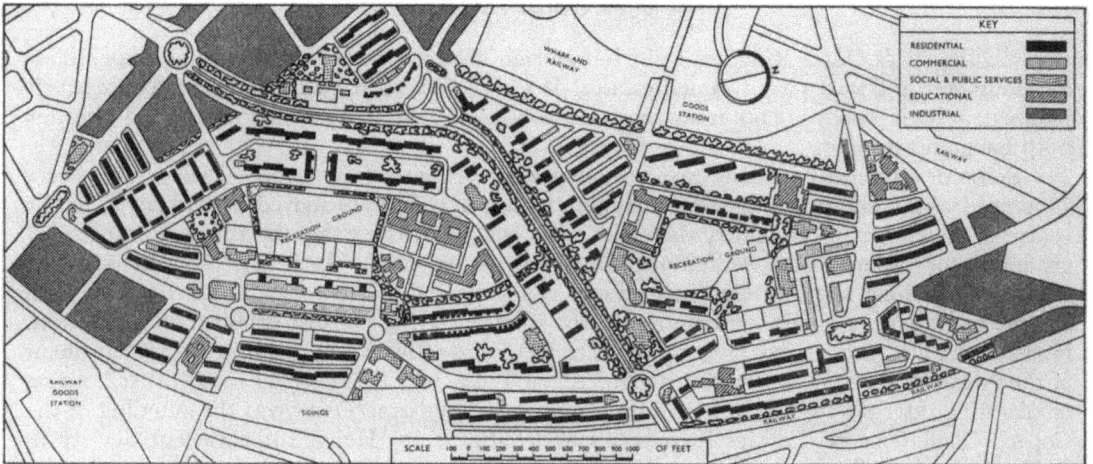

improved and made habitable. Birmingham was also the first city in England to put into operation a Town Planning Scheme under the 1909 Town Planning Act.

FIGURE 3

DENSITY OF POPULATION IN BIRMINGHAM *

BIRMINGHAM
AVERAGE
20
PEOPLE PER ACRE

EACH ☥ REPRESENTS 5 PEOPLE PER ACRE

CENTRAL WARDS

MIDDLE RING

OUTER RING

OUTER RING

CENTRAL WARDS

MIDDLE RING

OUTER RING

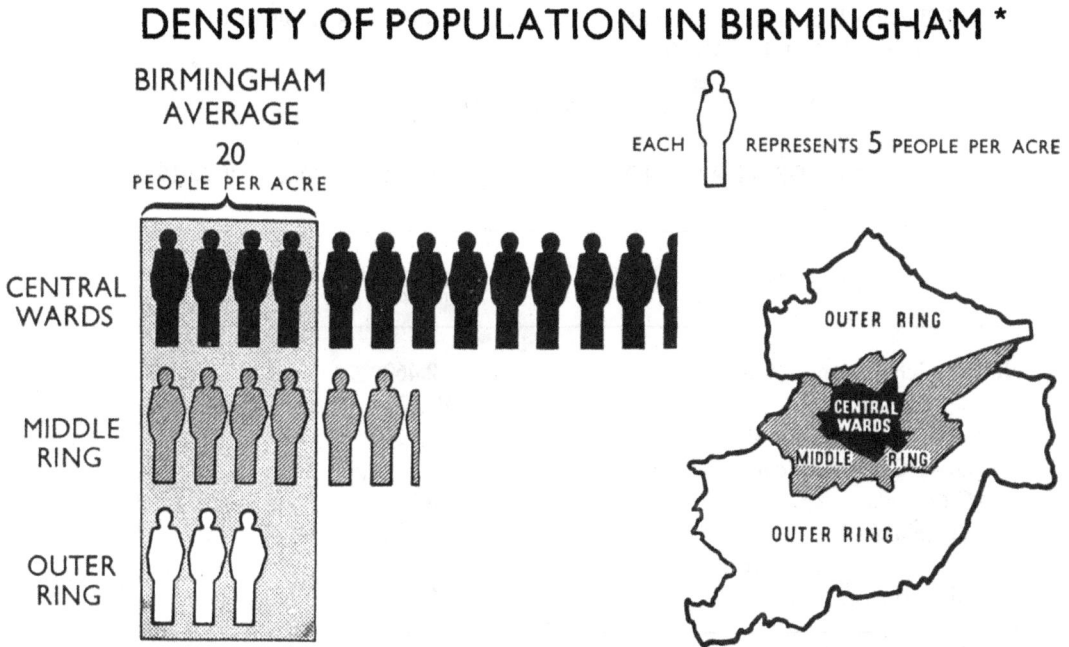

* See note to Table III, page 15.

In spite of the fact, however, that in 1938 a third of the population of the city was living in new houses which had been built since 1918, there are still 6,429 houses within the city boundary without separate water supply, 34,965 without separate water closet accommodation and 142,523 without bathrooms. Many families are not only living in overcrowded conditions but also lack the ordinary amenities of an accepted standard of living. In June, 1949, the number of families on Birmingham's waiting list for Corporation houses stood at 47,553. New registrations, however, come in at the rate of 700 a week, and only the most urgent cases can receive attention, families removed from dangerous buildings and infective tuberculosis cases necessarily taking priority.

These bad housing conditions are not unrelated, of course, to problems of juvenile delinquency. A lad recently brought before the Birmingham Juvenile Court for playing in the street was found to be living two miles from a playing-field. Young people with no space for pursuing hobbies and interests in their own homes cause the police considerable trouble, especially at week-ends and during school holidays, when a good deal of damage is done to property. 2,840 persons under the age of seventeen were brought before the Birmingham Juvenile Court in 1948, and, while bad housing is by no means the only cause of juvenile delinquency, it is certainly a contributory factor.

Before the end of the second World War, Birmingham had planned the re-development of five districts covering an area of 12,000 acres near the City centre. Under the 1947 Town and Country Planning Act, every Local Authority is given three years in which to prepare development schemes, and Birmingham's plans will ultimately cover 51,000 acres. The first area to be re-developed will include Duddeston and Nechells. (See map, page 10). Sites are already being cleared and it is hoped that building will begin shortly. Of the 6,800 houses in this area, 5,000 were unfit for human habitation in 1937 and a further 500 were overcrowded—many of them clustered around factories and workshops. The scheme (as shown in the plans on page 16) provides for the complete re-planning of the area. Dwelling houses and factories will be segregated, new traffic and estate roads planned, and two major open spaces provided.

SCHOOL

The following table gives information about the number of schools in Birmingham and the number of children attending them:

TABLE IV

CHILDREN ATTENDING BIRMINGHAM SCHOOLS, JULY, 1949

Type of School	No. of children on books	No. of Schools
Nursery Schools and Classes	2,460	20*
Primary Schools	98,271	270
Secondary Modern Schools	39,166	87
Secondary Grammar Schools		
City	5,897	11
Voluntary	2,804	5
Secondary Technical Schools	2,115	5
Special Schools	2,839	24

* In addition, there are 56 Nursery Classes attached to Primary School Departments,
or operating in separate Buildings.

The number of young people aged fourteen and over engaged in full-time education is shown in the following table, though these figures do not include children who attend private schools, or students at Universities and Training Colleges.

TABLE V

YOUNG PEOPLE AGED 14 AND OVER ENGAGED IN FULL-TIME EDUCATION

Age	No.
14	13,516
15	2,131
16	689
17	363
18	59
19	4
TOTAL	16,762

Due mainly to the large increase in the birth rate in recent years, there is likely to be a serious shortage of school accommodation in Birmingham. Before the war the average annual intake into Birmingham schools was about 15,000. During the six years ended 31st December, 1947, the number of births in the city was:

TABLE VI

NUMBER OF CHILDREN BORN IN BIRMINGHAM 1943-8*

1943	20,195
1944	22,539
1945	20,008
1946	22,935
1947	23,935
1948 (est.)	20,531

* Deducting those whose parents resided outside the city.

The result of this large increase in the birth rate is that, as compared with 31st July, 1948, the Education Committee is likely to be confronted with the task of accommodating approximately 16,000 additional school children by the 31st July, 1951, and another 8,000, i.e. a total of 24,000 by 31st July, 1952.

Because of the interruption of building owing to the economic conditions resulting from the war, the Education Committee will probably find it impossible to secure permission to create 24,000 additional school places during the next few years, even if sites, labour and material are available. At a recent meeting of the Education Committee, therefore, the chairman issued a warning that in some parts of the city where the Education Committee could rent existing premises they would be compelled to do so, whilst in other parts of the city where no existing buildings were available the Committee would have no alternative but to transport children to any schools in the city where vacancies still remained. Much as the Education Committee dislikes these temporary expedients there is, unfortunately, no alternative if all children of compulsory school age are to be educated.

Children and young persons at school have regular medical examination and all the facilities provided under the 1944 Education Act, including milk and meals. 158,160 meals are supplied each week to 221 Schools. Two Residential Open-Air Schools and two Open-Air Day Schools are provided for delicate children, and there are schools for all other handicapped children.

Plans for County Colleges as required under the 1944 Education Act have already been submitted to the Minister of Education. The Education Committee estimates a need of twenty-one Colleges for 41,000 young people aged 15, 16 and 17 (the suggested location of these Colleges is shown in the map on page 144) and proposes to build at the rate of two Colleges per year (beginning in 1949), each college to accommodate 360-400 students per day. These colleges are to be used for part-time Technical, Commercial or Art education until such time as attendance at County Colleges becomes compulsory. Separate Colleges, provided on a national or regional basis, are recommended for young persons from Special Schools needing treatment for blindness or deafness. Birmingham proposes to centre in the County Colleges the work at present being done with the under-eighteens in the Evening Institutes and Senior Colleges.

The work of the Youth Employment and Welfare Department is described in a later chapter of this Report.

The City's Evening Institutes have recently celebrated the silver jubilee of their activities since the re-organization in 1923-4 of the earlier 'Night Schools'. In view of the new conditions created by the 1944 Education Act the Education Committee has determined that, in future,

preliminary courses for junior students should last for one year only and demand a minimum attendance of only two nights per week. The new Pre-Senior Courses are carefully designed to prepare young people so that they may, at the age of sixteen, enter a variety of senior vocational courses in Technical and Adult Institutes. To provide for those young people who cannot easily be persuaded of the advantage of vocational study, Evening Institutes now offer a wide range of practical, social and recreational activities. The greatest importance is attached to this development and it is hoped that as a consequence more and more young people will find satisfaction within the Institutes of the City.

The geographical distribution of Evening Institutes in the city is shown in the map below.

FIGURE 4

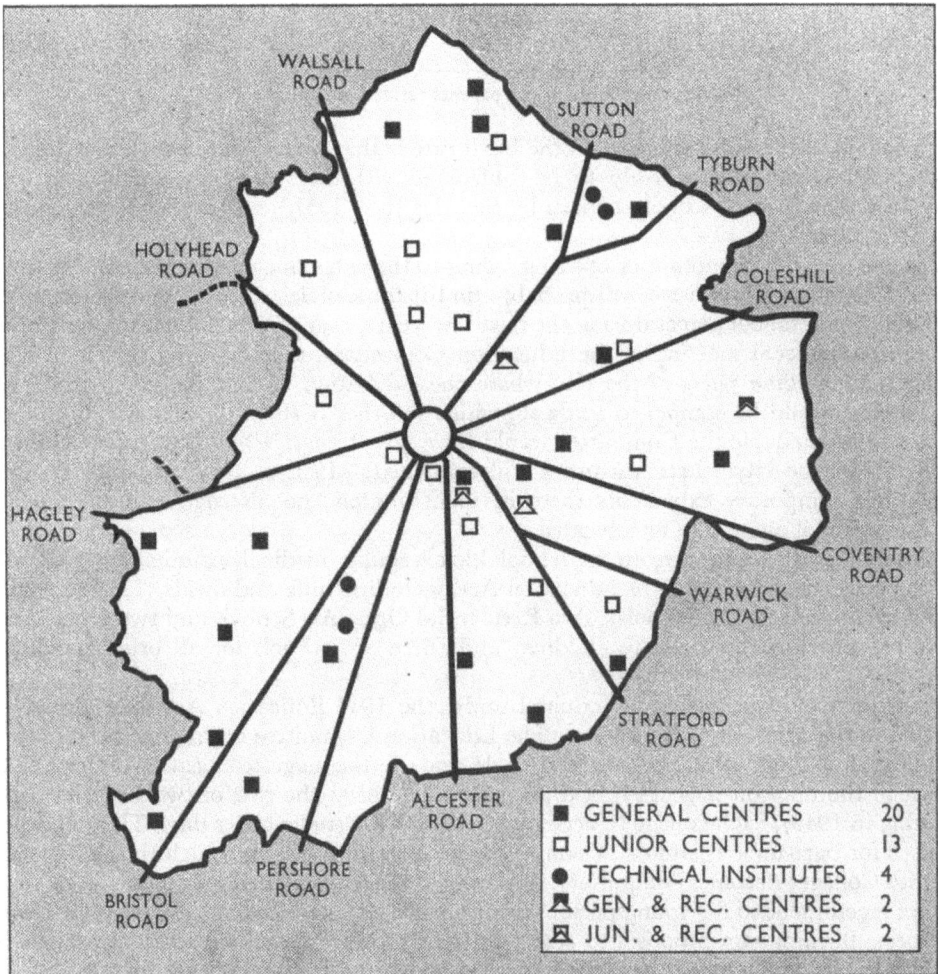

■ GENERAL CENTRES	20
□ JUNIOR CENTRES	13
● TECHNICAL INSTITUTES	4
⚒ GEN. & REC. CENTRES	2
⚒ JUN. & REC. CENTRES	2

LOCATION OF EVENING INSTITUTES AND L.E.A. RECREATIVE CENTRES

LEISURE

The greater part of this Report, of course, is devoted to a discussion of the leisure-habits of the young people of the city, and all that we propose to do at this point is to comment on a few of the amenities which are available in the area.

Cinema-going is easily the most popular leisure-time interest among young people, and there are in Birmingham eighty cinemas, with a total seating capacity of approximately 110,000. The city boasts three theatres (including the well-known Birmingham Repertory Theatre) and three music halls. There are over a hundred amateur dramatic societies, of which the most widely known is that associated with the Crescent Theatre.

In the following chapter we indicate the extent to which the seventeen swimming baths, the billiard saloons and the dance halls are patronized by young people. In addition to three public dance halls, premises permanently licensed for dancing include 101 institutes and church rooms, 12 public baths, and 123 hotels and licensed premises. There is also provision for dancing in 13 public parks and occasional licenses are granted from time to time for dancing in 126 schools. Other entertainments of increasing popularity are ice-skating, roller-skating, and speedway racing. There are 1,389 licensed premises in the city, but our observations and inquiries would lead us to the conclusion that only a minority of Birmingham's young people frequent these houses.

Special performances are given for young people by the City of Birmingham Symphony Orchestra and the Orchestra co-operates with the Education Authorities in the musical education of schoolchildren. A recent development has been the promotion of concerts in which young people are given the opportunity of taking part in orchestral concerts arranged for audiences of their own age.

The Central Public Library and a separate Commercial Library attract many students and research workers. There are twenty-five branch libraries in the suburban areas. All of them have a children's section and there are about 56,000 borrowers between the approximate ages of ten and sixteen. During the year ended 31st March, 1948, 910,524 books, of which 638,000 were fiction, were borrowed by these young people. The Central Library includes a comprehensive music section of 10,444 volumes and 7,200 books in foreign languages. Near the Library is the Museum and Art Gallery, opened in 1885, which attracts an average of 5,000 visitors per week. The Art Gallery is famed for its pre-Raphaelite collection, and among many well-known works of art are landscapes by David Cox, who was a native of the city.

In a later chapter we shall be discussing the provision of parks and playing-fields in the city. Unplanned building in the past left little space for parks or gardens. In the city as a whole there are 3·8 acres of open country per 1,000 of the population. This compares quite favourably with the situation in other cities, but these open spaces are very unevenly spaced. During school holidays playgrounds are open in the central wards as these are the least well-provided with playing-fields and parks. One of the finest open spaces in the Midlands is the Lickey Hills, within a fivepenny tram-ride of the city centre. This covers almost 520 acres and rises to 998 ft. above sea level. In view of the fact that the National Playing-fields Association suggests six acres per 1,000 population for playing fields alone, much remains to be done, especially for the children and young persons living in the central wards. Under the new planning schemes every boy and girl will live within reach of an open space, but during the intervening years some will have nowhere but the streets and drab courts of the central wards in which to play.

Birmingham, moreover, has spread so far that people living in the centre of the city have to travel miles to reach open country, and people in the suburbs have long journeys to make if they wish to enjoy the cultural amenities of the city. Because of bad planning in the past there is little sense of belonging to a community and many of the new areas are far from self-contained. Under the new planning schemes the city will eventually be divided into more manageable self-contained areas with playing-fields, swimming baths and open spaces within reach of every young person in the city. Above all, however, more houses are needed, so that no boy or girl will be compelled to live under the conditions existing in many parts of Birmingham today.

A Dressmaking Class.

Instruction in Wireless Transmission and Reception.

BIRMINGHAM EVENING INSTITUTES

Classes in many practical, cultural and recreative subjects, conducted in an informal atmosphere, are provided by the Birmingham Education Authority, usually in school buildings.

CHAPTER III

'TWENTY QUESTIONS'

In an endeavour to obtain information from young people themselves, we prepared a list of *Twenty Questions* (see pages 36-7, 40-1) which were answered by over 1,300 adolescents living in the city. From this number we selected a thousand (1,004 to be precise) as representing a fair sample of the total youth population. This sample is made up of 500 boys and 504 girls, the Local Education Authority having advised us to assume that the city's youth population is approximately equally divided between the sexes. (See Chapter V). We discovered in the course of our inquiry that about 55 per cent of the boys and 33 per cent of the girls are attached to youth organizations. Our sample of 500 boys, therefore, is made up of 280 who are attached and 220 who are not, the corresponding figures for the girls being 167 and 337. These young people, also, were drawn from all parts of the city and each age group from fourteen to nineteen inclusive is represented in approximately equal numbers. A complete analysis of the sample is given in Table VII.

TABLE VII

ANALYSIS OF 1,004 REPLIES TO 'TWENTY QUESTIONS' INQUIRY

	Still at School	Industrial Jobs	Other Jobs	In the Forces	Total
Unattached Girls ...	75	136	126	—	337
Attached Girls ...	33	62	72	—	167
Total Girls ...	108	198	198	—	504
Unattached Boys ...	60	64	56	40	220
Attached Boys ...	55	95	110	20	280
Total Boys ...	115	159	166	60	500

It was a comparatively easy matter to obtain completed questionnaires from members of youth organizations. All types of unit are represented. The 280 attached boys come from church clubs (95), other clubs (152), pre-Service units (34), Scouts and Rovers (20), Brigades (12), and political units (6). The 167 girls represent church clubs (43), other clubs (93), Guides and Rangers (15), G.T.C. and W.J.A.C. (11), Red Cross or St. John units (11), Brigades (7) and political units (7). It will be seen that about 15 per cent of these boys and girls belong to more than one organization.

To offer one illustration of the varied occupations represented among these young people, a group of twenty-nine boys all of whom are sixteen years of age, all engaged in industrial occupations, and all attached, is made up as follows: turner, warehouse assistant, press worker, electrical assistant, metal worker, carpenter, driver's mate, gas fitter, die sinker, motor builder, trolleyman, body builder, machine operator, wood pattern maker, garage worker, confectionery worker, property repairer, driller, motor mechanic, two machine feeders, two toolmakers, three printers and three engineering apprentices. These same boys belong to church clubs (5), boys' clubs (2), an industrial club (1), Old Scholars' clubs (2), an Evening Institute club (1), other clubs (10), pre-Service units (6), the Boys' Brigade (1), the Scouts (1), and the Crusaders (1). Only one boy in this particular group happens to belong to two units—a boy who is a Scout and who belongs to an open club.

Thirty-one sixteen-year-old attached boys employed in 'other jobs' include eleven clerks, three butchers, three apprentice draughtsmen, two electricians, two display artists, two salesmen, a display junior, a window dresser, a builder, a gardener, a painter, a laboratory assistant, a P.O. messenger and an assistant to an Inspector of Weights and Measures. Four of these boys belong to more than one youth organization. Eight of them belong to church clubs, two to L.E.A. clubs, two to Co-operative clubs, one to an industrial club, one to a Y.M.C.A., and seventeen to other or unspecified clubs. Two of them are Scouts, one belongs to the Sea Cadets, and one to the Young Unionists.

The membership of youth organizations in our city is made up of young people who are engaged in a wide diversity of occupation. A very different situation would have been revealed if our inquiry had been conducted in an area with a more restricted occupational interest.

It was an easy matter also, to obtain questionnaires from young people still at school, and we are grateful to the teachers of twelve secondary modern schools, six grammar schools, two technical schools and one Day Continuation College who co-operated with us by distributing questionnaires to their pupils.

It was a very much more difficult task to obtain 557 questionnaires (337 from girls and 220 from boys) which we could confidently regard as a fair sample of the city's unattached youth population, and we are not completely satisfied that we can claim that the 557 questionnaires we finally selected do in fact represent a true sample. Sources from which they were obtained, however, include forty-one factories and workshops, six retail shops, three chain stores, municipal, insurance and newspaper offices, a motor bus company, the City Transport Department, British Railways, an R.A.F. station and an Army Camp, two remand hostels, a girls' hostel, the City Libraries, Evening Institutes, hospitals and the Chamber of Commerce. We are grateful to many welfare officers, heads of departments, personnel officers and others, some of whom went to great trouble to assist us. Personal contact was made with young people in public dance halls, billiards saloons, milk bars and amusement arcades, and one or two probation officers distributed questionnaires to some of their young charges. All questionnaires were anonymous, no name or address being asked for, and still further to ensure anonymity every boy or girl was given an envelope in which the questionnaire could be sealed.

It will be seen therefore that we ourselves made every effort to obtain as wide a sample of the city's youth population as possible. We realize, however, that any inquiry made by the questionnaire method must be selective to this extent that it misses those people who never will consent to write answers to printed questions. One member of our staff spent an evening at a largely attended dance at a community centre where, during the course of the evening, he was individually introduced to sixteen nineteen-year-old boys. Each of these boys accepted a questionnaire and a stamped addressed envelope, but only one was returned. The following Sunday afternoon he distributed an equal number of questionnaries among boys of the same age at a largely attended Church Youth Fellowship, and all were returned. This does not mean that our sample is overloaded with representatives of church organizations (these units are indeed, under-represented), but it does mean that it has been much more difficult to obtain the co-operation of the more socially irresponsible. It may possibly be—we do not know—that there is a bottom 10 per cent of unattached young people whom we have failed to reach. The statistics we offer in this chapter need to be read, therefore, in the light of this possible qualification.

It would be quite impossible, in the space at our disposal, to offer a complete account of the findings of this *Twenty Questions* investigation. It would be interesting to take each question and to compare the answers given by boys and girls, by attached and unattached, by younger and older adolescents, by those in industrial and those in clerical occupations, by those who left school at fourteen and those who stayed at school longer. Such an undertaking, however, is not possible, and we must be content to summarize some of our more important findings under such headings as Use of Leisure, Attitude to School, Employment, Pocket Money, Church Attendance, Reading, Radio Listening, Holidays, etc. References to this investigation are also scattered throughout this Report.

LITERACY

One further general comment of a preliminary character, however, should be made. Among the first comments made by those who have looked through these questionnaires have often been: 'What dreadful writing' or 'What appalling spelling'. Remarks of this kind, of course, are not applicable to all the questionnaires, but to a very considerable extent such comments are justified. These young people represent, we know, the generation whose education was often interrupted during the war years, and very many of them left school at fourteen. Many of these young people have had little or no need to use a pen since they left school. When every allowance has been made for these facts, we are still surprised that so many young people cannot spell the name of the Sunday newspaper which they claim to read every week, and that so many, asked how they employed a certain evening, give such answers as 'whent no were', 'whent to the cinima', or 'to the pictuers'. One boy 'when a work' (went a walk?), while other answers include 'went to Jim', 'knight school', 'listened to the whiles', 'road my bike', 'play billyards' and 'mesed arowend'. It is particularly surprising that so many young people cannot spell the name of the job they do. The sixteen-year-old gardener who told us that his occupation was 'gorneden' was presumably of very low intelligence, but we do not think that this explanation applies to several 'machien workers', 'mecanics' and 'fileing clarks', or to the fifteen-year-old girl 'buffy hand', to the sixteen-year-old 'wateress' or to several boy 'plummers'. There is perhaps some excuse for a number of 'bus conductresses, electricians and assistants of various kinds who found difficulty with these long words. One sixteen-year-old boy is employed, he says, in 'odd gobs'. One seventeen-year-old girl works in a factory but her ambition in life is to become a 'bally dancer'. Asked to give the title of the last book they read, one or two young people replied, 'I don't no'.

THE USE OF LEISURE

Our inquiry included some questions about work and education, but its primary purpose was to elicit information about the way in which young people employ their leisure hours. We asked them to state how often they went dancing, to the cinema, to a youth organization, etc. (more than once a week, once a week, once a month, occasionally, or never). We asked also for information about their activities on the previous Saturday and Sunday and on each evening of the previous week. This more precise inquiry appears to have given us more reliable information than has the more general question, though we must say that on the whole we are impressed with the care taken by young people to give us information, and with the apparent honesty of their replies. A summary of the information obtained in answer to the above questions will be found in the eight Tables on pages 28-33. In Table VIII will be found a summary of the number of evenings spent by attached and unattached boys and girls at home, at cinema, at dance halls and in youth organizations. Boys who belong to youth organizations go to them on an average two evenings a week (see Tables IX-XVI) while girl members attend rather less than three evenings a fortnight. Unattached young people go to the cinema a little more than do those who belong to youth organizations, but on the other hand they spend rather more evenings in their homes. It will be seen that unattached boys are represented as spending an average of 0·2 evenings a week at a youth organization, and unattached girls an average of 0·1. The explanation of this apparent anomaly is that some of these young people belong to social clubs of various types which we have not regarded as falling officially within the Youth Service.

TABLE VIII

HOW BIRMINGHAM YOUNG PEOPLE EMPLOY THEIR EVENINGS

	Number of evenings a week			
	At Home	At Cinema	At Dance Hall	At Youth Organization
Attached Girls	2·3	1·1	0·5	1·4
Unattached Girls... ...	3·1	1·5	0·5	0·1
Attached Boys	1·6	1·3	0·4	2·0
Unattached Boys... ...	2·5	1·4	0·4	0·2

A general discussion of the leisure habits of unattached boys and girls will be found in Chapter VIII, but at the moment we would invite readers to note that the unattached girls from whom our information was obtained spend more than three evenings in their homes each week, and two evenings at cinema or dance hall. The unattached boys spend two-and-a-half evenings in their homes and rather less than two evenings at cinema or dance hall. Before the sight of several hundred young people standing in a cinema queue is allowed to prompt any loose generalizations about 'cinema addicts', one should remember that there are even more hundreds of young people who are in their homes.

ATTITUDE TO SCHOOL

We invited young people to tell us how old they were when they left school and whether or not they would have preferred to stay on at school beyond this age. The answers given to these questions are summarized in Table XVII. 62 per cent of the boys and 68 per cent of the girls had no desire to remain longer at school. The percentage of those who would have preferred a still longer education tends to decline among those who in fact did enjoy the extra years at school. Four girls who left school at fourteen answer 'yes' with the qualification 'if it was a secondary school'. Three girls and one boy declare that they left school when they were thirteen.

EMPLOYMENT

We asked young people to tell us how many jobs they had had since they left school. Answers to this question reveal a very general stability of employment. This is a tribute to the success of the work of the Birmingham Youth Employment Department, although we would not appear to suggest that it is always regrettable when a boy or girl changes his or her occupation. There will always be a few unstable people who cannot hold a job for long, but only twenty-six girls and fifteen boys in the whole sample have had five jobs or more. In Tables XVIII and XIX will be found an analysis of the answers to this question. Among those who completed our questionnaire there is a greater stability of employment among those who remained at school

Mixed dances under proper instruction and supervision are valuable social agents.

Hundreds of young people take part in inter-club competitions organized by the Birmingham Youth Committee, Birmingham Table Tennis League and other bodies.

POPULAR PASTIMES
Table tennis and dancing are probably the most popular indoor pastimes in mixed clubs.

27

TABLE IX

WHAT 280 'ATTACHED' BOYS SAY ABOUT THEIR LEISURE HABITS

	More than once a week	Once a week	Once a month	Occasionally	Never
Dancing	28	67	13	76	96
Cinema	127	92	14	46	1
Church	29	66	14	88	83
Watching football in winter ...	31	92	13	79	65
Horse races	—.	—	—	7	273
Greyhound races	—	—	—	8	272
Public house	7	3	1	18	239
Youth Organization	162	75	3	14	—
Rambling and hiking	4	7	16	146	107
Cycling	61	31	16	117	55
Amusement arcade	1	5	4	104	166
Cafés and milk bars	29	17	8	145	81
Speedway	3	18	15	68	176
Theatre	—	9	30	160	81

TABLE X

WHAT 220 'UNATTACHED' BOYS SAY ABOUT THEIR LEISURE HABITS

	More than once a week	Once a week	Once a month	Occasionally	Never
Dancing	26	39	7	41	107
Cinema	96	80	7	30	7
Church	12	38	5	77	88
Watching football in winter ...	20	69	11	55	65
Horse races	—	2	3	12	203
Greyhound races	—	1	2	7	210
Public house	7	3	2	41	167
Rambling and hiking	10	8	10	84	108
Cycling	45	23	19	95	38
Amusement arcades	4	3	4	79	130
Cafés and milk bars	31	14	6	101	68
Speedway	5	22	12	47	134
Theatre	6	12	28	121	53

TABLE XI

WHAT 167 'ATTACHED' GIRLS SAY ABOUT THEIR LEISURE HABITS

	More than once a week	Once a week	Once a month	Occasionally	Never
Dancing	38	39	3	55	32
Cinema	51	70	5	38	3
Church	27	37	11	64	28
Watching football in winter ...	7	14	4	36	106
Horse races	—	—	—	—	167
Greyhound races	—	—	—	5	162
Public house	—	—	—	16	151
Youth Organization	88	68	—	11	—
Rambling and hiking	3	4	5	101	54
Cycling	20	12	3	82	50
Amusement arcades	1	—	1	50	115
Cafés and milk bars	9	12	6	82	58
Speedway	2	9	1	26	129
Theatre	2	9	14	102	40

TABLE XII

WHAT 337 'UNATTACHED' GIRLS SAY ABOUT THEIR LEISURE HABITS

	More than once a week	Once a week	Once a month	Occasionally	Never
Dancing	50	67	13	115	92
Cinema	155	117	15	43	4
Church	19	59	13	178	68
Watching football in winter ...	6	28	7	93	203
Horse races	—	—	1	15	321
Greyhound races	2	1	1	19	314
Public house	3	5	—	51	278
Rambling and hiking	5	3	7	160	162
Cycling	50	17	6	167	97
Amusement arcades	5	2	2	116	212
Cafés and milk bars	28	17	13	209	70
Speedway	1	20	10	75	231
Theatre	7	28	39	215	48

TABLE XIII

HOW 280 'ATTACHED' BOYS SPENT THEIR SPARE TIME DURING A NORMAL WORKING WEEK

	SUNDAY			Mon.	Tue.	Wed.	Thur.	Fri.	SATURDAY		
	Morn.	Aft.	Evg.	Evenings					Morn.	Aft.	Evg.
At home	58	63	66	59	67	63	54	46	35	47	45
In bed	30	2	—	—	—	—	—	—	18	—	—
Homework	10	—	4	11	14	10	8	4	11	5	4
Total at home ...	98	65	70	70	81	73	62	50	64	52	49
At work or on duty ...	15	4	4	10	6	6	8	9	123	26	6
Evening Institute, Technical School, music lesson, etc.	—	—	—	23	17	19	6	10	1	—	—
At school	—	—	—	2	2	—	—	—	—	—	—
Youth Organization ...	21	7	36	81	102	92	116	110	10	6	25
Church	46	33	60	—	3	4	1	3	—	1	5
Library, lecture or meeting	—	—	—	1	1	—	4	1	2	—	1
Visiting	4	16	15	7	4	7	13	12	—	3	16
Walk	26	27	18	5	5	13	11	13	5	6	7
Watching or playing football	29	40	—	—	4	—	1	1	22	126	1
Tennis, cricket, etc. ...	10	15	—	7	5	1	7	4	3	26	2
Dance	—	—	10	11	6	3	11	12	—	—	58
Cinema	—	47	52	46	30	38	29	37	1	5	80
Cycling	16	20	7	2	—	6	3	—	5	7	2
Outings and excursions...	4	—	1	1	—	—	1	—	2	3	3
Swimming...	5	—	—	3	1	1	—	1	1	5	2
Gardening	3	—	—	1	—	—	—	—	—	1	—
Billiards	—	2	3	2	—	2	3	4	—	—	3
Roller- or ice-skating ...	—	—	—	1	1	—	1	1	1	1	4
Boxing	—	—	—	—	—	—	—	—	—	—	1
Concert or jazz concert	—	1	2	1	1	1	1	—	—	1	3
Speedway	—	—	—	1	—	—	—	—	—	—	3
Theatre, pantomime or music hall	—	—	—	1	1	4	2	4	—	—	6
Whist drive	—	—	—	—	—	1	—	—	—	—	—
Shopping	—	—	—	2	1	—	—	—	31	10	—
Bonfire night	—	—	—	—	—	—	—	5	—	—	—
Canteen or milk bar ...	—	—	—	1	—	—	—	—	—	—	1
Public house	—	—	1	1	—	1	1	1	—	—	1

TABLE XIV

HOW 220 'UNATTACHED' BOYS SPENT THEIR SPARE TIME DURING A NORMAL WORKING WEEK

	SUNDAY			Mon.	Tue.	Wed.	Thur.	Fri.	SATURDAY		
	Morn.	Aft.	Evg.	Evenings					Morn.	Aft.	Evg.
At home	62	50	63	66	75	74	70	67	25	33	47
In bed	23	7	—	—	—	—	—	—	10	1	1
Homework	6	15	10	18	19	17	18	10	7	3	2
Total at home ...	91	72	73	84	94	91	88	77	42	37	50
At work or on duty ...	20	6	8	9	13	6	10	7	81	22	5
Evening Institute, Technical School, music lesson, etc.	—	—	—	17	17	17	9	10	—	—	—
Church	21	11	19	1	—	—	1	4	—	1	—
Library, lecture or meeting	—	—	—	2	2	—	3	2	5	1	2
Visiting	6	15	23	10	12	12	8	9	1	5	11
Walk	18	21	12	13	13	10	13	7	6	13	12
Watching or playing football	19	25	—	1	3	2	3	2	22	85	—
Tennis, cricket, etc. ...	2	3	—	2	1	1	2	—	—	4	—
Dance	—	—	9	11	6	14	6	17	—	1	34
Cinema	—	28	46	40	22	24	33	43	3	6	70
Cycling	16	17	8	5	4	10	6	3	4	12	1
Outings and excursions ...	5	6	4	1	1	1	1	1	5	9	5
Swimming...	3	—	—	—	1	1	1	—	—	1	—
Gardening	7	2	—	—	—	1	—	1	6	1	—
Billiards	1	3	4	2	1	6	6	3	—	1	1
Roller- or ice-skating ...	—	—	—	1	4	1	1	3	—	—	2
Boxing	—	—	—	1	1	—	—	—	—	—	—
Concert or jazz concert...	—	1	2	—	1	—	2	3	—	1	2
Band or orchestra practice	—	—	—	1	2	—	1	—	—	—	1
Social club, works club, etc.	—	—	1	5	9	10	13	8	—	1	2
Pigeons	1	2	—	—	—	—	—	—	1	1	—
Speedway	—	—	—	—	—	—	—	—	—	—	2
Theatre, pantomime or music hall	—	—	—	2	1	1	2	5	—	1	5
Whist drive	—	—	—	—	1	—	—	—	—	—	1
Shopping	—	—	—	—	—	—	—	—	35	12	—
Canteen or milk bar ...	—	—	—	1	1	—	3	2	—	—	3
Carnival, fair, etc. ...	—	—	—	2	—	—	1	—	—	—	2
Public house	1	—	1	2	—	—	—	—	—	—	2

31

TABLE XV

HOW 167 'ATTACHED' GIRLS SPENT THEIR SPARE TIME DURING A NORMAL WORKING WEEK

	SUNDAY			Mon.	Tue.	Wed.	Thur.	Fri.	SATURDAY		
	Morn.	Aft.	Evg.	Evenings					Morn.	Aft.	Evg.
At home	108	54	39	52	64	60	65	59	55	47	49
At work	—	—	1	1	—	—	—	—	60	19	—
Evening Institute, Technical School, music lesson, etc.	—	—	—	9	11	5.	6	4	—	—	—
Youth Organization ...	1	2	21	44	53	36	42	31	—	—	7
Church, choir, etc. ...	27	26	32	6	3	2	11	5	1	1	3
Library, lecture or meeting	1	1	—	1	1	—	2	1	1	1	1
Visiting, parties, etc. ...	12	28	22	6	10	11	11	8	—	8	15
Walk	12	20	13	9	3	10	5	6	2	9	1
Watching football ...	1	5	—	—	—	—	—	—	—	7	—
Netball	—	—	—	—	—	—	—	—	6	1	—
Dance	—	—	12	10	6	11	2	10	—	—	39
Cinema	—	24	24	23	13	23	14	28	—	4	43
Cycling	1	3	—	2	—	—	1	1	—	2	—
Outings and excursions ...	—	—	1	—	1	—	—	2	2	1	1
Rambling	1	1	1	—	—	—	—	—	—	—	—
Swimming...	1	—	—	1	—	2	1	1	1	—	—
Roller- or ice-skating ...	—	—	—	1	—	1	1	3	—	2	1
Watching boxing... ...	—	—	—	—	—	—	—	1	—	—	—
Concert	—	1	—	—	—	1	2	2	—	—	—
Theatre, pantomime or music hall	—	—	—	—	—	3	4	3	—	—	3
Shopping	—	1	—	—	—	—	—	—	40	—	—
Carnival, fair, etc. ...	—	—	—	—	—	1	—	—	—	3	1
Baby minding	—	1	—	2	2	1	—	1	1	—	3
Visiting cemetery ...	2	—	—	—	—	—	—	—	—	—	—
Selling savings stamps ...	—	—	—	—	—	—	—	1	—	—	—

TABLE XVI

HOW 337 'UNATTACHED' GIRLS SPENT THEIR SPARE TIME DURING A NORMAL WORKING WEEK

	SUNDAY			Mon.	Tue.	Wed.	Thur.	Fri.	SATURDAY		
	Morn.	Aft.	Evg.	Evenings				.	Morn.	Aft.	Evg.
At home	232	149	150	171	153	179	155	163	91	85	90
At work	5	3	3	9	9	7	7	4	121	36	4
Evening Institute, Technical School, music lesson, etc.	—	—	—	24	17	18	18	8	—	1	—
Church, choir, etc. ...	46	19	29	2	4	3	4	1	1	—	1
Library, lecture or meeting	1	—	—	4	2	2	2	1	—	1	2
Visiting, parties, etc. ...	13	45	51	20	23	30	31	27	3	18	24
Walk	18	40	21	11	14	18	8	12	—	9	7
Watching football ...	1	3	—	—	—	—	1	—	—	5	—
Netball, tennis, gardening	4	1	—	—	—	—	—	—	—	5	—
Dance	—	1	18	12	16	18	12	22	—	3	83
Cinema	—	50	64	59	54	41	68	46	—	17	96
Cycling	5	8	4	—	2	2	3	1	1	4	2
Outings and excursions ...	6	6	2	3	2	—	2	10	4	12	5
Swimming...	1	—	—	4	4	1	3	5	1	1	2
Roller- or ice-skating ...	—	—	1	6	1	6	2	8	1	2	5
Concert	—	2	1	2	3	1	1	6	—	1	1
Works or Social club ...	—	—	10	3	6	5	10	6	—	—	1
Speedway	—	—	—	—	—	—	—	1	—	—	4
Theatre, pantomime or music hall	—	—	—	3	8	4	8	9	—	—	12
Whist drive	—	—	—	—	1	1	—	—	—	—	1
Shopping	1	—	—	—	1	—	—	1	112	135	5
Carnival, fair, etc. ...	—	—	—	—	—	—	—	1	—	—	6
Baby minding	—	—	1	—	4	3	1	1	—	—	1
Visiting cemetery ...	—	3	—	—	—	—	—	—	—	—	—
Selling savings stamps ...	—	—	—	—	—	—	—	1	—	—	—
Dog Show...	—	—	—	—	—	—	—	—	—	1	—
Public house	—	—	2	1	—	1	—	2	—	—	1

NOTE: The slight discrepancy in the total figures for each column is due to the fact that in some cases two occupations have been included for the same evening, and in some instances no information was given us.

TABLE XVII

ANSWERS TO THE QUESTION 'WOULD YOU HAVE PREFERRED TO STAY ON AT SCHOOL BEYOND THE AGE AT WHICH YOU LEFT?'

School Leaving age	BOYS		GIRLS	
	Yes	No	Yes	No
14	91	111	93	180
15	29	58	24	47
16	15	54	5	25
17	10	9	3	1
18	2	3	1	—

until fifteen or longer than among those who left school at fourteen. The former, however, are in the main ex-secondary school pupils, and we doubt whether it is possible to conclude from our findings that the raising of the school-leaving age to fifteen will necessarily lead to a greater stability of employment. With two exceptions, however, every boy or girl in our sample who has had five jobs or more left school at fourteen. The exceptions are a sixteen-year-old shorthand typist who left school at fifteen and who is already in her tenth job, a packer in a cycle factory who is on probation from the Courts and who remained at school until her fifteenth birthday and who, not yet sixteen, is now in her fifth job.

Other girls who have had an exceptionally large number of jobs include a fifteen-year-old tea packer who has had six (she would like to become a hairdresser), a sixteen-year-old shop assistant who has also had six, two seventeen-year-old cardboard box makers who are in their sixth and seventh jobs, an eighteen-year-old 'printer' who has had six, and an eighteen-year-old 'conductoress' who has had eight. Two coffee packers aged seventeen and eighteen have had five and six jobs respectively, while another at seventeen has had six. An eighteen-year-old warehouse worker has had nine, and another who has had 'lots' would like to become a dressmaker. All these girls left school at fourteen and most of them are unattached.

TABLE XVIII

AVERAGE NUMBER OF JOBS HELD BY BOYS

School-leaving age	Present age				
	15	16	17	18	19
14	2·0	2·35	2·0	2·0	2·62
15	1·1	1·33	1·47	1·33	1·25
16	—	1·0	1·2	1·38	1·36
17	—	—	1·0	1·1	1·0

More of the boys than of the girls were in full-time education until they were fifteen or over, and there are considerably fewer of them who have held a large number of jobs. These few include an eighteen-year-old painter and decorator who has worked with eight firms but whose aim in life is still to remain in the decorating business, a soldier of the same age who has had nine jobs, and a polisher, also eighteen, who has held eight. The record, however, is held by a nineteen-year-old soldier who claims to have had no less than seventeen jobs and whose aim in life is to become a bricklayer.

TABLE XIX

AVERAGE NUMBER OF JOBS HELD BY GIRLS

School-leaving age	Present age				
	15	16	17	18	19
14	2·2	1·92	2·05	2·53	2·34
15	1·12	3·0	1·5	1·33	2·43
16	—	1·1	1·0	1·0	1·0
17	—	—	1·0	—	1·7

351 girls and 326 boys enjoy their present job, while forty girls and fifty-two boys do not. 127 girls and 59 boys, however, think that the job they are doing is a blind alley, while 264 girls and 307 boys do not. In spite of the fact that so many young people enjoy their work, 19 per cent of the girls and 22 per cent of the boys would like to change their present job. It is evident that a number of those who enjoy their work would nevertheless like a change.

We further asked the question: 'What job in life do you aim to do?' Answers to this inquiry, though of great interest, do not permit of easy classification. About fifteen per cent of the girls (we expected more) answer 'get married', 'have a home of my own', or 'become a wife and mother'. Quite a number of girls, as might be expected, have stage or film ambitions. One eighteen-year-old factory girl wants to become an air hostess. A nineteen-year-old girl packer answers: 'I wish I knew'. This girl stayed at school until she was seventeen, and says of her present job 'I endure it'. She does not belong to any youth organization because, she says, 'I am not a good mixer'.

The ambitions of the boys are more varied, though on the whole they do not range outside the sphere of the boys' present employment. This would appear to offer confirmation of the fact that most of these boys are happy and content in their work. A 'bus conductor aims at becoming a 'bus driver, a factory hand aims at becoming a foreman, and a plumber's mate a plumber. One boy has no higher aim in life, if his answer is to be treated seriously, than to become a 'driver's mate on a pop lorry'. Other answers include a professional footballer (several boys), a Member of Parliament (a boy who spends most evenings in political activity), a dance band pianist, a scoutmaster, and a P.T. instructor. While quite a number of girls, as we have seen, want to become good wives, just one boy answers 'a good husband'. A fourteen-year-old schoolboy wants to become a slaughterman, a nineteen-year-old airman wants to become a turf accountant, and a 'bus conductor of the same age wants to become an Egyptologist and is reading books about this subject.

A considerable amount of time is taken by young people in travelling. Asked 'How long does it take you to travel from home to work', the answers given average twenty-eight minutes

TWENTY QUESTIONS

· On this and on the opposite page are shown two completed questionnaires. These particular examples were not used in the Survey, but they illustrate the low standard of literacy of many of the young people in the city.

1—(a) Age 16 10 MONTH   (b) Sex MAIE

2—Occupation G.P.O MESSINGER

3—(a) How old were you when you left school ?   14 YEAR
   (b) Would you have preferred to stay on at school beyond this age ?   No

4—How many jobs have you had since you left school ?   ONE

5—(a) Do you enjoy your present job ?   YES
   (b) Were any unpleasant tricks played on you when you first started work ?   YES
   (c) Do you think your job is a blind alley ?   No
   (d) Do you wish to change your present job ?   YES
   (e) What job in life do you aim to do ?   ENGINEER

6—How long does it take you to travel from home to work ?   40 MINS

7—Do you live
   (a) with parents ? YES   (c) in lodgings ? NO
   (b) with relations ? No   (d) in a hostel ? No

8—Do you attend
   (a) Day Continuation School ? YES   (c) Technical Classes ? No
   (b) An Evening Institute ? No

9—What did you do
   (a) Last Saturday morning ?   WORK
   (b) Last Saturday afternoon ?   STAY HAT HOME
   (c) Last Saturday evening ?   STAY HAT HOME
   (d) Last Sunday morning ?   STAY HAT HOME
   (e) Last Sunday afternoon ?   WENT TO THE PICTUER
   (f) Last Sunday evening ?   phY BILLARDS
   (g) Last Monday evening ?   WENT TO THE PICTUER
   (h) Last Tuesday evening ?   STAY AT HOME
   (i) Last Wednesday evening ?   STAY AT HOME
   (j) Last Thursday evening ?   STAY AT HOME
   (k) Last Friday evening ?   STAY AT HOM

10—Do you belong to any clubs or youth organisations ?
   (a) If so, what ?   NO
   (b) When you go, what do you most enjoy doing ?   No
   (c) If you don't belong to any club or youth organisation, why don't you ?   No
   (d) If you once belonged to a youth organisation, but left it, why did you leave ?

11—Do you think there should be
   (a) separate clubs for boys ? YES   (c) mixed clubs ? No
   (b) separate clubs for girls ? YES

12—What do you do—pay board or receive pocket money ?   S BE NIT
   (a) How much a week do you have for yourself ?   5/
   (b) How much do you spend per week on
     (i) Cigarettes ? No   (iv) Cinemas ? /
     (ii) Dances ? No   (v) Betting or Gambling ? N
     (iii) Drinks ? No

[see other side

13 (a) What is the title of the last book you read ? Bill Boyd
   (b) Did you read it
     (i) less than a week ago ? No   (iii) less than six months ago ? No
     (ii) less than a month ago ? No   (iv) more than six months ago ? No
   (c) Do you borrow books from any library ? No

14—(a) What Sunday newspapers do you read fairly regularly ? PICTORAL
   (b) What newspapers or magazines or comics do you read fairly regularly ? DANO

15—What Radio programme do you listen to fairly regularly ? Paul Taiple

16—Do you fill in Football coupons
   (a) regularly ? No   (b) occasionally ? No
   Do you bet in any other way ?
   (a) on horses ? No   (c) on cards ? No
   (b) on dogs ? No

17—(a) What games or sports do you play regularly ? CRIKIT
   (b) What games or sports do you watch regularly ? N

18—Have you ever been
   (a) Camping in tents ? YES   (e) To the sea-side ? No
   (b) To a Holiday Camp ? YES   (f) Abroad ? No
   (c) To a Youth Hostel ? No   (g) To any other kind of holiday ? YES
   (d) To London ? N
   To which of these did you go last year ? Hole Feet

19—How often do you go (put a tick in the appropriate column)

	More than once a week	Once a week	Once a Month	Occasionally	Never
Dancing					✓
Cinema		✓			
Church					✓
Watch Football in Winter					✓
Horse Races					✓
Greyhound Races					✓
Public House					✓
Youth Organisation					✓
Rambling and Hiking					✓
Cycling					✓
Amusement Arcade					✓
Cafe and Milk Bars					✓
Speedway					✓
Theatre				✓	

Any other amusements or entertainment you attend regularly   No

20—Which of the following do you think the most important
   An interesting job ? ___   Health ? ✓
   Friends ? ___   Intelligence ? ___
   Good looks ? ___   Money ? ___

[See other side

See also pages 40 and 41.

TWENTY QUESTIONS

1—(a) Age *18 years* (b) Sex *girl*

2—Occupation *capstan machine*

3—(a) How old were you when you left school ? *14 years*
   (b) Would you have preferred to stay on at school beyond this age ? *No*

4—How many jobs have you had since you left school ? *1*

5—(a) Do you enjoy your present job ? *They sent me*
   (b) Were any unpleasant tricks played on you when you first started work ? *for a right hand spanner.*
   (c) Do you think your job is a blind alley ?
   (d) Do you wish to change your present job ? *No*
   (e) What job in life do you aim to do ? *Model*

6—How long does it take you to travel from home to work ? *½ hour*

7—Do you live
   (a) with parents ? *No*   (c) in lodgings ?
   (b) with relations ? *My sitter* (d) in a hostel ?

8—Do you attend
   (a) Day Continuation School ? *No*   (c) Technical Classes ? *No*
   (b) An Evening Institute ? *No*

9—What did you do
   (a) Last Saturday morning ? *pitures*
   (b) Last Saturday afternoon ? *stayed in*
   (c) Last Saturday evening ? *pitures*
   (d) Last Sunday morning ? *when walk*
   (e) Last Sunday afternoon ? *when walk*
   (f) Last Sunday evening ? *stayed*
   (g) Last Monday evening ? *when to work*
   (h) Last Tuesday evening ? *pitures*
   (i) Last Wednesday evening ? *stayed in*
   (j) Last Thursday evening ? *stayed in*
   (k) Last Friday evening ? *stayed in*

10—Do you belong to any clubs or youth organisations ?
   (a) If so, what ? *No*
   (b) When you go, what do you most enjoy doing ? *Did once*
   (c) If you don't belong to a club or youth organisation, why don't you ?
   (d) If you once belonged to a youth organisation, but left it, why did you leave ? *they where silly*

11—Do you think there should be
   (a) separate clubs for boys ?   (c) mixed clubs ? *Mixed*
   (b) separate clubs for girls ?

12—What do you do—pay board or receive pocket money ? *pay board*
   (a) How much a week do you have for yourself ? *10 shillings*
   (b) How much do you spend per week on
   (i) Cigarettes ? *None*   (iv) Cinemas ? *4 shillings*
   (ii) Dances ?   (v) Betting or Gambling ? *None*
   (iii) Drinks ? *none*

[See other side]

See also pages 40 and 41.

---

13 (a) What is the title of the last book you read ? *little woman*
   (b) Did you read it
     (i) less than a week ago ?   (iii) less than six months ago ?
     (ii) less than a month ago ?   (iv) more than six months ago ? *2 years*
   (c) Do you borrow books from any library ? *yes*

14—(a) What Sunday newspapers do you read fairly regularly ? *New of world*
   (b) What newspapers or magazines or comics do you read fairly regularly ? *Silver star*

15—What Radio programme do you listen to fairly regularly ? *up pole*

16—Do you fill in Football coupons
   (a) regularly ? *No*   (b) occasionally ? *No*
   Do you bet in any other way ?
   (a) on horses ? *No*   (c) on cards ? *No*
   (b) on dogs ? *No*

17—(a) What games or sports do you play regularly ? *rounds*
   (b) What games or sports do you watch regularly ?

18—Have you ever been
   (a) Camping in tents ? *No*   (e) To the sea-side ? *Torquay*
   (b) To a Holiday Camp ? *No*   (f) Abroad ?
   (c) To a Youth Hostel ?   (g) To any other kind of holiday ?
   (d) To London ? *✗✗*
   To which of these did you go last year ? *Torquay.*

19—How often do you go (put a tick in the appropriate column)

	More than once a week	*Once a week	Once a Month	Occasionally	Never
Dancing	✓			✓	
Cinema	✓	4 times			
Church					✗
Watch Football in Winter					✗
Horse Races					✗
Greyhound Races					✗
Public House				✓	
Youth Organisation		✓			
Rambling and Hiking		✓			
Cycling					
Amusement Arcade					
Cafe and Milk Bars					
Speedway					
Theatre				✓	

Any other amusements or entertainment you attend regularly *garden*

20—Which of the following do you think the most important
   An interesting job ?   Health ? ✓
   Friends ?   Intelligence ?
   Good looks ?   Money ? ✓

[See other side]

for the girls and twenty-four minutes for the boys. It would appear that something approaching one hour a day is spent in travelling to or from work. Seventy-six girls and fifty-one boys say that they spend an hour-and-a-half a day or more in travelling to and from work.

In view of the accusation which has been recently made in some quarters that initiation tricks of a degrading and unpleasant character are sometimes played on young people when they first enter employment, we asked the question: 'Were any unpleasant tricks played on you when you first started work?' We realize this question is capable of such varied interpretation as to render it largely valueless, and though fifty-four girls and one hundred boys answer 'yes', we do not know what significance may be attached to these replies. The answer was given by young people engaged in a wide range of employment both clerical and industrial, and we think very often the boy or girl had innocent practical jokes in mind. We have evidence on the other hand that more undesirable practices are not entirely unknown.

POCKET MONEY

We asked young people to tell us how much a week they had for themselves. By all the standards of earlier generations they certainly have a great deal of money to spend. We suspect that some young people have put down the total amount of their wages, without deducting what they pay for board. Sometimes, too, fares have to be paid and meals bought out of 'pocket money'. When these allowances have been made the amount of money which young people can spend as they please is still large. There are some wide variations—ranging among fourteen-year-old boys from a shilling to fifteen shillings, and among seventeen-year-old girls from four shillings to ninety shillings. One fifteen-year-old labourer has £2 a week of which he spends 15s. on cigarettes, 5s. on dancing, 2s. 6d. on the cinema and 2s. 6d. on betting. A fifteen-year-old electrician has 30s. of which he spends 10s. on cigarettes, 5s. on dances and 7s. 6d. at the cinema. A seventeen-year-old factory girl has 35s. for herself and spends 5s. on drinks and 7s. on gambling. An eighteen-year-old boy polisher claims to have £4 a week for himself. He spends £1 to 25s. on cigarettes and takes a girl to the pictures five times a week. A nineteen-year-old girl clerk has 38s. and spends 7s. on cigarettes, 11s. on dances and 5s. 6d. at the cinema. On the other hand, an eighteen-year-old girl clerk says 'My young man pays for everything and I save'. A summary of the information we obtained about pocket money is given in Table XX. We have excluded from this table boys and girls aged fifteen and over who are still at school. The average pocket money of fifteen-, sixteen- and seventeen-year-old schoolgirls and boys is about four shillings a week.

TABLE XX

POCKET MONEY

Age	BOYS		GIRLS	
	Range	Average per week	Range	Average per week
14	1s. 0d. – 15s.ᵗ	4s. 3d.	1s. 0d. – 10s.	3s. 3d.
15	2s. 9d. – 40s.	9s. 2d.	3s. 0d. – 30s.	6s. 4d.
16	3s. 6d. – 40s.	11s. 1d.	5s. 0d. – 35s.	11s. 4d.
17	2s. 6d. – 47s.	14s. 6d.	4s. 0d. – 90s.	15s. 6d.
18	5s. 0d. – 80s.	21s. 0d.	3s. 0d. – 50s.	21s. 9d.
19	10s. 0d. – 80s.	28s. 0d.	7s. 6d. – 60s.	26s. 10d.

SMOKING

Of boys aged sixteen and over, 45 per cent of the unattached and 43 per cent of the attached spend money weekly on cigarettes, the average expenditure in the two groups being 6s. 10½d. and 5s. 6½d. respectively. Among the girls of the same age 29 per cent of the unattached smoke regularly, their average expenditure being 5s. 5½d., but only 17 per cent of the attached girls spend money on cigarettes every week and the average amount spent is 4s. 4d. Few boys or girls under the age of sixteen tell us that they spend money on tobacco every week, but these include one fifteen-year-old girl who spends 5s., and the labourer mentioned above who says his weekly expenditure on cigarettes is 15s.

BETTING AND GAMBLING

Only 5 per cent of the girls and 13 per cent of the boys say that they spend money weekly on betting or gambling, though 12 per cent of the girls and 23 per cent of the boys say they indulge occasionally. Amounts spent range from a penny to ten shillings a week, the average, among those who do bet, being about eighteenpence. The number of young people who indulge in these activities is shown in Table XXI. Half the girls who say they bet on horses, dogs and cards add 'occasionally'.*

TABLE XXI

BETTING AND GAMBLING

| | Number filling up Football coupons | | Number Betting on | | |
	Regularly	Occasionally	Horses	Dogs	Cards
167 Attached Girls	1	15	11	1	12
337 Unattached Girls ...	10	38	44	8	41
280 Attached Boys	21	34	20	5	41
220 Unattached Boys	17	27	20	5	36

DRINKING

Twenty boys and eight girls say they go to the public house once a week or more, and fifty-two boys and sixty-seven girls say they go occasionally. The number of boys and girls who mention a visit to a public house in their account of the previous week's activities is extremely small. Only nine girls—and these all unattached—say that they spend money weekly on drink. Among these are a girl of sixteen and one of seventeen who each spend 5s. Another girl says 'my boy friend pays'. Of boys aged eighteen and nineteen, 16 per cent spend money on drink every week, their average expenditure being 5s. 9d. A fifteen-year-old butcher's boy says he goes to a public house more than once a week, where he drinks beer and cider, while an eighteen-year-old student answers: 'nothing for months on end and then as much as a pound in a night'. One nineteen-year-old sailor spends 30s. a week on drink, and another sailor of the same age says that his weekly expenditure is 40s.

*As we go to press we learn from various sources of an increase in the promotion of football sweepstakes in offices and factories. We also hear of several clubs in which such sweepstakes take place regularly, the club leaders themselves participating.

TWENTY QUESTIONS

1—(a) Age 16½   (b) Sex MALE

2—Occupation LABORATORY ASSISTANT

3—(a) How old were you when you left school ? 15½
   (b) Would you have preferred to stay on at school beyond this age ?

4—How many jobs have you had since you left school ? 1

5—(a) Do you enjoy your present job ? YES
   (b) Were any unpleasant tricks played on you when you first started work ? NO
   (c) Do you think your job is a blind alley ? NO
   (d) Do you wish to change your present job ? NO
   (e) What job in life do you aim to do ?

6—How long does it take you to travel from home to work ? 1 hr

7—Do you live
   (a) with parents ? YES   (c) in lodgings ?
   (b) with relations ? YES   (d) in a hostel ?

8—Do you attend
   (a) Day Continuation School ?   (c) Technical Classes ? YES
   (b) An Evening Institute ? YES

9—What did you do
   (a) Last Saturday morning ? GO TO WORK
   (b) Last Saturday afternoon ? FLY MODEL AIRCRAFT
   (c) Last Saturday evening ? SEE THE REDS SHOES
   (d) Last Sunday morning ? FLY MODEL AIRCRAFT
   (e) Last Sunday afternoon ? " " "
   (f) Last Sunday evening ? PLAY CHESS
   (g) Last Monday evening ? ATTEND NIGHT SCHOOL
   (h) Last Tuesday evening ? PLAY BADMINTON
   (i) Last Wednesday evening ? ATTEND A MODEL AERO CLUB
   (j) Last Thursday evening ? LISTEN TO THE RADIO
   (k) Last Friday evening ? SEE NIGHT TRAIN TO MUNICH

10—Do you belong to any clubs or youth organisations ?
   (a) If so, what ? MODEL AERO CLUB
   (b) When you go, what do you most enjoy doing ? CONVERSING
   (c) If you don't belong to any club or youth organisation, why don't you ?
   (d) If you once belonged to a youth organisation, but left it, why did you leave ? DUE TO A POLITICAL BIAS ON THE PART OF THE CLUB ORGAN.

11—Do you think there should be
   (a) separate clubs for boys ? NO   (c) mixed clubs ? YES
   (b) separate clubs for girls ? NO

12—What do you do—pay board or receive pocket money ? THE LATTER
   (a) How much a week do you have for yourself ? 15/-
   (b) How much do you spend per week on
      (i) Cigarettes ? 5/   (iv) Cinemas ? 3/6
      (ii) Dances ?   (v) Betting or Gambling ?
      (iii) Drinks ?

[See other side

See also pages 36 and 37.

Two further examples of completed questionnaires, showing a higher standard of literacy.

13 (a) What is the title of the last book you read ? THE LIFE OF CASANOVA
   (b) Did you read it
      (i) less than a week ago ?   (iii) less than six months ago ? YES
      (ii) less than a month ago ?   (iv) more than six months ago ?
   (c) Do you borrow books from any library ? YES

14—(a) What Sunday newspapers do you read fairly regularly ? EXPRESS, NEWS OF WORLD
   (b) What newspapers or magazines or comics do you read fairly regularly ?

15—What Radio programme do you listen to fairly regularly ? MUCH BINDING IN THE MARSH

16—Do you fill in Football coupons
   (a) regularly ? NO   (b) occasionally ? NO
   Do you bet in any other way ?
   (a) on horses ?   (c) on cards ?
   (b) on dogs ?

17—(a) What games or sports do you play regularly ? BADMINTON & CHESS
   (b) What games or sports do you watch regularly ?

18—Have you ever been
   (a) Camping in tents ?   (e) To the sea-side ? YES
   (b) To a Holiday Camp ? YES   (f) Abroad ? YES
   (c) To a Youth Hostel ?   (g) To any other kind of holiday ?
   (d) To London ? YES
   To which of these did you go last year ? SEA - SIDE

19—How often do you go (put a tick in the appropriate column)

	More than once a week	Once a week	Once a Month	Occasionally	Never
Dancing					✓
Cinema	✓				
Church					✓
Watch Football in Winter					✓
Horse Races					✓
Greyhound Races					
Public House				✓	
Youth Organisation					✓
Rambling and Hiking					✓
Cycling			✓		
Amusement Arcade					
Cafe and Milk Bars				✓	
Speedway					✓
Theatre			✓		

Any other amusements or entertainment you attend regularly

20—Which of the following do you think the most important
   An interesting job ?   Health ?
   Friends ?   Intelligence ?
   Good looks ?   Money ?

[See other side

TWENTY QUESTIONS

1—(a) Age *18 yrs* (b) Sex *FEMALE*
2—Occupation *BUS CONDUCTORESS.*
3—(a) How old were you when you left school? *14 yrs*
   (b) Would you have preferred to stay on at school beyond this age? *YES.*
4—How many jobs have you had since you left school? *THREE*
5—(a) Do you enjoy your present job? *YES.*
   (b) Were any unpleasant tricks played on you when you first started work? *NO*
   (c) Do you think your job is a blind alley? *NO*
   (d) Do you wish to change your present job? *NO*
   (e) What job in life do you aim to do? *GET MARRIED.*
6—How long does it take you to travel from home to work? *1. HOUR.*
7—Do you live
   (a) with parents? *yes* (c) in lodgings?
   (b) with relations? (d) in a hostel?
8—Do you attend
   (a) Day Continuation School? (c) Technical Classes?
   (b) An Evening Institute?
9—What did you do
   (a) Last Saturday morning? *IN AS. WORKING.*
   (b) Last Saturday afternoon? *STAYED. HOME.*
   (c) Last Saturday evening? *STAYED. HOME.*
   (d) Last Sunday morning? *WENT. FOR. A. BICYCLE. RIDE.*
   (e) Last Sunday afternoon? *WENT. VISITING.*
   (f) Last Sunday evening? *ODEON. PICTURE. HOUSE.*
   (g) Last Monday evening? *STAYED. HOME.*
   (h) Last Tuesday evening? *"   "   SEWING*
   (i) Last Wednesday evening? *ICE. SKATING.*
   (j) Last Thursday evening? *STAYED. HOME. WASHED. HAIR.*
   (k) Last Friday evening? *BABY. WATCHING*
10—Do you belong to any clubs or youth organisations?
   (a) If so, what?
   (b) When you go, what do you most enjoy doing?
   (c) If you don't belong to any club or youth organisation, why don't you? *PREFER. NOT. TO. MIX.*
   (d) If you once belonged to a youth organisation, but left it, why did you leave?
11—Do you think there should be
   (a) separate clubs for boys? *YES* (c) mixed clubs? *YES.*
   (b) separate clubs for girls? *YES.*
12—What do you do—pay board or receive pocket money? *15/o BOARD.*
   (a) How much a week do you have for yourself? *£4*
   (b) How much do you spend per week on
     (i) Cigarettes? (iv) Cinemas?
     (ii) Dances? (v) Betting or Gambling?
     (iii) Drinks?

[See other side]

See also pages 36 and 37.

13—(a) What is the title of the last book you read? *FOREVER. AMBER*
   (b) Did you read it
     (i) less than a week ago? ___ (iii) less than six months ago? *YES*
     (ii) less than a month ago? ___ (iv) more than six months ago? ___
   (c) Do you borrow books from any library? *NO*
14—(a) What Sunday newspapers do you read fairly regularly? *SUNDAY. PICTORIAL. DAILY. MIRROR*
   (b) What newspapers or magazines or comics do you read fairly regularly?
15—What Radio programme do you listen to fairly regularly? *FAMILY. FAVORITES. PLAYS*
16—Do you fill in Football coupons
   (a) regularly? (b) occasionally? *Yes*
   Do you bet in any other way?
   (d) on horses? (c) on cards?
   (b) on dogs?
17—(a) What games or sports do you play regularly? *ICE-SKATING, HORSE. RIDING*
   (b) What games or sports do you watch regularly? *TENNIS*
18—Have you ever been
   (a) Camping in tents? (e) To the sea-side? *YES*
   (b) To a Holiday Camp? (f) Abroad? *FRANCE. HOLLAND*
   (c) To a Youth Hostel? (g) To any other kind of holiday?
   (d) To London? *YES*
   To which of these did you go last year? *D.*
19—How often do you go (put a tick in the appropriate column)

	More than once a week	Once a week	Once a Month	Occasionally	Never
Dancing				Yes	
Cinema		Yes			
Church					NO
Watch Football in Winter					
Horse Races				Yes	
Greyhound Races					NO
Public House					NO
Youth Organisation					NO
Rambling and Hiking	Yes				
Cycling					NO
Amusement Arcade	NO	NO	NO	NO	NO
Cafe and Milk Bars					
Speedway					NO
Theatre		YES			

Any other amusements or entertainment you attend regularly

20—Which of the following do you think the most important
   An interesting job? Health? *YES*
   Friends? Intelligence?
   Good looks? Money?

[See other side]

CHURCH ATTENDANCE

The inquiry produced some interesting information about church attendance. (See Table XXII) Not only were young people asked to tell us how often they attended church, but we were able to compare their answers to this question with the information given us about the way in which the previous Sunday was employed.

It appears that young people either attend church very regularly or not at all. No less than 242 girls and 165 boys state that they attend church 'occasionally' (girls seem to be rather less willing than boys to admit that they attend church 'never'), but only ten of these particular girls (about 4 per cent) and twelve (about 7 per cent) of these boys did in fact attend on the previous Sunday. We conclude, therefore, that 'occasionally' largely refers to such events as weddings and funerals. We conclude that 67 per cent of boys and girls attend church seldom or never. We have evidence that many of them have never attended a church service in their lives. On the other hand, 28 per cent of the girls and 29 per cent of the boys claim to attend church once a week or more, and over 26 per cent of the girls and over 24 per cent of the boys did in fact attend on the previous Sunday. The churches are in effective and regular contact with a quarter of the youth population of the city. There is a considerably higher proportion of attendance among those young people who are attached to youth organizations than among those who are not, although our sample has by no means been weighted on the church side. We were interested to discover that the percentage of attendance among unattached young people did not appear to decrease in the higher age groups.

In view of the fact that considerably less than a quarter of the total adult population is in regular association with the church, it would seem either that the churches are losing young people in their early twenties (rather than in their late teens), or that we may anticipate an increasing influence of the church when those who are now young people become adult. We have attended a number of churches in our city where the evening congregation consisted almost entirely of young people in their teens.

TABLE XXII

CHURCH ATTENDANCE
(expressed in percentages)

	Once a week or more	Went last Sunday	Once a month	Seldom or Never
Unattached girls	23·1	21·9	3·6	73·0
Attached Girls	38·3	36·5	6·6	55·1
Combined Girls	28·1	26·5	4·7	67·0
Unattached Boys	22·7	17·2	2·3	75·0
Attached Boys	33·9	30·7	5·0	61·0
Combined Boys	29·0	24·8	3·8	67·2
Combined Boys and Girls	28·6	25·8	4·2	67·1

RADIO LISTENING

Our inquiries suggest that there is very little group-listening on the part of young people in youth organizations. Very few units even possess a wireless set. On the other hand, there appears to be a considerable amount of home listening by both girls and boys. We asked the question, 'What radio programmes do you listen to fairly regularly?' In reply to this question

| Family Favourites |
| Have A Go |
| Up The Pole |
| Plays |
| Dick Barton |
| Dance Music |
| Saturday Night Theatre |
| Band Parade |
| Stand Easy |
| Much Binding |
| Take It From Here |
| Curtain Up |
| Music Hall |

FIGURE 5

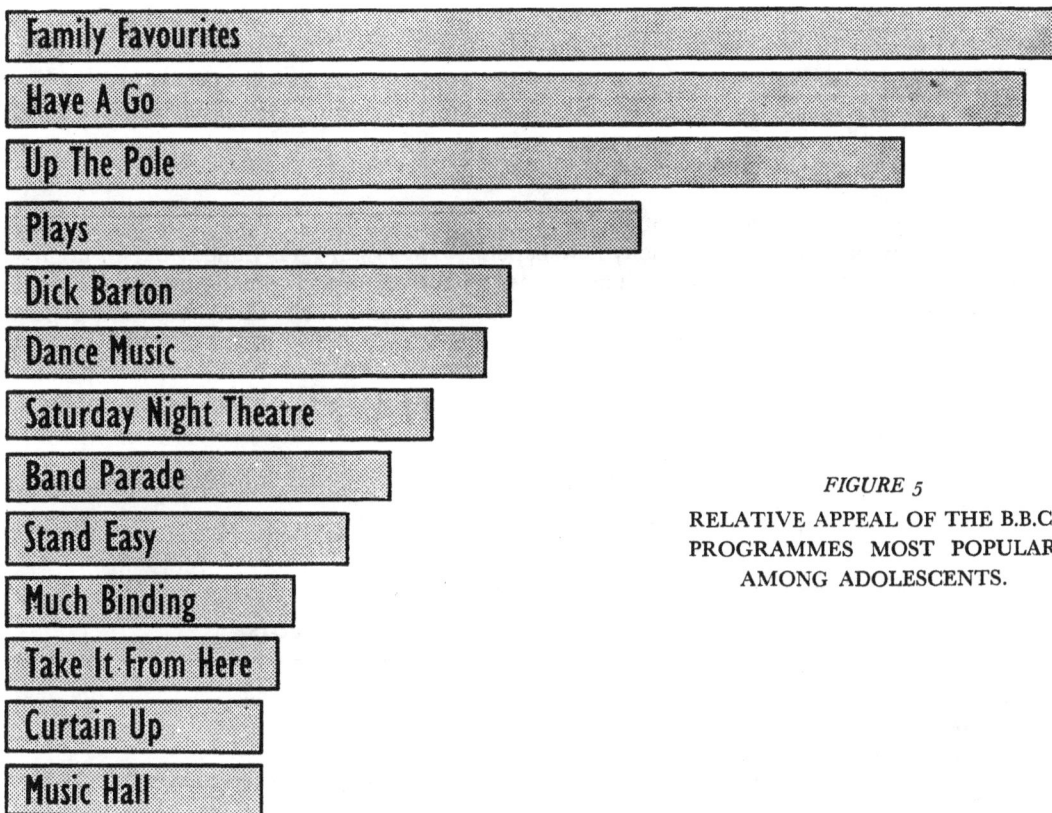

RELATIVE APPEAL OF THE B.B.C.
PROGRAMMES MOST POPULAR
AMONG ADOLESCENTS.

programmes were named by 85 per cent of the boys and 95 per cent of the girls. Of the minority, four said 'we have no wireless' and the remainder either answered 'do not listen' or they left the question without reply. There is more listening by the 'unattached' than by the attached, the non-listeners including 20 per cent of the attached boys and only 8 per cent of the unattached, 8 per cent of the attached girls and 4 per cent of the unattached.

The most popular programme is *Family Favourites*, this being very closely rivalled by *Have*

TABLE XXIII

RADIO LISTENING

167 Attached Girls		337 Unattached Girls		280 Attached Boys		220 Unattached Boys	
Family Favourites ..	32	Family Favourites ..	60	Have a Go ..	25	Up the Pole ..	21
Have a Go ..	26	Have a Go.. ..	51	Up the Pole ..	24	Have a Go ..	17
Up the Pole ..	22	Up the Pole ..	38	Sat. Night Theatre	22	Family Favourites	16
Band Parade ..	9	Plays	38	Plays	19	Take it from Here	14
Sat. Night Theatre	9	Band Parade ..	26	Much Binding ..	18	Dick Barton ..	13
Dick Barton ..	9	Dick Barton ..	20	Dick Barton ..	17	Plays	11
Stand Easy.. ..	8	Donald Peers ..	15	Family Favourites	15	Stand Easy ..	10
Curtain Up ..	8	Sat. Night Theatre	14	Stand Easy ..	15	Jazz Club ..	10

a Go, the third place being taken by *Up the Pole*. In Table XXIII will be found a list of the most popular programmes. Plays are enjoyed by many young people. No less than fifty-two different regular programmes are mentioned by girls and forty-two by boys. Talks scarcely appear at all and the Third Programme and religious services are each mentioned only once. Only two boys and one girl mention the news.

READING

The first comment to be made about the reading habits of young people is that a very large place appears to be taken by the Sunday newspaper. No less than 1,443 Sunday papers are read regularly by our 1,000 young people. The choice of paper is no doubt made by parents rather than by the young people themselves, and as will be seen from Table XXIV the most popular papers are *News of the World, Sunday Pictorial* and *The People*. Very few young people appear not to read a Sunday paper and a few mention as many as five or six. Boys mention 764 papers and girls 679. *The Observer* and the *Sunday Times* muster seventeen readers among the boys and only five among the girls.

TABLE XXIV

SUNDAY NEWSPAPER READING BY YOUNG PEOPLE

GIRLS		BOYS	
News of the World	214	News of the World	195
Sunday Pictorial	171	Sunday Pictorial	166
The People	128	The People	147
Sunday Mercury	53	Sunday Mercury	72
Sunday Dispatch	29	Sunday Express	60
Sunday Express	28	Sunday Dispatch	39
Sunday Graphic	14	Empire News	30
Reynolds News	13	Sunday Graphic	16
Sunday Chronicle	13	Sunday Chronicle	11
Empire News	11	Reynolds News	11
The Observer	3	Sunday Times	9
Sunday Times	2	The Observer	8

Apart from Sunday newspapers, 337 unattached girls mention 96 other different publications, the *Daily Mirror* claiming forty readers and all other daily morning or evening papers together only fifty. Publications like *Woman's Own, Woman*, and *Woman's Weekly* have together a total circulation among these girls of 102. Next on the list come *Dandy* (29), *Beano* (21), *Girls' Crystal* (21), *Picture Post* (12), *Red Star* (11), *Red Letter* (10), and *Film Fun* (10). Several eighteen- and nineteen-year-old girls read nothing at all except *Beano* and *Dandy*. Religious publications are mentioned by three girls, and among periodicals which each receive one mention only are *New Statesman, Children's Newspaper*, and *Punch*. One sixteen-year-old schoolgirl reads twelve weekly publications and an eighteen-year-old nursery nurse mentions nine.

Of the fifty-three periodicals mentioned by 167 attached girls, only twenty-one are named more than twice, the most popular being the *Daily Mirror* (30), *Woman* (23), *Woman's Own* (14), *Dandy* (13) and the *Birmingham Mail* (10).

220 unattached boys read eighty-three different newspapers or periodicals. At the top of the

list is the *Daily Mirror*, mentioned by forty-six boys, various Birmingham papers are read by forty-seven and all other daily newspapers together only total 28. *Dandy, Picture Post, Cycling, Wizard, Hotspur,* and *Champion* are each mentioned by about ten boys. Only two boys read any religious publication. Among periodicals mentioned only once are the *Radio Times* and *Punch*.

Seventy of the 280 attached boys read the *Daily Mirror*, but other newspapers are more frequently mentioned than they are by unattached boys. Local newspapers appear on 61 lists and other morning newspapers on 56, five boys reading *The Times*. Among popular periodicals are *Wizard* (24), *Hotspur* (18), *Rover* (15), *Adventure* (14), and *Champion* (11), but an interesting feature is the occasional mention of such publications as *The Soldier, Sea Cadet, Air Reserves Gazette, The Scout, Scouter, Table Tennis Review, Flight, Boxing Magazine,* and *Amateur Photographer,* and a number of other publications which are concerned with crafts and hobbies. One seventeen-year-old chocolate worker gives the names of no less than fifteen periodicals which, he says, he reads regularly.

We asked the questions: 'What is the title of the last book you read?' and 'Did you read it less than a week ago, less than six months ago, more than six months ago?' The most regular readers appear to be among the unattached girls, forty-five per cent of whom have read a book within the last week, although one in five of the books mentioned by these girls seem to be romances of the paper-covered variety. About a quarter of the boys and about one-fifth of the girls have not read a book during the last six months and many of them write down: 'Don't read', 'Can't remember', 'Have not read a book for ages', 'No time for reading', or 'Not interested in books'. In reading through the titles of the last book read by young people the outstanding fact which becomes apparent is the influence of the cinema on reading habits. The titles which recur again and again are those of books which have been filmed. *Forever Amber* is mentioned by sixteen young people and *No Orchids for Miss Blandish* appears on a number of lists, but other books which receive quite frequent mention are *Rebecca, Gone with the Wind,* and *London Belongs to Me*. Quite a number of young people mention *Great Expectations, Oliver Twist, David Copperfield,* and *Jane Eyre,* and here also the influence of the cinema is apparent. School and adventure stories are more popular among attached than among non-attached young people, more of whom read classical and modern fiction. The explanation of this fact, as we shall see in a later chapter, is that the great majority of those who are attached are to be found in the younger age-groups. Twenty-one boys mention books on technical subjects, and thirty-three mention books about sport—both types of books being almost unrepresented among the girls. In Table XXV will be found an analysis of the information obtained about the length of time since the last book was read and in Table XXVI will be found an attempted classification of the type of book which is mentioned by these young people.

TABLE XXV

ANSWERS TO THE QUESTION 'HOW LONG AGO DID YOU LAST READ A BOOK'

	A week ago	Less than a month ago	Six months ago	More than six months ago	No answer or 'never read books'
	per cent	per cent	per cent	per cent	per cent
200 Attached Boys	38	23	12	5	22
167 Attached Girls	33	31	14	6	16
220 Unattached Boys	39	24	13	5	19
337 Unattached Girls	45	22	13	5	15

TABLE XXVI

BOOKS READ BY YOUNG PEOPLE

	Unattached Boys	Unattached Girls	Attached Boys	Attached Girls
	per cent	per cent	per cent	per cent
Classical Fiction	14	14	9	14
Modern Fiction	15	27	8	19
Adventure and School Stories ...	10	15	20	14
'Thrillers'	14	4	15	11
Paper-covered romances, etc. ...	9	19	6	21
Sport...	7	—	8	—
Technical Subjects	3	—	5	—
Other Non-Fiction	9	6	7	5
'Do not read'	19	15	22	16

TABLE XXVII

HOW YOUNG PEOPLE SPENT THEIR LAST YEAR'S HOLIDAY

Type of Holiday	337 Unattached Girls	167 Attached Girls	220 Unattached Boys	280 Attached Boys
Camping in tents	20	23	27	96
Butlins, etc...	27	16	17	17
Youth Hostelling	10	15	17	25
Seaside	148	65	81	83
Summer School or Conference ...	—	7	—	—
Country	17	15	12	—
Abroad	11	6	11	14
Went to London last year ...	34	18	32	26
Caravan	3	—	—	—
Touring	1	—	—	—
Yachting	—	—	1	—
Climbing	—	—	1	—
Day trips	1	—	—	2
No holiday last year	50	21	36	43
Never had a holiday	8	4	1	3

HOLIDAYS

Our inquiry also furnished information about the type of holiday enjoyed by young people. We invited them to tell us where they went for their holidays last year. Seventy-one girls and seventy-nine boys declared that they had no holiday at all last year. We presume that this means that they did not go away from Birmingham for their holidays. Twelve girls and four boys say that they have never been camping, to a holiday camp, to a youth hostel, to London, to the sea-side or abroad. On the other hand, many of these young people, especially among the boys, had several holidays during the year—one nineteen-year-old 'bus conductor says that he went camping, to the sea-side, to London and abroad. An eighteen-year-old girl factory storekeeper says she went travelling with a fair. The most interesting result of this inquiry, however is that while 34 per cent of the attached boys went camping in tents, the percentage among unattached boys was only 12. Fewer girls go camping in tents, but among them, too, the percentage among those who are attached is more than double that among the unattached. An analysis of the way in which the previous year's holiday was spent by these young people will be found in Table XXVII (see opposite page).

SUMMARY

The general picture presented by this inquiry is depressing. It is even more depressing if it be true that there is a 'bottom 10 per cent' of unattached young people who are not represented among these questionnaires. It has astonished us that the standard of writing and spelling among so many of these young people should be so poor, and that the reading of so many should be limited to 'comics'. It is almost astounding that in the list of radio programmes to which these young people listen there should be only one mention of the Third Programme and only one mention of religious services. Although a quarter of these young people attend church, only ten of them read any kind of religious newspaper or magazine. But then, there is scarcely a 'serious' publication of any kind which can claim more than half a dozen of these young people among its readers. Exceptions to this statement are perhaps provided by *Picture Post*, which is read by sixteen girls and twenty-one boys, and by some of the popular women's weeklies.

The results of this inquiry, however, are not without their encouraging features. There is a remarkable stability of employment among these young people. Only a minority of them indulge in gambling or in drinking. More of them attend church than is commonly supposed, and about 15 per cent of them are attending classes in Evening Institutes. It is not true to say, as some do, that young people 'are never at home', because they do spend several evenings every week, either in their own homes or visiting the homes of their friends. Cinema attendances, also, while very frequent (three times a fortnight) are not as frequent as is sometimes loosely alleged by those who talk about young people 'going to the pictures every night'. The cinema, indeed, has led to a revival of interest in some of the great classical fiction of our language. Some excellent titles are to be found among books read by some of these young people. A nineteen-year-old factory girl mentions *War and Peace*, and a storekeeper of the same age has read *The Seven Pillars of Wisdom*.

The general impression, however, that is left by a perusal of these thousand completed questionnaires is that of the sheer intellectual poverty of these young people. The majority of them have left school and are not taking advantage of any form of part-time education. Two-thirds of them do not wish that they could have remained at school longer than they did.

It is impossible to question the need of a Service of Youth. Our investigation, however, does not on the whole give us much encouragement to believe that the interests of attached young people, as revealed by their reading and listening, are on a much higher cultural level than are those of the unattached. Obviously, it is a *better* Youth Service that is needed.

47

Netball is played indoors on winter evenings.

Billiards, Snooker and Bagatelle on miniature tables.

A BOYS' AND GIRLS' CLUB

Youths and girls meet on separate evenings, but also hold joint activities.

CHAPTER IV

THE PATTERN OF THE LOCAL YOUTH SERVICE

THE PATTERN OF THE YOUTH SERVICE in Birmingham presents a structure which will delight the hearts of those who rejoice in variety and in the spontaneity of voluntary effort, but which will be the despair of those who, in the interests of efficiency or of administrative tidiness, would like to see a uniform 'nationalized' Youth Movement. At the present time large contributions to the welfare of young people are being made both by the Education Committee, and by the Voluntary Organizations (including the Churches). An increasing contribution is being made by Industry. The political parties are officially outside the Youth Service, but their growing interest in youth work cannot be disregarded in any attempt to assess the total educational and recreational provision which is available for young people.

EARLY HISTORY

The beginnings of the history of voluntary effort in Youth Service in Birmingham are probably to be found in a meeting held at 'The Hotel' on 7th July, 1782. On this occasion a Sunday School Association was formed—Birmingham being quick to follow the lead of Robert Raikes, who opened the first Sunday School in Gloucester in 1781—and before the end of that year twelve schools for boys and twelve for girls were opened in different districts in the town. The first annual report records that a total of 14,000 scholars were then under instruction. Of £429 subscribed, £248 had been spent on the 'salaries of masters and mistresses' and £76 on 'books and stationery'. As it was a rule that all children should attend church on Sundays, the Dissenters soon began to establish their own schools. In 1787 the Unitarians opened a school where no sectarian doctrines were taught and a more general education was offered. In the same year a school was opened in connexion with the Congregational Chapel in Carr's Lane. The Baptists at Cannon Street and the Methodists at Cherry Street established their first Sunday Schools in 1795. These schools grew very rapidly, and some of them were attended by over a thousand children.* In 1838 the Birmingham Statistical Society for the Improvement of Education estimated that of an approximate population of 45,000 children between the ages of five and fifteen, 21,824, or 48·5 per cent, were receiving instruction in Day or Sunday Schools, and 23,176, or 51·5 per cent, were receiving no instruction at all. The average period of attendance at a Day School was 3·3 years, and at a Sunday School, 3·7 years. Of school conditions, the Report has this to say about the common Day Schools, which were, admittedly, the schools in which overcrowding was the worst:

> Ventilation is very little attended to in these schools: and in some cleanliness is equally neglected. There is generally a much greater number of children crowded together than in Dame Schools: and the effluvia rising from the dress of the scholars mingled with the close air, exhausted of its oxygen and unfit for the purpose of comfortable or healthy respiration renders any long continuance in the school intolerable to a person not accustomed to it.†

A large effort of imagination is required to recall the intolerable conditions in which boys and girls in our city grew up only a century ago. The following quotation is taken from a letter from Rev. Thomas Nunns, M.A. (perpetual curate of Saint Bartholomew's Chapel), written in 1842 to the Rt. Hon. Lord Ashley:

* *A Century of Birmingham Life,* J. A. Langford.
† Journal of the Statistical Society of London, April, 1840.

The first, worst and most glaring evil, and the source of innumerable other evils under which the working classes here labour, and which tends to depress their condition and degrade their character, perhaps most, I conceive, is—*The early age at which children, both boys and girls, are admitted to work in manufactories* . . . . children can find employment in very many manufactories at the early age of seven, and still more at that of eight. At that tender age, then, they enter upon the business of life. Their education is completed. They begin to provide for themselves. What knowledge they afterwards pick up is necessarily very small.

A further evil consequent on the employment of children in factories was 'the utter ignorance of females arrived at womanhood, in all the departments of domestic economy'. The writer went on to say that at seven years of age a boy was paid a shilling a week and a girl sixpence, and that these amounts rose to 3s. 6d. for a boy and 2s. 5d. for a girl at the age of twelve.

An extract from a Report of the Birmingham Society for the Protection of Young Females and the Suppression of Juvenile Prostitution, published in 1840,* reads as follows:

The Provisional Committee find from statistics that have been laid before them, that in the town and neighbourhood of Birmingham there are upwards of 700 infamous houses, in each of which from 1 to 12 young females are kept for licentious purposes, and in many of which juvenile and even infantine prostitution is carried on. They find also that in addition to these there are numerous houses of assignation where boys and girls from eight to fourteen years of age are encouraged to spend the whole night together, the boys being thus trained to a course of immorality and crime, the girls to degradation and ruin.

About the middle of the century provision was being made for the first time to meet some of the needs of young people on weekdays as well as on Sundays, and some voluntary organizations in the city can look back upon a very considerable history. The Birmingham Y.M.C.A., which has recently celebrated its centenary, was formed in October, 1849, and from the very commencement was interested in the welfare of lads. Special attention was given to those parading the streets, to the newsboys and the telegraph boys. Rooms were opened on Sunday evenings to provide a place of meeting. Classes were held in French, English, Arithmetic, 'Phonography' and Art. All sorts of activities were promoted for the young people of the town, one of the most outstanding being the annual Assault-at-Arms in the Town Hall. This was preceded in the very early days by a series of lectures, which were also given in the Town Hall. These lectures were being arranged during the first year of the Association's existence. In 1903 the Association moved to its present commodious premises in Dale End, where a special part of the building was reserved as a Youths' branch.

One of the first organizations to address itself to the needs of girls appears to have been the Y.W.C.A., which commenced its work in 1868 in one of the side streets of Birmingham. At first its provisions were limited to Bible classes, but it was not long before it branched out into other activities, such as the provision of classes in cookery. From the original centre there sprang fifteen branches, some of which today are among the best youth clubs in the city.

One of the earliest boys' clubs was the Rugby School Boys' Club, founded in 1859 in the earliest days of the Club movement. Its establishment was due to the interest of a number of Old Rugbeians whose first premises were in Moseley Road, Balsall Heath. The present building in Elkington Street was opened by Dr. Gore while he was Bishop of Birmingham, and it was for many years the only building in the city which had been specially built for club purposes. The history of the Bromsgrove School Boys' Club goes back to 1895 when masters and boys of the school initiated work in Aston. Both these clubs eventually became branches of the Birmingham Boys' and Girls' Union—first known as the Birmingham Street Boys' Union—the object of which was defined in 1913 as being to deal with 'the problem of the boys and girls who spend their childhood upon the streets subject to influences of a degrading character. It is estimated that there are about 15,000 such children in the city and that it is from their ranks that the loafers, hooligans, criminals and unemployables are mainly recruited'. The Birmingham Boys' and Girls' Union today is an Association of eight clubs with splendid central headquarters at Kyrle Hall, Sheep Street, in one of the poorest parts of the city, and while perhaps the aims would not

* Birmingham Central Library, Reference 520458.

be defined today in the phraseology of 1913, the traditions of the past would appear to be well maintained. This Union has been the medium through which the Midland Public Schools have organized their Mission Clubs. Before the second world war there were Bromsgrove, Old Edwardians, Rugby, Summerfields, Trent and Wrekin. Of these, Summerfields Club at Kyrle Hall is the only one which has an unbroken history since 1909. Bromsgrove and Rugby have been re-opened since the war and it is hoped that King Edward's School, Trent College and Wrekin College will soon re-establish their Mission Clubs which were such virile branches of the Union.

The Boys' Brigade, which was founded by Sir William Smith of Glasgow in 1883, is the parent of all uniformed voluntary organizations, and the first company to be formed in Birmingham was established in 1890 in connexion with the Camp Hill Presbyterian Church Sunday School. As the other uniformed organizations came into being, most of them speedily established units in Birmingham.

The Birmingham Association of Girls' and Mixed Clubs has recently celebrated its jubilee, and, in view of the frequent assertion that youth work began as an ambulance service or as a rescue agency, it is interesting to recall that it was laid down in 1898 that 'the purpose of the Union shall be to promote and encourage the mental, moral and spiritual welfare of girls in the area'. The Birmingham Federation of Boys' Clubs came into being in 1928 to co-ordinate the activities of all boys' clubs in the city. A full-time secretary was appointed two years later.

The continuing vitality of voluntary effort and its capacity for experiment is illustrated by the most interesting growth of the Stonehouse Gang Group of clubs, the direct result of a newspaper reporter's experiences in the city's Juvenile Court. One of the factors in juvenile delinquency, he came to believe, was the fascination which the gang idea has for boys between the ages of twelve and sixteen, and he set out to divert this fascination into channels of Christian citizenship. The Stonehouse Gang Group began in December, 1938, with only two boys. It experimented carefully for two years before admitting more than ten lads into membership, but after that its popularity increased steadily and there are now five units in Birmingham and the total membership approaches the thousand mark. In technique it has similarities with several other youth movements. In much of its activity it functions as a boys' club; in its emphasis on 'good turns' and its crew system (organized in a similar way to patrols) it has copied the Scouts; in its Christian emphasis it has much in common with the Boys' Brigade—but to these things it has added distinctive features of its own—disciplinary courts with boy magistrates, 'full gang assemblies', at which all the officers and crew leaders have to give regular accounts of their stewardship to the full membership and face questions and criticism, and a particular emphasis on adventure in its wider activities.

STATUTORY PROVISION

The history of Statutory provision in Birmingham goes back to the School Care Committees which were set up as a result of the Education (Choice of Employment) Act of 1910 in an endeavour to improve the social conditions and the industrial opportunities of Elementary School boys and girls. 'The Education Committee joined hands with the Employment Exchange so that the two problems could be tackled together: even then it was realized that finding a boy employment could not be divorced from caring for his leisure time and providing him with proper social and recreative activities.'*

In 1924 the Education Committee took over entire responsibility for Juvenile Employment, including vocational guidance, placement in industry, and Unemployment Insurance administration, as well as the after-care work associated with it. The whole of the city was covered by a network of After-Care Committees, and every boy and every girl leaving school was given individual advice in the choice of a career and information as to what the voluntary organizations could do for them in their spare time. Parallel with this activity, the Juvenile Organizations Committee (which had been established in 1918) was co-ordinating the work of the various

* *Report of the City's Education Committee on its work for Youth*, presented to the City Council, Oct., 1944.

voluntary bodies. In 1927 the then full-time secretary of this Committee became a member of the Chief Education Officer's staff, and the J.O.C. became a sub-committee of the Juvenile Employment and Welfare Committee. Twelve years later, with the outbreak of war in 1939 and the publication of Circular 1486, the J.O.C. was extended and its functions greatly increased, and it was re-named the Youth Committee.

THE PRESENT STRUCTURE

(A) *The Birmingham Youth Committee.* There are two outstanding features of the present pattern of the Youth Service in Birmingham. In the first place the Local Authority has fully accepted the principle of partnership with the Voluntary Organizations. In the second place, the education, the employment and the leisure of young people are treated as one problem. The Youth Committee, as we have seen, is a Sub-Committee of the Youth Employment and Welfare Committee, which is itself a Sub-Committee of the Education Committee.

FIGURE 6

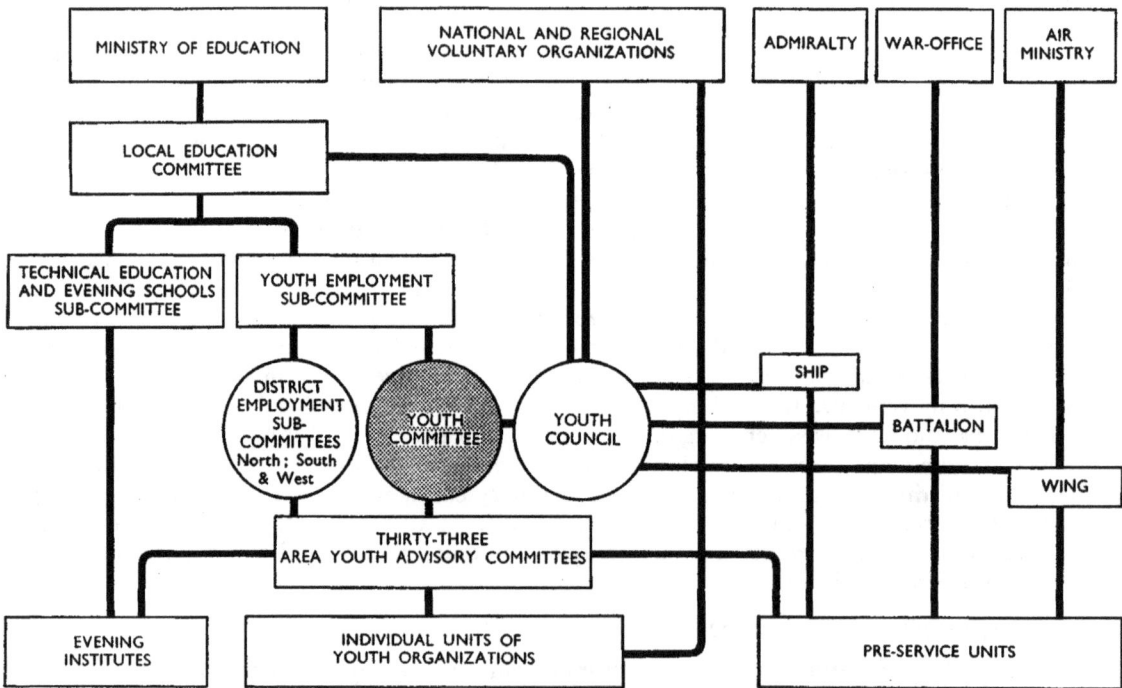

THE STRUCTURE OF THE BIRMINGHAM YOUTH SERVICE

This identification of the Youth Service with the Youth Employment Service seems to be very unusual, and we are not aware of any other Authority in the country where the Youth Committee stands in a similar relation to the Youth Employment Committee, though we have heard of one Midland town where the posts of Youth Employment Officer and Youth Officer are combined.* Even in those areas where the Local Education Authority has exercised its powers to maintain Youth Employment Bureaux, there is usually but slight contact between the Youth Employment Department and the Youth Committee. In any event before the passing of the Employment and Training Act of 1948, only 104 out of 315 Local Education Authorities had exercised these powers. As a result of this recent Act, there has been set up a Youth Employment Service, the purpose of which is to help every boy and girl passing from school life into the

* As we go to press with this Report we learn that one large County Authority is about to combine the Youth Employment and the Youth Services.

world of work. There is a Central Youth Employment Executive, responsible to the Ministry of Labour and National Service. The Service can be operated locally either by the Education Authority or by the Ministry of Labour and National Service. In Birmingham the Service is of course provided by the Education Authority, which is grant-aided by the Ministry of Labour and National Service.

The unique feature of the administrative pattern in Birmingham is the subordination of the Youth Service to the Youth Employment Service. It is contended by some that Youth Service suffers when its administration is in the hands of those whose main interest is in the employment, rather than in the leisure, of young people, and that for this reason less direction and inspiration has been given by the Authority to the development of the Youth Service in Birmingham than in some other cities. However this may be, it does appear to us that there is nearly everything to be said for the closest collaboration, at every administrative level, among those who are concerned with the working conditions and with the leisure of young people.

For administrative purposes, the city is divided into thirty-three areas, in each of which there is a Local Youth Advisory Committee concerned both with the employment and with the leisure of young people. These Committees are served by fourteen assistant organizers who give vocational guidance to young people and who co-ordinate recreational activities for young people in their own areas. The membership of these Committees includes representatives of schools, Evening Institutes and Voluntary Organizations in the area, together with ministers, clergy, social workers and representatives of local industries. The duties with which these committees are charged include the compilation of information about youth organizations in the district, the maintenance of contact with school-leavers, after-care work and the promotion of special events. The Committee also provides a means whereby the attention of the Youth Committee itself may be drawn to any local need such as the provision of playing-field facilities for youth organizations in the area. It must be confessed that a scheme which seems admirable on paper does not always work out successfully in practice, and in some parts of the city there has been some dissatisfaction with these Area Committees. It would appear that in some cases their work is hindered by the uncooperative attitude of many leaders of youth organizations. We return to a discussion of this problem later in our Report.

TABLE XXVIII

CONSTITUTION OF THE YOUTH COMMITTEE

Organization	Number of Representatives
Education Committee	6
Voluntary Organizations	6
Social and Education Organizations ..	2
Sports and Services	2
Religious Bodies	3
Industry	2
Teachers	2
Other Interested persons	1
Total	24

53

There appears to be closer co-operation between the Authority and the Voluntary Organizations at higher administrative levels. A diagrammatic representation of the pattern of administration will be found in Fig. 6. There is a large Youth Council, the membership of which is composed of representatives of the Education Committee, the Voluntary Organizations, the Churches, and Industry. This Council, which meets once a year, elects representatives to the Youth Committee, the membership of which is distributed as shown in Table XXVIII.

The Youth Committee normally meets monthly and appoints one sub-committee to deal with applications for grant-aid and another to plan future policy.

(B) *The Education Committee and Voluntary Organizations.* Of Birmingham's total population of 1,076,230,* the number of those who are between fourteen and twenty years of age was 81,976. An increasing number of these are coming under the direct responsibility of the Education Committee. 16,762 are engaged in full-time education, while 21,626 are taking advantage of various forms of part-time education, this latter number being made up as follows:

TABLE XXIX

YOUNG PEOPLE ENGAGED IN PART-TIME EDUCATION

Institution		No. Attending
Day Continuation Schools		3,016
Technical, Commercial or Art Courses		5,399
Evening Institutes, under 17	5,212	
,, ,, 17-20	3,662	
	———	8,874
L.E.A. Classes in Clubs		4,337
Total		21,626

With the eventual raising of the school-leaving age to sixteen and with the opening of the County Colleges the above figures will increase until they eventually include every boy and every girl under the age of eighteen. The new problems which this situation will create for the Voluntary Youth Organizations are discussed in a later chapter.

The Birmingham Education Committee has been most careful not to put difficulties in the way of the Voluntary Youth Organizations, but rather to assist them in every possible way. In 1944 it outlined the principles by which it was guided in the following terms:

In the past the voluntary bodies have played a great and important part in making provision for the needs of youth, and the Education Committee have been most anxious that any increase in their own youth work shall not be at the expense of voluntary effort, but shall break new ground. The devotion, thought and time given by voluntary agencies to the provision of youth facilities has been unsparing, and it is hoped will go forward with even greater enthusiasm and keenness. As the demands of youth work have grown, so the voluntary bodies have required more assistance, and the Committee have been anxious to find ways in which help could be given without unduly increasing the control of the Local Authority.

The policy here laid down appears to us to have been faithfully implemented, and there is,

* See note to Table III, page 15.

in the main, a happy relationship between the two main partners in the Youth Service. In connexion with a few schools there are Old Scholars' Clubs, and there is a growing tendency for Evening Institutes to set aside one evening for recreative activities, but nowhere does the Authority appear to have initiated work which could be regarded as competing with that of voluntary bodies. In 1948 Grouped Courses in Evening Institutes were reduced from three to two evenings a week because it was felt that 'insistence upon three nights' attendance per week is too much to ask young people who work full-time in industry and does not allow them opportunity to develop other interests in home, Club, Church, etc.' From time to time the Chief Education Officer circularizes the leaders of voluntary organizations asking them to avoid fixing major club meetings on evenings on which grouped course subjects are taken in Evening Institutes.

In view of the suggestion made by Mr. L. J. Barnes* that the provision of a routine Youth Service should increasingly become a statutory responsibility, and that the voluntary organizations should concentrate on 'experimentation, the trying-out of new methods, the opening-up of new fields', and work of a 'piloting or pioneering' nature, it is interesting to notice that in our city the L.E.A. has shared also in experimental work. The voluntary organizations tend on the whole to follow a rather stereotyped method and programme. The organizer of one movement said to us: 'You need visit only one of our units, because when you have seen one you have seen them all'. Nevertheless, some of the work which has been directly initiated by the Birmingham Education Committee has been experimental to a degree. Few things that we have seen have interested us more than the successful attempt of the Authority to make contact with 'unattached' young people (described below and in Chapter VIII), and the work that is carried on in the centre known as 'Conway'.

'Conway' represents an effort on the part of the Authority to strengthen the hands of the leaders of youth organizations in the Sparkbrook area by enabling them to offer to their members a larger programme than their own resources would permit. One of the most striking features of the Youth Service in Birmingham is the comparatively small membership of the individual unit. There appears to be a gross total—not allowing for those who belong to more than one organization—of 42,970 young people distributed among 1,384 units or an average membership per unit of only thirty-one.† It may be that a comparatively small unit, so long as it is not too small, can give something to its members which a larger Youth Centre cannot provide, but a small unit meeting perhaps one evening a week and in restricted premises must necessarily be able to offer its members only a limited programme. At 'Conway' a large range of activities is offered to *bona fide* members of all youth organizations in the vicinity, these members being able to attend 'Conway' only on those evenings when their own unit is not meeting. Membership cards must be renewed each month by the Club leader, the purpose of this requirement being to prevent a member leaving his own Club and continuing to attend 'Conway'. (see Fig. 7, 'Conway' Membership card). If a boy changes his club, his 'Conway' membership lapses for one month. Altogether there is a total membership of 172 boys and 111 girls who represent some forty local units. There is an average nightly attendance of about seventy. Each evening's programme includes two organized activities (every member must attend at least one 'activity' either at his own club or at 'Conway') and a 'surprise item', in addition to provision for recreational pursuits. On the occasion of our own visit, a cookery class and a German language class were taking place. The Centre is staffed entirely by L.E.A. Instructors, there being no voluntary helpers. A supply of camp equipment and a library of gramophone records is being accumulated for loan to other organizations associated with the Centre. This is a most effective way in which an Authority can assist the Voluntary Organizations, where so often there are no facilities available for the provision of such activities as Drama, Physical Training, or Cookery, and it is to be regretted that in some instances the value of this service has not always been appreciated by the leaders of the voluntary organizations concerned.

* *The Outlook for Youth Work*, Chaps. 1 & 2.

† *See further, next chapter.*

FIGURE 7

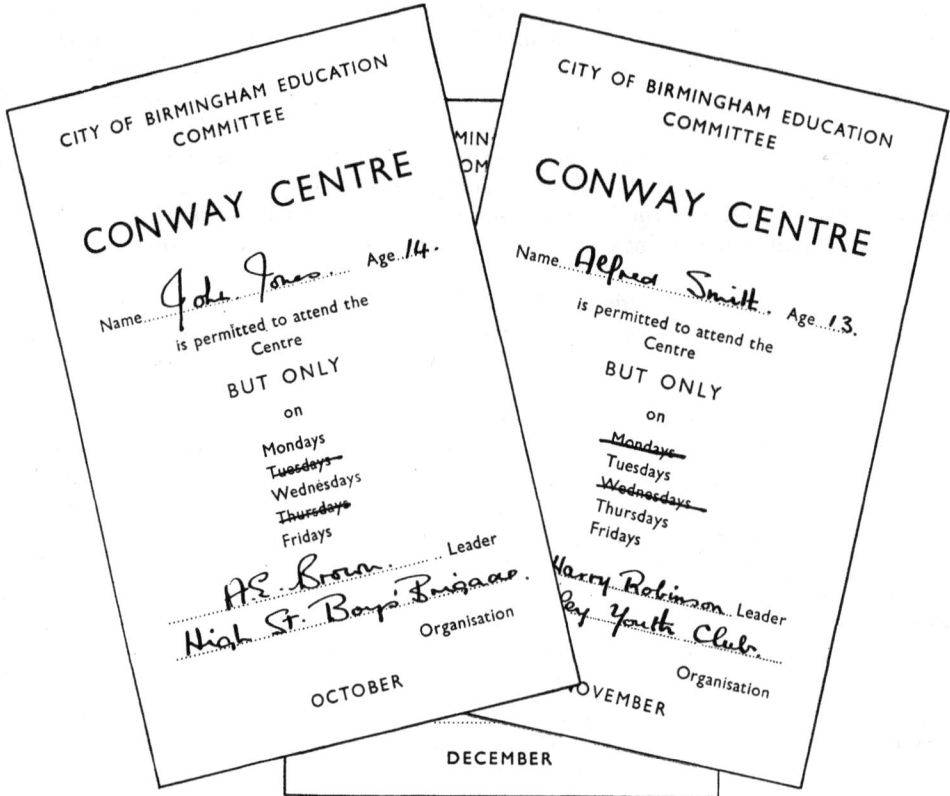

EXAMPLES OF 'CONWAY' CENTRE MEMBERSHIP CARDS

ASSISTANCE TO VOLUNTARY BODIES

The assistance which the Education Committee offers to the Voluntary Organizations may be summarized as follows:

(a) *Grants*

During the financial year 1947-48 grants totalling £2,810* were made to thirty-eight units of youth organizations towards the cost of equipment, rent of premises, or salaries of leaders. In addition, grants were offered towards the cost of three training courses arranged by voluntary bodies. Grants for capital expenditure are made direct from the Ministry on the recommendation of the Local Education Committee, and during the year in question three grants totalling £900 were recommended in this way.

(b) *Use of School Premises, Playgrounds and Playing-fields*

Youth organizations are offered the use of school premises for their activities, the only charge being half of the caretaker's fee. 159 schools are used in this way by 535 units of youth organizations. Some of these units are children's rather than youth organizations and in some cases the playground alone is used; but it may be said that one quarter of the youth organizations in the city meet on school premises. The Education Committee is very catholic in its hospitality, and organizations which meet on school premises include Clubs, pre-Service units and uniformed organizations of all kinds, and such varied groups as Bands of Hope, Table Tennis Clubs, Mutual Improvement Associations, Model Aeroplane Clubs, Latter Day Saints, Good Templars, Campaigners and Boxing Clubs. In only a few cases is it possible to allow youth organizations the use of school playing-fields. It is estimated that the cost to the Education Department of

---

* If this amount is compared with grants made by the Authority in other cities of comparable size, it is very small. It is to be remembered, however, the cost of services rendered to Youth Units in other ways is considerable.

granting the free use of schoolroom accommodation to youth organizations, including Play Centres, amounted to approximately £35,000 for the year 1948-9.

(c) *Instructors*

Youth organizations are offered the services of qualified instructors in a wide variety of subjects, which include Physical Training, Drama, Handicrafts, Discussion Groups, and Ballroom Dancing. During the winter session 1947-48, 263 classes were supplied with instructors through the Technical Education and Evening Schools Sub-Committee. The total number of enrolments during that period was 4,337 and the number of student-hours 129,418.

(d) *Assistant Leaders*

Twenty-four men and women, who constitute a panel of paid assistant club leaders, are working in clubs in order to meet the shortage of adult personnel, and their fees are paid by the Education Committee. It has been decided, however, not to add to the present panel of these paid assistant leaders. In November, 1947, Alderman A. F. Bradbeer, the then Lord Mayor, made an appeal in the Press for additional helpers in voluntary youth work. Thirty-five replies were received in response to this appeal, and of this number twenty-six attended for an interview with members of the Youth Committee. Finally, twenty-nine were put in touch with youth organizations in which they showed interest, most of them expressing a desire to help in club work rather than in connexion with any of the uniformed organizations. In order to give them an outline of what might be required of them a short training course of one night a week for six weeks was held at the Education Office.

(e) *Equipment and Food Permits*

Where permits or coupons are required for the purchase of sports equipment, band instruments or sports clothing (this last is no longer necessary) assistance is offered by the Youth Committee. Applications for food licences for club canteens have been approved in respect of 570 youth units.

(f) *Orchestral Concerts*

For several years in succession special concerts for young people have been sponsored by the L.E.A. and given in the Town Hall by the City of Birmingham Orchestra. These concerts are for young people between 15 and 20 years of age, and there is normally an attendance of 1,500. In addition, three concerts are given every year at the headquarters of various youth organizations themselves. Under the title 'Platform for Youth', a series of six recitals by young people for young people were given in the early months of 1949. There was no charge for admission, but programmes were on sale each evening at 6d. each. The recitals were intended for young people between 14 and 20 years of age, and, while there was little demand for tickets from youth organizations, there was a heavy demand from Grammar and Secondary Modern Schools. Tickets were issued on the understanding that the holder would attend the whole series of concerts or would return the ticket for use by another person. The concerts were excellent, and many of the youthful artists reached a very high standard.

(g) *Sports and Games*

The Youth Committee promotes Football, Cricket, and Netball Leagues. 100 teams took part in Football Leagues, 32 in Cricket Leagues, and there were 16 teams in the Girls' Netball League.

(h) *The Approach to the 'Unattached'*

An interesting attempt on the part of the Authority to make provision for the 'unattached' is described in Chapter VIII. The Education Committee has also co-operated with the Catering and Entertainments Committee by providing supervisors for a number of Civic Restaurants which have been thrown open to young people in the evenings.

(j) *Handbook for Youth Leaders*

In 1945 the Birmingham Education Committee published an excellent *Handbook for Youth Leaders* which was described in a Ministry of Education publication, *Further Education*, as 'an admirable example of its kind'.

THE VOICE OF YOUTH

One criticism we wish to offer of the pattern of Youth Service administration in our city is that little appears to be provided for the voice of youth to be heard or for the exercise of any effective leadership on the part of young people themselves outside the limits of their own particular organization.

One exception is in the Kingstanding area where a Youth Parliament was set up in 1941. The chairman and secretary of the Local Advisory Committee act as adult advisers to this

Parliament. Any requests or suggestions which the Youth Parliament wishes to make to the Youth Committee must go through the Local Youth Advisory Committee. The Youth Parliament has interviewed and arranged socials for school-leavers, organized week-end conferences and short courses on leadership, and has carried through an annual rally for the young people of the area. Inter-club activities have also been arranged. The young people themselves seem very keen, but their leaders are not always sufficiently alive to the value of this kind of inter-club co-operation. The success of such a venture, of course, is largely dependent upon the goodwill of the leaders.

The fact that Birmingham can only show one experiment of this kind is all the more surprising when we recall that the Youth Councils or Youth Parliaments which have come into being in many parts of the country are generally regarded as being one of the most valuable features of the Youth Service.* Some of these developments are of particular interest. In Wolverhampton, for instance, there is a Council of Youth which is composed of elected members—all of whom must be under twenty-one—of all local youth organizations. This Council provides a Forum in which young people may have an opportunity of discussing all matters relating to the Youth Service. It has promoted conferences, training courses and 'youth weeks': it staffed a Safety Exhibition at the Civic Hall, and one of its chief responsibilities is the publication, six times a year, of *Wolverhampton Youth* which is written by youth for youth. The Council is represented on the Borough Youth Advisory Committee.

In 1942 the young people of Luton established their own Youth Council, which is represented on the Youth Committee itself by two Youth Councillors who have full voting powers. The most successful achievement of the Luton Youth Council was a Survey, in 1947, of all the leisure-time facilities available for young people in the town—a Survey the results of which were published in a report issued with an attractive cover designed by an eighteen-year-old girl. The results of an even more ambitious Survey of Youth opinion carried out by the Tynemouth Youth Council were published in a report which also appeared in 1947.

Youth Councils of this kind not only provide an almost essential link between youth and maturity, but they can give a real introduction to civic administration and a training in self-government, while they have the added advantage that they can bring together young people from many types of organization in discussion and in action. Any such association in which young people of varied backgrounds can co-operate is surely of the highest value, though the suggestion will not be welcomed by possessive leaders of highly introverted units.

It may well be, of course, that the creation of a Youth Council in a city as large as Birmingham, and with some 1,400 youth units, presents problems which would not arise in a smaller place. We wonder, however, whether the work of the Local Youth Advisory Committees might not be better done if some at least of their responsibilities could be handed over to young people themselves. To a further discussion of this problem and of the whole question of the larger part which youth might play in service to the community we return in the final chapters of this Report.

Mention should perhaps be made at this point of the Birmingham Youth Forum, a group which, though without any official recognition, does provide a common ground on which trade unionists, Young Communists, University undergraduates and members of church organizations are able to meet for joint discussion. This Forum, which has been in existence for some ten years, has about two hundred members, with an average attendance, at a monthly meeting, of about half that number. Members must be under thirty, but the average age is probably no more than twenty. The Forum is open both to individual members and to young people nominated by any youth organization in the city. There is an adult chairman (who incidentally, was partly responsible for the creation of the Kingstanding Youth Parliament) who reports that the success of the Forum may be largely due to the fact that it has, in the main, confined its activities to the provision of a platform on which young people may learn both to articulate their own opinions and to be tolerant towards the views of others.

* *Service of Youth Today*, P.E.P., April, 1948.

THE CONTRIBUTION OF INDUSTRY

Birmingham is, in the main, a city of small firms and there appear to be few industrial undertakings which promote their own Youth Clubs. Only one firm provides premises specially designed for club use and employs full-time professional club leaders. There are a few other firms, however, with Youth Clubs, and in some instances welfare officers or personnel managers give a proportion of their time to club leadership. Pre-Service units are associated with a number of the larger undertakings, and other firms which have no pre-Service unit of their own allow their employees an extra week's holiday if they are members of such a unit, to enable them to attend camp. There are a great many firms in connexion with which there are football and cricket or other sports or social clubs providing recreational facilities for all employees, regardless of age. We have not regarded such clubs as falling within the scope of our Survey, although they do cater for large numbers of young people. A few of the larger undertakings own their own sports grounds.

Birmingham is geographically divided between two Co-operative Societies, each of which promotes an extensive programme of social and educational activity among children and young people, this work coming under the direction of an Education Committee with a full-time Education Secretary. A feature of the Co-operative Youth Clubs is that they are staffed by paid part-time leaders. Most of these clubs are grant-aided by the L.E.A. to the extent of half the salaries of these part-time leaders, and they are otherwise financed by grants from the Co-operative Education Committees. One of these Committees, for instance, has an annual income of about £9,000, of which about 25 per cent is spent on Children's and Youth work.

Some industrial undertakings also make a direct or indirect contribution to further education of a more formal character. In our city, 5,399 young people under the age of twenty are released by their employers to attend Technical, Commercial or Art courses, the actual figures being:

TABLE XXX

YOUNG PEOPLE RELEASED FROM INDUSTRY FOR EDUCATIONAL PURPOSES

	Boys	Girls
Commercial Classes	48	124
Technical Classes	4,567	153
Art Classes	487	20
TOTAL ..	5,102	297

In addition, 3,016 young people are released by their employers to attend Day Continuation Classes. The Bournville Day Continuation College which is attended by nearly 2,000 students drawn from 57 firms and other undertakings, is very widely known. The attendance at Day Continuation Classes and Technical Colleges made possible for young people by some of Birmingham's most progressive undertakings often serves as an introduction to further training promoted by the firms themselves. Some industrial and business houses have their own training schemes through which young people with ability may qualify for skilled jobs and rise to positions of responsibility. In certain instances it is the policy, as far as possible, to fill all technical, supervisory and managerial positions from the ranks. There are instances where progressive small firms work together in groups for the promotion of training schemes. The aim of one such

SEASIDE CAMP: *One Birmingham industrial concern has held an annual camp for its factory and office youths since 1901.*

PLAY PRODUCTION: *Boys' and girls' clubs catering for factory and office workers co-operate in a joint activity.*

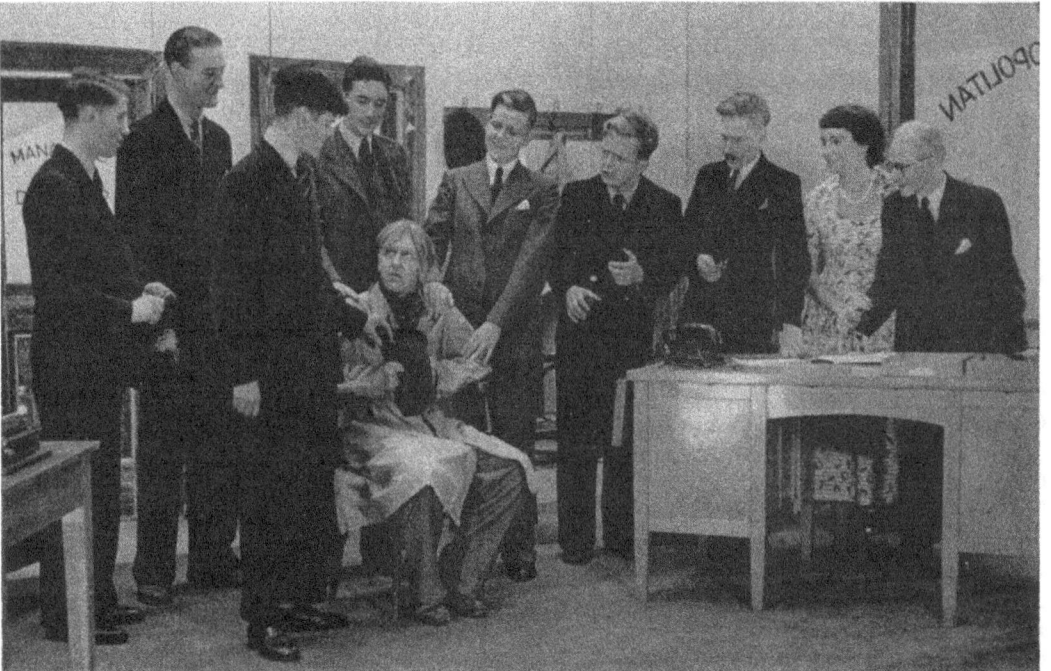

group is that 'every youth in our employ shall be given encouragement and opportunity to develop to the limit of his ability'.

Training varies from brief initiation schemes for new employees of from one day to two weeks' duration to a variety of apprenticeship schemes. Owing to the large number of engineering companies in the area there are many engineer apprentices. Training for these boys usually leads to National Certificates and sometimes to University degrees. Some firms cover the whole expense of training and offer scholarships which are tenable at a University. One undertaking owns its own hostel for young apprentices who come from all over the world.

There are more training schemes for boys than for girls owing to the fact that the short working life of the girl makes an expensive training an uneconomic proposition. One large factory we visited, however, had a shorthand and typing school—largely attended by girls—in charge of a full-time instructor, and a large retail store has a two-year training course for both boy and girl employees.

One of Birmingham's largest firms has its own education department with a full-time education officer. This department makes possible many opportunities of further education for boy and girl employees. Not only do all the boys and girls employed by this firm attend a Day Continuation College until they reach the age of eighteen at least, but for those employees with ability there is a variety of training schemes and the provision of special scholarships which are tenable at Universities and other places of further education.

In spite of all these provisions, however, there are still many firms which are unable or unwilling to release their young people for training. There are, as we have already seen, over ten thousand firms which employ less than twenty people, and a large number of young people in the distributive trades will remain outside any effective educational provision until those sections of the 1944 Education Act which refer to County Colleges are carried into effect.

In an attempt to arouse the interest of young people, most Trade Unions offer an associate membership to workers under the age of sixteen. The Birmingham Trades Council has appointed a Committee to deal with all matters connected with youth in industry. This Committee is known as the Youth Advisory Council and has a membership of nineteen, representing fourteen Trade Unions, and its objects include the protection of the interests and industrial welfare of young people, the promotion of education in the principles of Trade Unionism, and the provision of social activities designed to attract young people to the Unions. The Committee recently carried out a survey of young people engaged in undesirable occupations, but found that the number so employed was very small. In January, 1948, the Committee united with a number of other bodies to establish a Youth Crisis Committee, the work of which, however, fell through.

THE CONTRIBUTION OF THE CHURCHES

The churches have for long played a very large part in the service of childhood and youth. In our city all the Brigades and most of the Scouts and Guides are associated with a place of worship. The churches have also promoted a good many of the more recent club developments, and approximately half the Youth Clubs in Birmingham are associated with one or other of the religious denominations. It would appear indeed that about half the youth organizations in the city meet on church premises. It is to be borne in mind also that there are undoubtedly a great many small church groups which are linked up with no larger organization, and the members of which, therefore, are not included in any published statistics.

In connexion with the Church of England Diocesan Council of Religious Education there are two parallel Committees, a Sunday School Council which is concerned with work among children up to the age of fourteen, and a Youth Council which co-ordinates all activities among young people over that age. This organization is staffed by voluntary workers, except that there is one whole-time Sunday School adviser.

The many activities of the Free Churches among children and young people are given general direction from their various denominational Youth Departments, and more specific leadership from County or District denominational Youth Committees. In our city they are also

61

co-ordinated by the Birmingham Youth and Sunday School Union, which has a central office and a full-time secretariat. This Union also owns a large centrally situated book-shop, and a holiday house in the country which is used throughout the year for Conferences and Study Week-ends.

The Birmingham Roman Catholic District Youth Committee superintends all the youth work of the Catholic Church in the three Deaneries in the city. The organizer is a priest who is given a small parish in order that he may devote the major part of his time to youth work. He works from a headquarters where training courses are conducted, and a number of sports leagues are organized by his committee.

The Anglicans and Free Churches come together with many of the voluntary youth organizations in the Birmingham Christian Youth Council. This body makes arrangements for the observance of Empire Youth Sunday, and it organized the local 'Follow-up' of the World Conference of Christian Youth at Oslo, 1947, and of the Ecumenical Conference at Amsterdam, 1948. Otherwise its activities are not extensive.

OTHER CONTRIBUTIONS

The three boys' pre-Service organizations—the Sea Cadet Corps, the Army Cadet Force, and the Air Training Corps—while within the Youth Service, fall into a separate category of their own in that they are closely associated with their respective Ministries, by which also they are substantially financed. The National Association of Training Corps for Girls has no such connexion with any of the Service Ministries, and is more properly regarded as one of the uniformed voluntary organizations than as a pre-Service movement.

Each of the four political parties has its own Youth Organization, but these are officially outside the Youth Service. We agree with the comment of a recent writer that:

> it is difficult to see how the political unit could be incorporated into the Youth Service, since the expenditure of public money in support of political parties cannot be tolerated, but the fact that they cannot belong to the Service tends to segregate the members of political groups from other adolescents. This is particularly unfortunate since they are probably drawn largely from the more serious minded. They may feel that they are penalized because they are interested in more than fun and games or even because they are attached to a particular political party.*

We were interested to discover that in a few areas in other parts of the country the Authority recognizes the political youth movements as forming a part of the Youth Service. They are not grant-aided at all, of course, but in other ways their members are encouraged to take part in activities promoted by the Authority.

The Standing Conference of National Voluntary Organizations provides, at the national level, the machinery for common action on the part of the voluntary bodies. This Conference is represented in Birmingham by a local organization which does not appear, however, to be very active.

SUMMARY

The facts which appear to us to stand out in this brief outline of the history and pattern of the Youth Service in our city are : first, that provision of any kind is still comparatively recent, and second, that many varied agencies are contributing in different ways to the implementation of the Service. It is clear that society is alive, as never before, to the needs and problems of youth, and Local Authority and Voluntary Organization, Church and Industry, private citizen and public body are all contributing, in their several ways, to the welfare of those who are the citizens of tomorrow. It is clear too, that adventure and enterprise are by no means to be found only in the past. There is work of a pioneering character to be seen at the present time. Everything that is alive is changing, and there can be nothing final or static about the present pattern of Youth Service in our city.

★ Service of Youth Today, P.E.P., April, 1948.

CHAPTER V

THE EXTENT OF THE LOCAL YOUTH SERVICE

THE REGISTRATION OF BOYS AND GIRLS of sixteen and seventeen, which took place at intervals from the beginning of 1942 until the end of 1945, produced for the first time accurate information about the leisure-time activities of boys and girls of these ages.

An analysis of the first 30,000 Birmingham registrations in 1942 revealed the following figures:

TABLE XXXI

ANALYSIS OF 30,000 REGISTRATIONS, 1942

	per cent
Receiving full-time education	2·9
Undertaking 'approved' activity	37·1
Unattached	60·0

A further analysis of the interests of those undertaking 'approved' activities gave the following information:

TABLE XXXII

ATTENDANCE OF YOUNG PEOPLE, AGE 16 AND 17, at 'APPROVED' ACTIVITIES, 1942

	per cent attending
Evening Institutes	5·9
Pre-Service Units	29·0
Civil Defence or Nursing Organizations ...	4·5
Other Youth Organizations	12·2

The larger figure (51·6 against 37·1) in Table XXXII is owing to the fact that some 14 per cent of the young people who registered were taking part in more than one 'approved' activity. There was also evident a greater popularity of the pre-Service units, especially for boys. Other organizations, in fact, could claim in their membership only about 12 per cent of the total 16-17 year-old population. There was also a significant difference between boys and girls. While about 46·9 per cent of the boys were 'unattached', the corresponding figure for the girls was 72·9 per cent.

An examination of the registration which took place about a year later shows a slight improvement, the figures being:

TABLE XXXIII

ANALYSIS OF REGISTRATION, 1943

	per cent
Receiving full-time education...	6·0
Undertaking 'approved' activity	40·9
Unattached	53·1

One striking fact which emerged from the interviews to which the unattached people were invited was that many of them had at one time been members of a youth organization, but had allowed their membership to lapse. It was discovered, indeed, that 62 per cent of the boys and 44 per cent of the girls had at some time or other been attached to one organization or another, but that of these members, 17 per cent of the boys and 56 per cent of the girls had lapsed by the time they reached the age of 16 or 16½. Some organizations were found to be more successful than others in retaining their members, as is shown by the following Table which indicates the number, out of every thousand members, who were retained by various organizations until the age at which young people registered. As organizations enrol members at different ages this Table is not to be regarded as offering a fair comparison of the retaining power of various movements, but it does show, as was pointed out at the time, that some of the organizations may have been under-estimating the developing maturity of their members.

TABLE XXXIV

NUMBER OF MEMBERS RETAINED OUT OF EVERY THOUSAND CONTACTED IN EACH TYPE OF ORGANIZATION

BOYS		GIRLS	
Part-time Education	966	Nursing Service	850
Civil Defence	955	Part-time Education	841
A.T.C.	901	Youth Clubs	810
Army Cadets	880	G.T.C. or W.J.A.C.	756
Youth Clubs	826	Y.W.C.A.	625
Boys' Brigade	786	G.L.B.	222
Y.M.C.A.	593	Girl Guides	155
Boy Scouts	531		

Those young people who were no longer in membership of any youth organization were asked why they had allowed their membership to lapse, and in over 30 per cent of the cases the reason given was that the boy or girl 'grew too old' or 'lost interest' or suggested that the organization no longer met his or her needs. This was particularly the case with the Guide, Scout and Brigade organizations.

Another fact which became apparent was that the boys' organizations both enrolled and retained a greater number of members than the girls' organizations. Clubs were found to be retaining 83 per cent of their boys and 81 per cent of their girls.

The then Chief Education Officer, summing up the situation in July 1943, in a report to the City Education Committee, to which we are indebted for this information, said:

> Even when we allow the widest possible margin to cover our lack of verification, we can only credit the 'approved' activities with being able to interest and maintain the interest of a section of about 45 per cent of our youth. This leaves us with a minimum of 55 per cent with whom as yet we have been able to do nothing, and the information we have regarding them is that 4·3 per cent could not undertake 'approved' activity even if they wanted to, and that the remaining 41·7 per cent have very little interest in the organizations. On carrying our analysis a step further we find that two-fifths of these 41·7 per cent have based their judgment on actual membership.

THE PRESENT POSITION

On 1st January, 1949, it was estimated that there were in Birmingham 81,976 young people between the ages of fourteen and twenty. We have been unable to discover how this number is divided between the sexes, but the Local Education Authorities have advised us to assume that there is an equal number of boys and girls, and also that the 16,762 who are known to be engaged in full-time education are also equally divided between the sexes.* This latter assumption is not unreasonable in view of the fact that the great majority of those who are engaged in full-time education are young people between the ages of fourteen and fifteen who are benefiting from the extra year at school.

Our investigations into the activities of these young people have produced the statistics shown in Table XXXV and Figure 8.

Perhaps the chief comment to be made about the above figures is that as the number of young people in full-time education includes 13,516 fourteen-year-olds and only 3,246 who are fifteen and over, it follows that if the inquiry had been concerned only with young people over the age of fifteen, the proportion of those 'unattached' (i.e. not taking part either in full-time or part-time education and not belonging to any youth organization) would have been rather higher than it is in these figures.

Our inquiries lead us to conclude that of the members of youth organizations 29 per cent of the boys and 35 per cent of the girls are still engaged in full-time education and that 20·4 per cent of the boys and girls† attend Evening Institutes or recognized classes in clubs with L.E.A. Instructors. The actual overlap is seen in the more detailed analysis in Table XXXVI.

Perhaps the most surprising fact about this Table is not only that considerably more girls than boys attend Evening Institutes, but also that the great majority of boys who do attend Evening Institutes are also members of youth organizations, and the number of otherwise unattached boys in attendance at Evening Institutes would appear to be very small. We were also surprised to discover how large a percentage of the members of youth organizations are still at school.

22,884 boys and 13,641 girls in the 14-20 age group belong to youth organizations. This represents 55·8 per cent of the boys and almost exactly one-third of the girls. These figures represent the nominal membership—the effective membership would be less.

It was extremely difficult to arrive at these figures, partly because most clubs have duplicate and even triplicate affiliations, so that there is a danger of counting the same boy or girl two or three times, and partly because a considerable number of young people belong to more than

---

* Neither the Registrar-General's estimates nor the annual census of the school population undertaken by the Education Committee's School Attendance Department provide information about the sexes separately. At the 1931 census, however, there was a small excess of females in the City's school-age population.

† The percentage appears to be approximately the same for boys and girls.

DISTRIBUTION OF YOUNG PEOPLE (aged 14-20) IN FULL—AND PART-TIME EDUCATION AND IN YOUTH ORGANIZATIONS

FIGURE 8

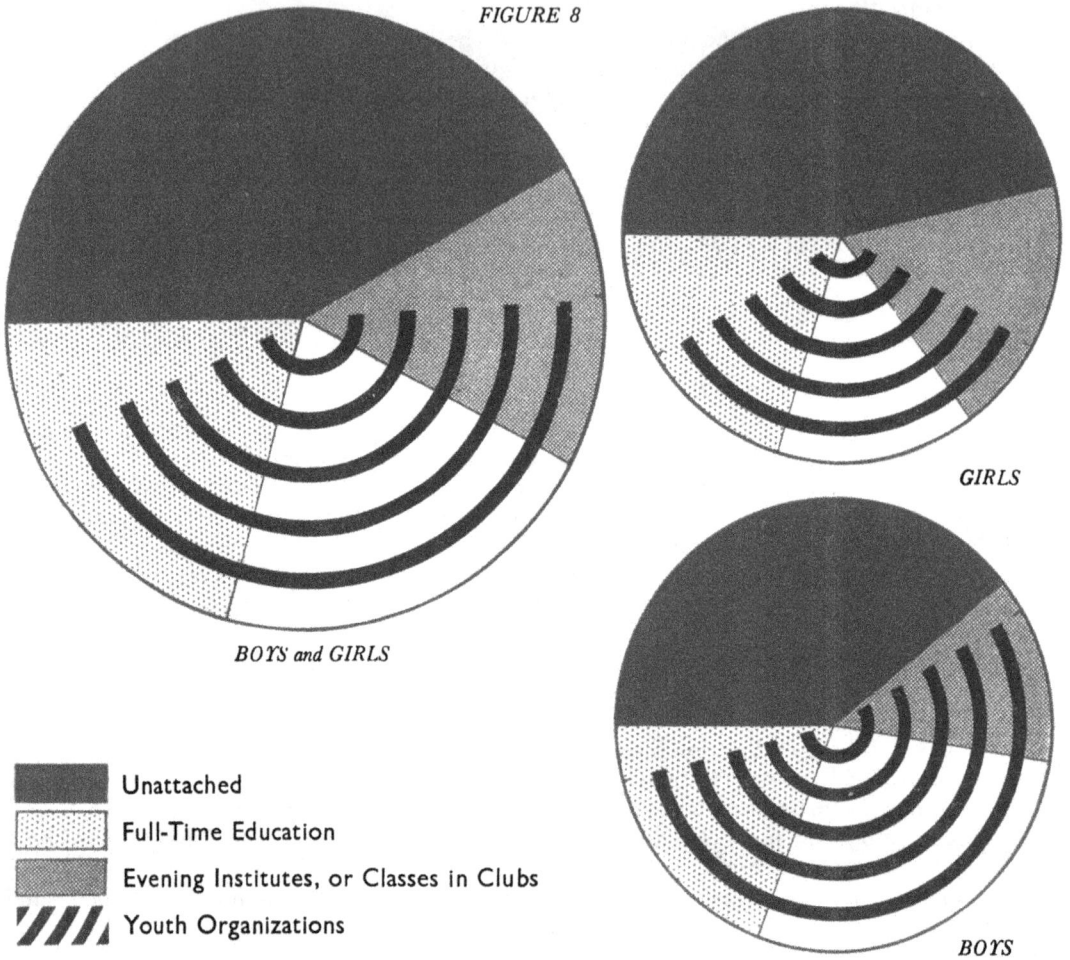

BOYS and GIRLS

GIRLS

BOYS

- Unattached
- Full-Time Education
- Evening Institutes, or Classes in Clubs
- Youth Organizations

TABLE XXXV

ACTIVITIES OF YOUTH POPULATION (AGE GROUP 14-20) 1st JANUARY, 1949

	BOYS		GIRLS		TOTAL	
	Number	per cent	Number	per cent	Number	per cent
In full-time education... ...	8,381	20·4	8,381	20·4	16,762	20·4
Attending Evening Institutes or classes in Clubs	5,631	13·7	7,580	18·5	13,211	16
Members of Youth Organizations	22,884	55·8	13,641	33·3	36,525	44·5
Unattached	15,396	37·5	18,943	46·2	34,339	41·9

TABLE XXXVI

ACTIVITIES OF BIRMINGHAM YOUTH POPULATION (AGE GROUP 14-20)
1st JANUARY, 1949
(Analysed in greater detail than in Table XXXV)

	BOYS	GIRLS	TOTAL
In full-time education, but not members of Youth Organizations	1,745	3,607	5,352
In full-time education and also attending Youth Organizations	6,636	4,774	11,410
Members of Youth Organizations, but not engaged in full-time education, and not attending L.E.A. classes	11,580	6,084	17,664
In Youth Organizations and attending Evening Institutes or classes in clubs	4,668	2,783	7,451
Attending Evening Institutes, but otherwise un-attached	963	4,797	5,760
Unattached	15,396	18,943	34,339
TOTAL	40,988	40,988	81,976

one organization. From a study of our *Twenty Questions* and as a result of our inquiries in organizations visited, we conclude that 15 per cent of the members of youth organizations belong to more than one unit. We were rather surprised to discover that quite 30 per cent of the girls in girls' organizations are members of a second movement; this suggests that the single-sex organization does not meet all the needs of the adolescent girl. The corresponding figure for boys in boys' organizations is approximately 20 per cent, and for boys and girls in mixed organizations approximately 10 per cent.

It will be noted that 37 per cent of the boys and 46 per cent of the girls are described as 'unattached'. It is not to be assumed, however, that all these young people are necessarily employing their leisure in negative or undesirable activities. We return to a discussion of these particular young people in Chapter VIII.

The above statistics include 3,016 young people who are in attendance at Day Continuation Schools, and 5,102 boys and 297 girls who are released by their employers to attend Technical, Commercial or Art Courses. Experience at the Bournville Day Continuation College would suggest that many of these young people are to be found among those who also attend Evening Institutes or youth organizations rather than among those who are otherwise 'un-attached'. Of 646 boys who attend this College, 232 also attend Evening Institutes and 492 are members of youth organizations. (179 of these boys actually attend Evening Institutes and Day Continuation Classes, and also belong to youth organizations.) The actual statistics supplied by this College are as follows:

TABLE XXXVII

YOUNG PEOPLE ATTENDING BOURNVILLE DAY CONTINUATION COLLEGE*

	BOYS		GIRLS	
	Number	per cent	Number	per cent
Attending College	646	—	895	—
Attending Evening Institutes ...	232	35·9	208	23·2
Members of Youth Organizations	492	76·1	456	50·9
Otherwise Unattached	101	15·6	439	49·0

* There are actually about 1,200 girls in attendance at this College, but our information was only obtained from the number indicated.

It would appear from these figures that one can conclude that attendance at Day Continuation Colleges stimulates a desire to take part in other activities, and that those people are right who envisage that the advent of the County Colleges will create a demand for additional Youth Service facilities.

We have evidence, on the other hand, that many of the 5,102 boys who are released by their employers to attend technical, commercial or art classes, and many engineering apprentices, do not belong to youth organizations. In our diagrammatic representation of the distribution of the youth population these boys are included, rather ambiguously, among the 'unattached'.

YOUTH ORGANIZATIONS
(A) Types of Organizations

There is in Birmingham an almost bewildering variety of youth organizations. Brigade Companies, Scout Troops, pre-Service Units and Clubs of all kinds exist in profusion. Within

TABLE XXXVIII

NUMBER OF YOUTH ORGANIZATIONS IN BIRMINGHAM AND NUMBER OF MEMBERS AGED 14-20

Organization	UNITS			MEMBERS	
	Boys	Girls	Mixed	Boys	Girls
Uniformed Voluntary	252	364	—	2,470	2,720
Boys' Pre-Service	54	—	—	3,657	
British Red Cross and St. John Ambulance Brigade	29	44	—	160	406
Political	—	—	63	895	1,155
Clubs	130	73	375	19,740	11,767
TOTAL	465	481	438	26,922	16,048

These figures represent gross totals—i.e. no allowance is made for young people who are members of more than one organization.

the city boundary there are about 1,400 units serving the needs of young people in the 14-20 age range. As these groups enrol a gross membership of about 43,000, the average membership per unit is little over 30. The most striking feature of the Youth Service, indeed, is that it consists of a very large number of small organizations of many kinds. The actual distribution is shown on the previous page.*

It is evident from these figures that the club is very much more popular than is any uniformed organization. It would also appear that the club is generally a larger unit, its average membership being about 55, while that of the uniformed organization is about 13. These figures, however, are a little misleading because we have excluded from our calculations all members under the age of 14, and the Brigades, Scouts and Guides usually have more members under this age than over. A few of the uniformed units included in these figures may possibly have no members at all over the age of 14. Of the 321 organizations visited by us, 291 had members in the 14-20 age range, and the average membership of these units and the average attendance at each meeting of the unit during the week of our visit are shown in the following Table:

TABLE XXXIX

AVERAGE MEMBERSHIP AND AVERAGE ATTENDANCE IN UNITS VISITED

Number and Type of Unit	Average Membership	Average attendance per meeting
82 Boys' ...	34	21
84 Girls' ...	32	12
125 Mixed ...	67	39

It is to be noted that included among these units were most of the city's very large organizations, a few indeed with membership running into the hundreds. In both columns any members under the age of fourteen have been ignored. If Sunday church parades and week-end out-door activities be excluded, the average overall attendance was 28 per meeting.

While it is true that there are something like 1,400 separate youth units at work in the city, it must not be assumed that these are all quite independent. Sometimes it happens that a group of organizations are integral parts of a larger community. This frequently happens in connexion with Church youth work. In association with the Weoley Castle Congregational Church, for instance, there is a Scout Group which includes Cubs, Scouts, Senior Scouts and Rovers; there are Brownies and Girl Guides; there are both boys' and girls' sections of the St. John Ambulance Brigade, the latter being further divided into junior and cadet nurses; there is a junior play-hour; there are junior and senior Youth Clubs, and there is a Sunday School graded into five departments, with five separate teachers' training classes meeting every week. In this instance we have listed the Scouts and Guides, the Youth Club and the two St. John Ambulance Brigades as separate units, making five in all, but it might be argued that the whole community is one youth centre, as indeed it is.

Pre-Service organizations are, as we should expect, considerably fewer and smaller today than they were during the war. Their membership now indeed is only about 40 per cent of what it was three or four years ago. The Girls' Training Corps and the Women's Junior Air Corps prefer not to be regarded as Pre-Service movements and are listed in Table XXXVIII among the uniformed voluntary organizations.

* More detailed statistics will be found in Table XLVIII (p.85).

FIGURE 9

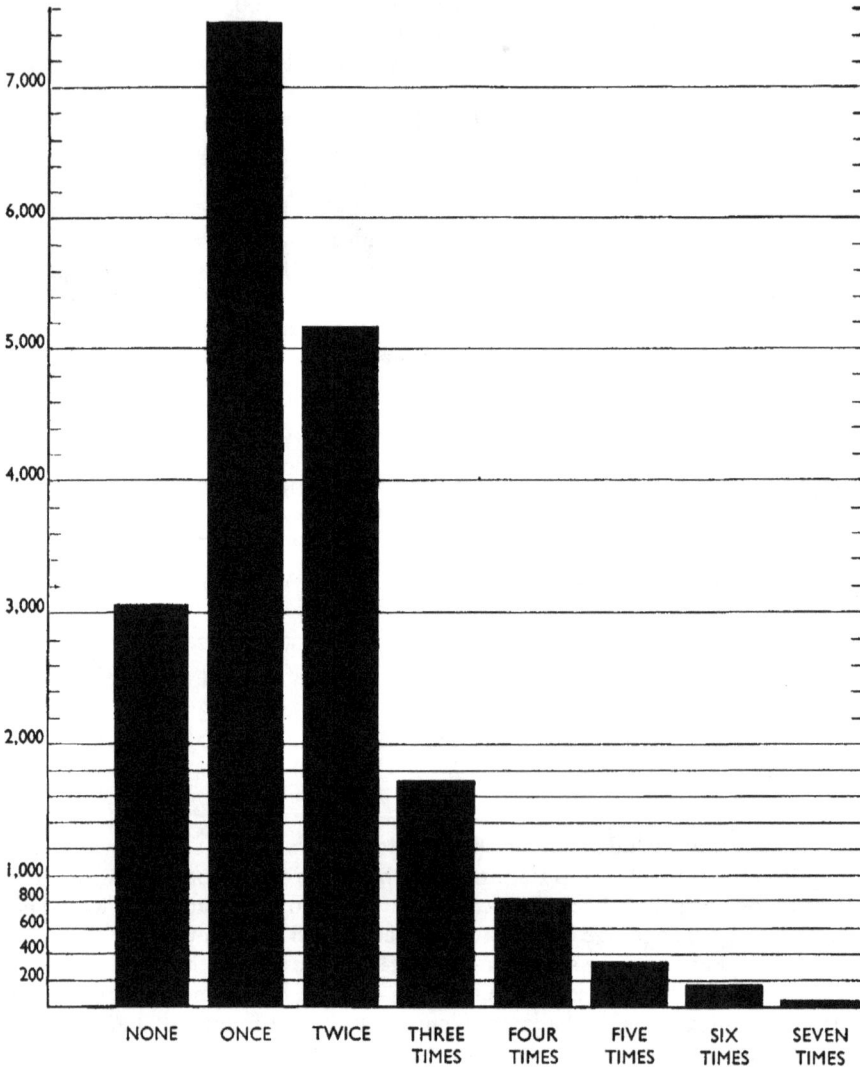

FREQUENCY OF ATTENDANCE

Analysis of one week's attendance by 18,753 members of youth organizations.

The only figures concerning the accuracy of which we have any considerable measure of doubt are those which refer to political youth organizations. Each of the political parties, as we have seen, has its youth movement, but the age-range usually goes up to thirty, and it is not easy to say how many of the members are under twenty. The figures we publish are those supplied by the political parties themselves. The statement that is sometimes made that Communism is spreading extensively among young people would not appear to be true of our city, even though we observed that a largely attended Communist rally in the Town Hall contained a considerable proportion of young people.

An analysis of the distribution of membership in the 14-20 age range between single-sex and mixed organizations, as follows:

TABLE XL

DISTRIBUTION OF MEMBERSHIP IN MIXED AND SINGLE-SEX ORGANIZATIONS

Organization	Boys in Boys' Units	Boys in Mixed Units	Girls in Girls' Units	Girls in Mixed Units
Uniformed Voluntary	2,470	—	2,720	—
Pre-Service	3,657	—	—	—
Red Cross and St. John Ambulance Brigade	160	—	406	—
Political	—	895	—	1,155
Clubs	6,003	13,737	1,860	9,907
TOTAL	12,290	14,632	4,986	11,062

These figures illustrate the much greater attraction of the mixed organization to the adolescent girl. We do indeed report the existence of 73 girls' clubs, but many of these are in fact 'twin' clubs closely associated with a boys' club, while others are little more than sewing circles. This figure of 73 also includes 22 units of the Girls' Friendly Society, with less than 100 members (in this age range) among them all. Apart from three large branches of the Y.W.C.A. the number of actual clubs for girls is very small indeed.

(B) Frequency of Meeting

Comparatively few youth organizations are open more than one or two evenings a week. A complete record of the activities of 291 units which are concerned mainly with young people in the 14-20 range gives the number of evenings a week on which they were open as follows:

TABLE XLI

FREQUENCY OF MEETING

Organization	Evenings per week						
	1	2	3	4	5	6	7
82 Boys' Units	23	12	17	13	9	3	5
84 Girls' Units	56	18	7	2	—	1	—
125 Mixed Units	31	35	11	12	13	11	12
TOTAL ...	110	65	35	27	22	15	17

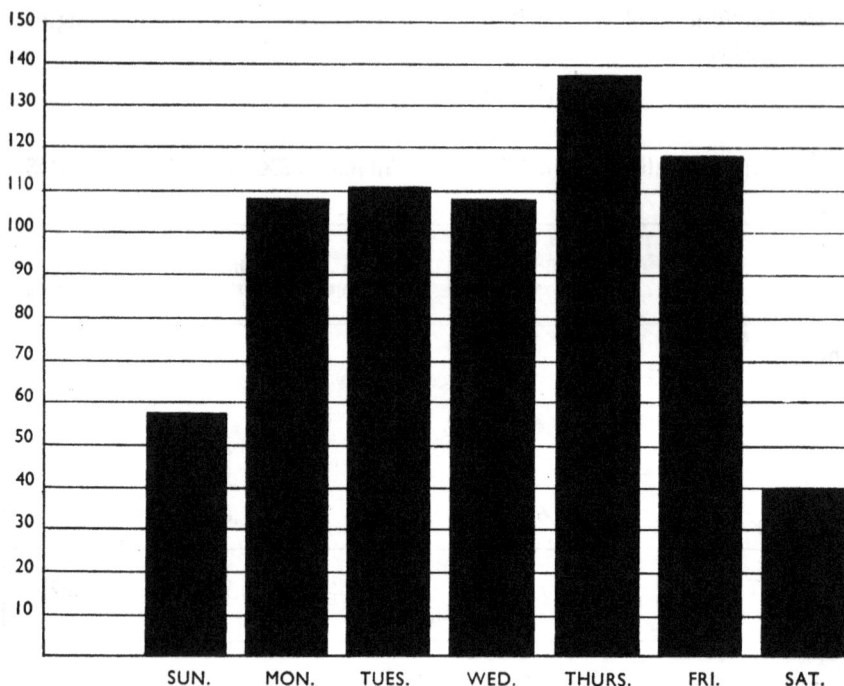

FIGURE *10*

THE
YOUTH SERVICE
THROUGH
THE WEEK

Showing how many of
the 291 units visited
(age range 14–19) were
open on each evening.
Church parades and
outdoor activities not
included.

It is not to be assumed, however, that if a unit is open five nights a week, any boy or girl could attend on each of these occasions. A large organization may be open almost every night, but one night may be reserved for girls, another for boys, and a third for junior members. Mixed organizations visited were found to offer nineteen evenings for girls only and twenty-eight for boys only.

(C) Attendance

An attempt was made to discover how often members attend. This information was difficult to obtain and in some cases our figures are only approximate, but, in the total age range 11-20, our inquiries produced the following statistics concerning 18,753 members:

TABLE XLII

FREQUENCY OF ATTENDANCE

Times a Week						
One	Two	Three	Four	Five	Six	Seven
7,490	5,164	1,702	815	315	159	77

These figures indicate that, in the week in question, 17 per cent of the members did not attend at all, 67 per cent once or twice, and only 16 per cent three times or more. It is to be borne in mind, however, that 15 per cent of these young people belong to more than one organization.

Attendance seems to be fairly evenly distributed over the different days of the week, except that attendance at indoor activities drops at the week-end. Attendances in the 14-20 age range were distributed as follows:

TABLE XLIII

INCIDENCE OF ATTENDANCE ON DIFFERENT DAYS OF THE WEEK

Number of Units and Number of Members	SUNDAY		MON.	TUES.	WED.	THURS.	FRI.	SATURDAY	
	Church Parade or Bible Class	Other Activities						Indoor Activities	Outdoor Activities
82 Boys' Units with 2,811 Members ...	647	264	745	657	553	777	1,106	132	752
84 Girls' Units with 2,717 Members ...	157	—	172	238	309	331	196	64	108
125 Mixed Units with 8,497 Members ...	787	1,420	2,104	2,134	2,276	1,832	2,043	1,858	888
TOTALS ...	1,591	1,684	3,021	3,029	3,138	2,940	3,345	2,054	1,748

The membership of these 291 organizations included almost as many girls as boys, but the more frequent attendance of the boys is evident from the following figures:

TABLE XLIV

ATTENDANCE OF BOYS AND GIRLS COMPARED

	SUNDAY		MON.	TUES.	WED.	THURS.	FRI.	SATURDAY	
	Church Parade or Bible Class	Other Activities						Indoor Activities	Outdoor Activities
Boys in Boys' Organizations (2,811 Members)	647	264	745	657	553	777	1,106	132	752
Boys in Mixed Organizations (4,269 Members)	377	775	1,052	1,117	1,249	972	1,113	1,005	825
Girls in Girls' Organizations (2,717 Members)	157	—	172	238	309	331	196	64	108
Girls in Mixed Organizations (4,228 Members)	410	645	1,052	1,017	1,027	860	930	853	63

AIR TRAINING CORPS CADETS: *Instruction in ground trades.*
Pre-Service organizations are amply supplied with equipment.

WOMEN'S JUNIOR AIR CORPS and AIR TRAINING CORPS: *Navigational*
training for a mixed group of youths and girls.   The W.J.A.C. is not a Pre-Service organization.

Two additional facts which emerge from these figures are that over nine times as many boys as girls take part in Saturday outdoor activities, and that no girls' organization whatever offered any Sunday activity other than of a devotional character. Facilities available at the week-end were as follows:

TABLE XLV

FACILITIES AT WEEK-ENDS

Number and type of Organizations	SUNDAY				SATURDAY			
	Church Parade or Bible Class		Other Activities		Indoor Activities		Outdoor Activities	
	Available for		Available for		Available for		Available for	
	Boys	Girls	Boys	Girls	Boys	Girls	Boys	Girls
82 Boys' Organizations	28	—	11	—	7	—	37	—
84 Girls' Organizations	—	13	—	—	—	3	—	6
125 Mixed Organizations	16	18	42	39	30	30	42	9

Whether the non-participation of girls in Saturday outdoor activities is due to the lack of opportunity or to the lack of demand may be a matter for investigation, but it is certainly striking to discover that only 15 of all the organizations visited offered girls any facilities of this kind at all.

Only 40 organizations visited offered Saturday evening indoor activities, but the fact that the average attendance was 51 as compared with an average overall for the whole week of 28, leads one to ask whether there is not a need for more Saturday evening facilities. The distribution of facilities on different evenings of the week is illustrated in Figure 10, page 72, in which no account is taken of church parades or outdoor activities.

(D) Distribution of Members in Age Groups

We obtained from 161 units a detailed statement of the number of members of each age from 14-19 inclusive. We do not know if these units can be taken as representative of the city's youth organizations as a whole, though they did include 43 non-church Youth Clubs, 34 Church Clubs, 20 Guide and Ranger Companies, 16 Scout groups, 19 Brigades and 7 boys' Pre-Service units.

The results of this investigation are shown in the Figures 11 and 12 (in neither case has any account been taken of members under the age of fourteen). The general overall picture is that of a gradual loss of members with each succeeding age group, though some organizations retain their members longer than others. All the uniformed voluntary organizations show a rapid decline in membership from the fourteenth birthday onwards, though it is interesting to note that the G.T.C., the W.J.A.C. and the Boys' Brigade (and, to a lesser extent, the Guides) all show a slight temporary recovery at the age of sixteen. In the clubs, membership is fairly evenly distributed among young people aged from 14-17, after which there is a rapid decline. The interesting feature of club membership is that there are more boys of the age of sixteen than of any other age. In the boys' Pre-Service units membership is fairly stationary until after the seventeenth birthday, when it falls rapidly. In the case of the boys the heavy loss of membership at eighteen and nineteen in all units is partly, but not altogether, accounted for by the fact of

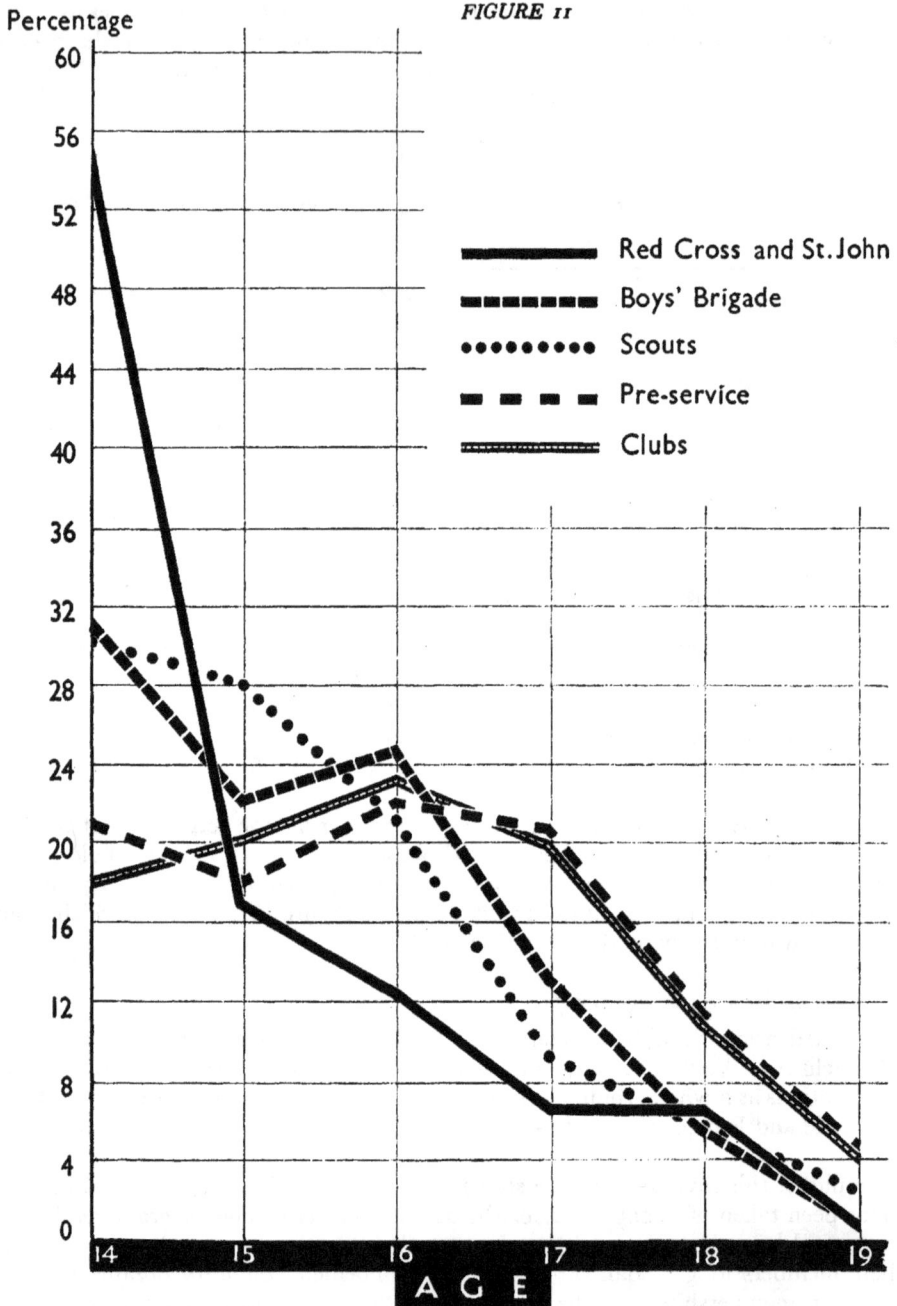

Percentage

FIGURE II

━━━━━━ Red Cross and St. John
■■■■■■■ Boys' Brigade
●●●●●●●● Scouts
▬ ▬ ▬ ▬ Pre-service
═════ Clubs

AGE

DISTRIBUTION OF BOYS BY AGE GROUPS IN VARIOUS ORGANIZATIONS
Showing the percentage of the total 14–19 year old membership in each age group.

conscription. Only a few political units were able or willing to give us this particular information, but such figures as we were able to obtain suggest that the political units report an increasing percentage of members in the higher age groups.

One fact whch emerges very clearly is that all the uniformed voluntary organizations lose a large proportion of their members in early adolescence. Our graphs do not take account of

76

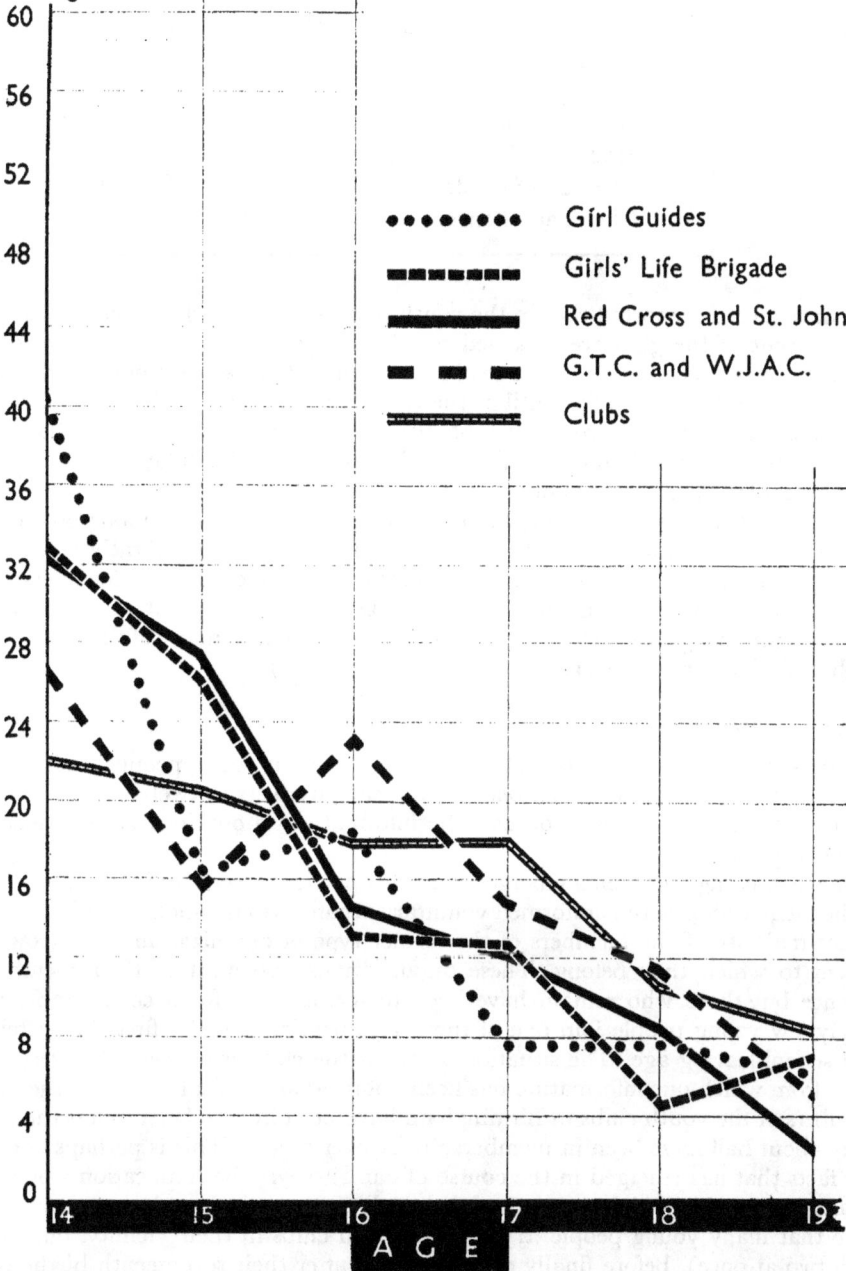

Percentage

FIGURE 12

•••••••• Girl Guides
▬▬▬▬▬ Girls' Life Brigade
▬▬▬▬ Red Cross and St. John
━ ━ ━ G.T.C. and W.J.A.C.
═════ Clubs

A G E

DISTRIBUTION OF GIRLS BY AGE GROUPS IN VARIOUS ORGANIZATIONS
Showing the percentage of the total 14–19 year old membership in each age-group.

members who leave these organizations before the age of fourteen. but if they had been included, the failure of these organizations to retain their members would have been even more startling. If the average number of members in each age group from 11-13 be compared with the average number of members of each age from 15-17, the percentage of members retained by these organizations is as follows:

77

TABLE XLVI

PERCENTAGE OF MEMBERS RETAINED BY UNIFORMED VOLUNTARY ORGANIZATIONS

	per cent
Boys' Brigade	36
Scouts and Rovers	31
Girls' Life Brigade	25
Guides and Rangers	25

We have already reported that in the youth population as a whole, 55 per cent of the boys and 33 per cent of the girls are attached to youth organizations. If these figures be further analysed, it would appear that at the age of fourteen about 45 per cent of the girls are attached, this percentage declining steadily until at the age of nineteen it is rather less than 20 per cent. The percentage for boys rises from about 65 per cent at fourteen to 70 per cent at sixteen, after which it begins to decline, falling rapidly after the seventeenth birthday to less than 40 per cent at eighteen and less than 20 per cent at nineteen.

These figures show a surprisingly high percentage of attachment among boys of fifteen and sixteen. It is to be remembered that these figures represent the nominal rather than the effective attachment. Our judgment is that, for an accurate assessment of effective membership, the gross membership figures of most organizations should be reduced by about 15 per cent. It is to be remembered also (as we make clear in our next paragraphs) that many of these boys only remain in membership for a very short time.

(E) Stability of Membership

Leaders of the same 161 units told us how many of their young people aged 14-20 had been in membership over two years, from one to two years, from six to twelve months, from three to six months and less than three months. The information so obtained is reproduced diagrammatically on page 79.

The outstanding fact which emerges from this particular inquiry is that there is a stability about the membership of the uniformed voluntary organizations which is not found in the clubs. The great majority of the members of the former type of organization have grown up in the movement to which they belong. These organizations lose most of their members in early adolescence but those who remain have been in membership for a considerable time. Comparatively few young people join one of these organizations for the first time after they have reached school-leaving age. The situation as far as the clubs is concerned is very different. If the clubs from which our information has been obtained are typical of others, then a quarter of the members of the youth clubs in Birmingham have been in membership less than six months, and only about half have been in membership for over a year. This is perhaps one of the most striking facts that has emerged in the course of our Survey. The implication would seem to be that many boys and girls join a youth club but do not remain long in membership. We have evidence that many young people 'try' all the youth clubs in their vicinity, one after another (or even two at once), before finally deciding, soon after their seventeenth birthday, that they have no more use for clubs. There is rather more stability, as one would expect, in the membership of clubs which are associated with Churches or with the Y.M.C.A. or Y.W.C.A. than there is in the membership of unattached clubs.

(F) Members under Fourteen

A summary of the total membership of boys and girls in the 11-14 age range is shown in the following table:

TABLE XLVII

MEMBERS OF YOUTH ORGANIZATIONS AGE 11-14

Organization	GIRLS	BOYS
Uniformed Voluntary	3,429	5,101
Red Cross and St. John	582	295
Clubs	3,741	4,726
TOTAL	7,752	10,122

The great majority of these children are members of single-sex organizations, as the strongest advocates of mixed clubs usually prefer a single-sex approach when dealing with the junior age

FIGURE 13

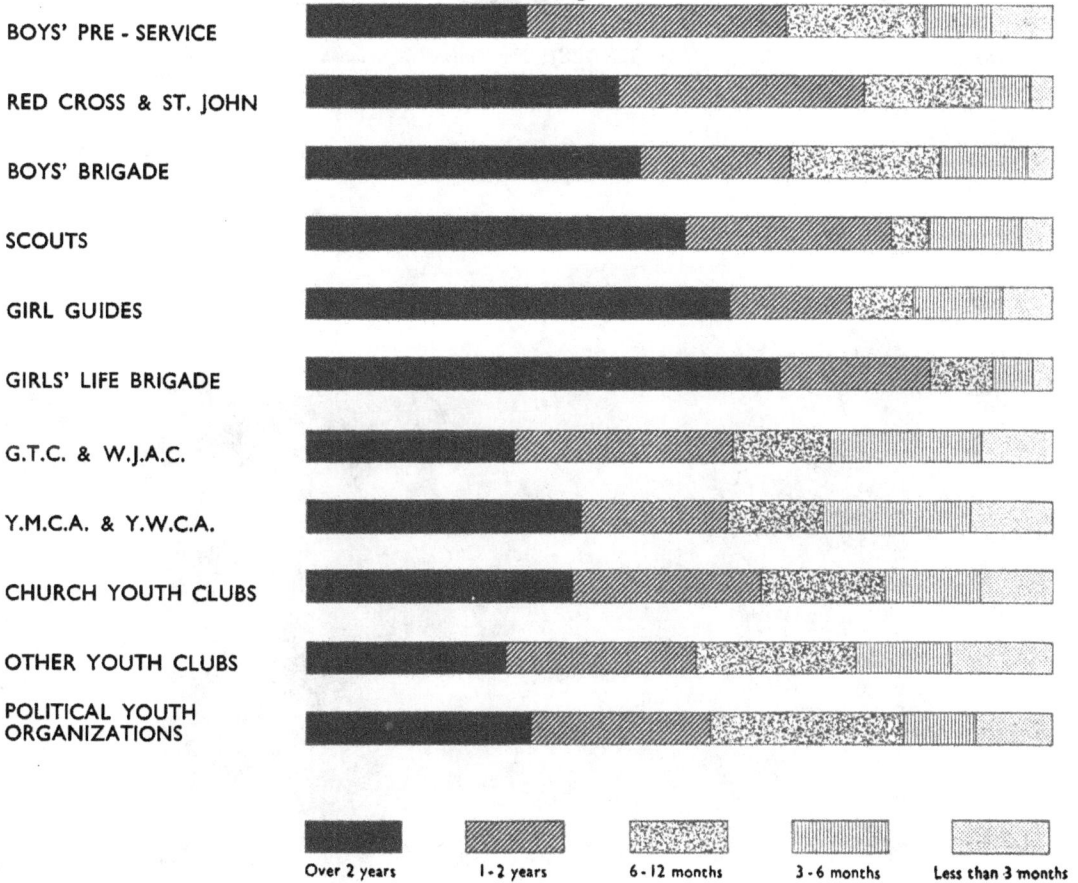

STABILITY OF MEMBERSHIP
The lengths of the shaded bars show the duration of membership (at the time of the Survey) of those belonging to various organizations.

79

A PERMANENT CAMPING SITE (GIRL GUIDES): *The National Association of Boys' Clubs, the Boy Scouts, and other youth organizations also have country houses and permanent camping facilities for their members.*

AIR RANGERS RECEIVING FLYING INSTRUCTION: *Girls too old for the Guides (16) can transfer to the Rangers, a few companies of which, e.g. Sea and Air Rangers, offer specialized activities in the informal atmosphere characteristic of the Movement.*

groups. The Co-operative Movement's children's organizations would appear to be the main exception to this rule. We doubt whether our information enables us to say how many units there are which cater for children of this age, but in the 321 units visited by us, 84 boys' organizations had an average 11-14-year-old membership of 30, and 82 girls' organizations had an average membership in the same age range of 27. Attendances were fairly evenly distributed over the days of the week, except for a very sharp drop on Saturday.

(G) Geographical Distribution

Readers will find on page 82 a map which illustrates the distribution of youth organizations throughout the city. The compilation of this map has been a task of extreme difficulty as often there appeared to be no source from which information could be secured. Even the secretaries of the Local Youth Advisory Committees were not always able to give us detailed information about the youth work which was being carried on in their own locality. There is a continual process of birth, death and resurrection among youth organizations, and this map, prepared in the closing weeks of 1948, will soon become out-of-date. The map indicates the position of 1,279 of the city's 1,384 youth units. About 75 per cent of these units have been pin-pointed, but the location of the remaining 25 per cent is indicated approximately only.

The general picture presented by this map confirms the impression that the Youth Service consists of a multiplicity of very varied units, most of which have only a comparatively small membership. It is to be borne in mind, however, as we have already pointed out, that in some instances a number of youth organizations not only use the same premises, but constitute together a larger total community.

The question may nevertheless be asked whether there are not in fact, too many units, and whether the needs of youth might not better be served by a smaller number of larger organizations. It is, therefore, with some surprise that one discovers that 16 per cent of the girls who are not members of any youth organization at all give as the reason for their non-attachment that there is 'no club anywhere near', that they 'don't know one', or that 'it is too far to go'. This kind of reason is offered rather more frequently by unattached girls than by unattached boys, but it is difficult to understand when one remembers that there are in the city 481 girls' and 438 mixed organizations, and that, in general, these appear to be fairly generally distributed in all districts.

As Birmingham covers an area of eighty square miles and has a youth population of about 82,000, there is an average distribution of seventeen youth organizations per square mile, and one for every sixty young people. A glance at the map will show that the density of youth units resembles very closely the density of population. While organizations of all types seem to be very generally distributed throughout the city, no area being noticeably either under- or over-provided with any particular type of unit, a few interesting features emerge. Both Northfield and Stechford have sixty-seven units, so large a figure for Northfield being particularly surprising. Hall Green, with the same population, has twenty fewer units. Acocks Green, with a much smaller population than Hall Green, has no less than sixty-three units—one for every forty-six young people living in the ward.

In the course of our inquiries we have often been assured that there is a noticeable lack of youth organizations in the new development areas on the outskirts of the city, but an examination of the map makes it difficult to justify this statement. The population in some of these districts, however, is increasing very rapidly, and it may well be that it is in these areas, rather than in the city centre, that there is inadequate provision. The distribution of the Youth Service in the central areas will eventually be greatly affected, of course, by the re-development and re-building proposals which we have discussed in an earlier chapter. In the second Table (Table XLIX) appended to this chapter will be found a list of the city's Municipal wards, with an estimate of the youth population in each, and a summary of the number of youth organizations we have been able to plot on the map.

FIGURE 14

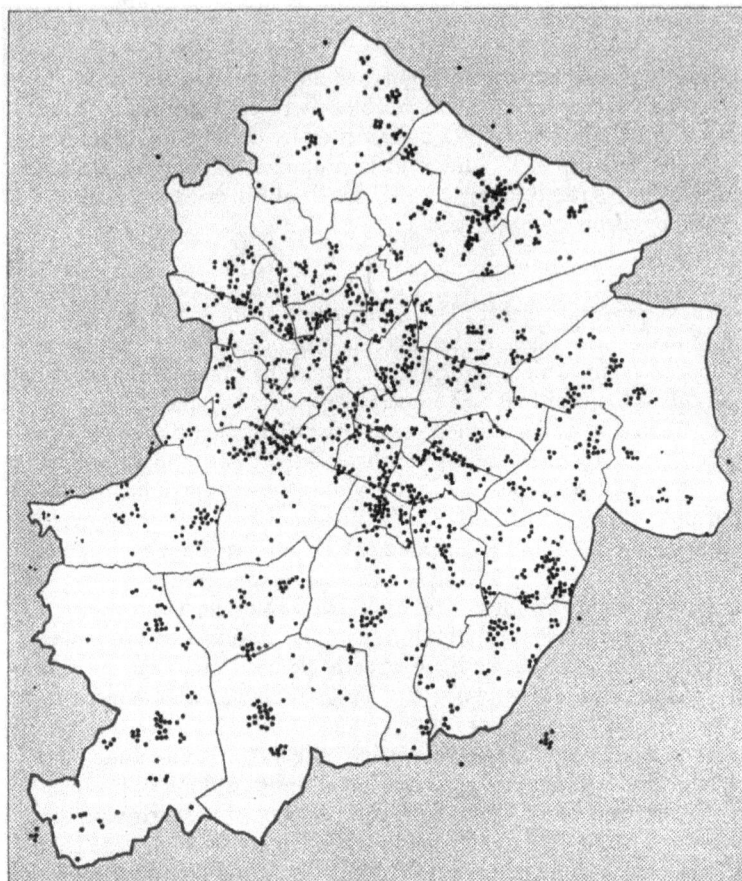

The map on the left indicates the position of 1,279 of the 1,384 youth organizations in the 14–20 age-range. It is clear that the Youth Service consists of a multiplicity of very varied units, most of which have a comparatively small membership.

Indicates position of an organization connected with an industrial concern.

A

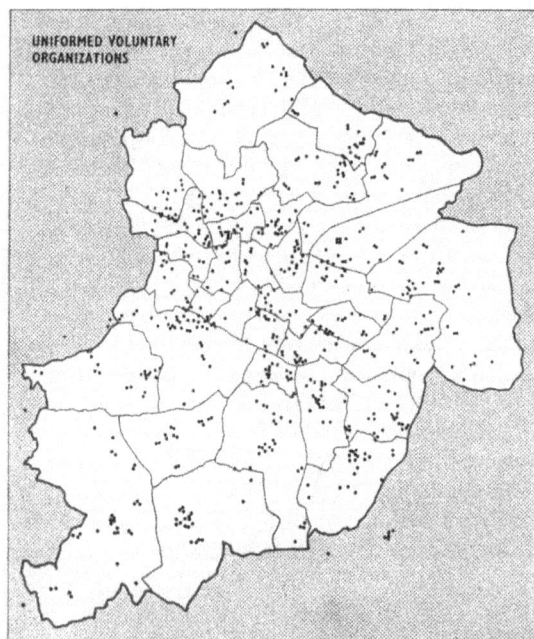

UNIFORMED VOLUNTARY ORGANIZATIONS

B

PRE-SERVICE ORGANIZATIONS

GEOGRAPHICAL DISTRIBUTION OF YOUTH ORGANIZATIONS

(A) UNIFORMED VOLUNTARY ORGANIZATIONS

Boys' Brigade, Girls' Life Brigade, Boy Scouts and Rovers, Girl Guides and Rangers, Girls' Training Corps and Women's Junior Air Corps, Camp Fire Girls, Church Lads' Brigade, Church Girls' Brigade.

(B) PRE-SERVICE ORGANIZATIONS

Sea Cadets, Air Training Corps, Army Cadets.

(C) BRITISH RED CROSS AND ST. JOHN AMBULANCE UNITS

Red Cross Cadets, St. John Ambulance Brigade Girl Cadets, St. John Ambulance Brigade Boy Cadets.

(D) POLITICAL YOUTH ORGANIZATIONS

Young Unionists, Labour League of Youth, Young Liberals, Young Communists.

(E) CLUBS

Boys', Girls' and Mixed Clubs of all kinds, Y.M.C.A. and Y.W.C.A., Community Centres, Evening Institutes and Recreative Centres.

E

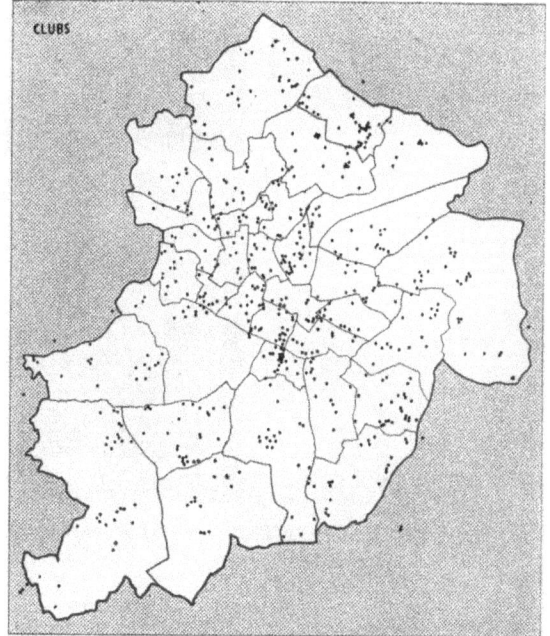

CLUBS

C

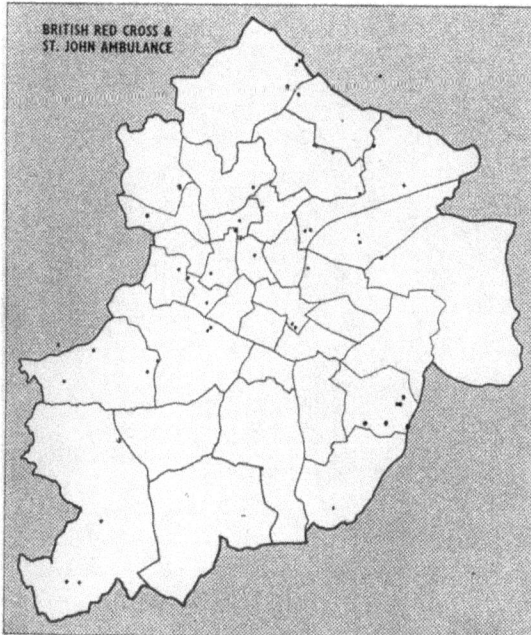

BRITISH RED CROSS & ST. JOHN AMBULANCE

D

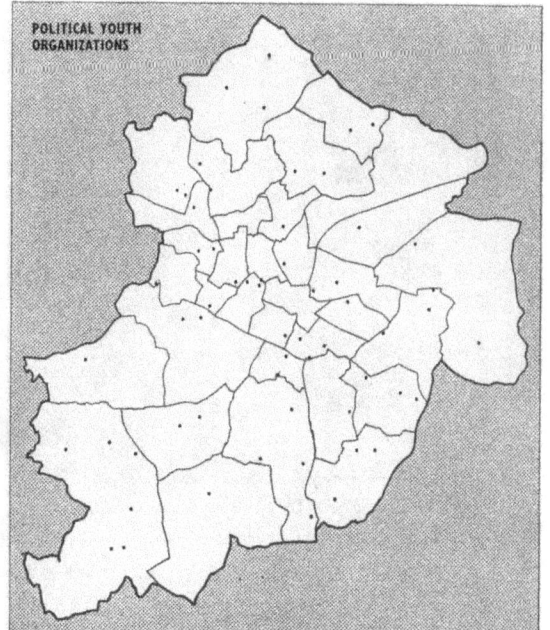

POLITICAL YOUTH ORGANIZATIONS

THE SCOUT MOVEMENT *embraces four age-groups: Cubs 8–11, Scouts 11–15, Senior Scouts 15–17½, Rovers 17½ and over.*

A ROVER MOOT: *In Rover units emphasis is laid on the application of Scouting principles to training for citizenship on more adult lines.*

TABLE XLVIII

DETAILED SUMMARY OF YOUTH ORGANIZATIONS IN BIRMINGHAM

ORGANIZATION	UNITS			MEMBERS			
	Boys	Girls	Mixed	Girls		Boys	
				11-14	14-20	11-14	14-20
Uniformed Voluntary							
Boys' Brigade	67					1,426	743
Life Boys...	46*					400	
Girl Guides		207		2,134	500 (age 14) 362 (age 15)		
Rangers		51			347 (age 16-20)		
Boy Scouts	178					3,135	500 (age 14) 794 (over 15)
Rovers							343
Girls' Life Brigade ...		58		1,250	550		
Church Lads' Brigade ...	7					140	90
Junior Girls' Training Corps and							
Girls Training Corps...		18			400		
W.J.A.C....		24			525		
British Camp Fire Girls		4		30	21		
Church Girls' Brigade ...		2		15	15		
Boys' Pre-Service							
Sea Cadets	4						250
Air Training Corps ...	19						2,030
Army Cadets	31						1,377
British Red Cross Society							
Red Cross Cadets ...	5	16		200	100	75	50
Young People in Adult Detachments					50		
St. John Ambulance Brigade							
Girl Cadets		28		382	256		
Boy Cadets	24					220	110
Political							
Young Unionists ...			42		920		615
Labour League of Youth			12		135		90
Young Communists ..			4		10		30
Young Liberals			5		90		160

Table continued on next page.

TABLE XLVIII—(continued)

DETAILED SUMMARY OF YOUTH ORGANIZATIONS IN BIRMINGHAM

ORGANIZATION	UNITS			MEMBERS			
	Boys	Girls	Mixed	Girls		Boys	
				11-14	14-20	11-14	14-20
Birmingham Association of Girls and Mixed Clubs		25	122	1,077	5,016	825	5,726
Birmingham Federation of Boys' Clubs	93		49			1,858	7,017
Midland Adult School Union	1	1	6	41	226	5	215
Birmingham Boys' and Girls' Union	4		4	93	142	185	290
Young Farmers' Club ...			1		9		5
Citizens' Clubs			5		122		78
Community Centres with Youth Centres			5		341		358
Settlements			2	256	190	198	196
Y.M.C.A.	2		6		91		689
Y.W.C.A.		3	7	386 (11-15)	774 (15-20)		323
Welsh League of Youth ...			1		12		18
Youth Service Corps ...		1	1		162		40
Religious (Non-Uniformed) Church of England Youth Clubs	4	3	87		2,698		2,757
Church of England Junior Youth Clubs ...	14*	13*	39*	707		1,128	
Free Church Youth Clubs	9	2	64	522	1,377	471	1,504
Girls' Friendly Society...		22		175	95		
Roman Catholic Youth Clubs	35	12		47	261	239	977
Young Christian Workers (Boys) ...	8						115
Young Christian Workers (Girls) ...		3			110		
Salvation Army	4	6	6	289	196	249	150

Table continued on next page.

TABLE XLVIII—(continued)

DETAILED SUMMARY OF YOUTH ORGANIZATIONS IN BIRMINGHAM

ORGANIZATION	UNITS			MEMBERS			
	Boys	Girls	Mixed	Girls		Boys	
				11-14	14-20	11-14	14-20
Jewish Youth Council ...			7	26	120	34	80
Old Scholars' Clubs ...	4	2	2		370		500
Unattached Industrial Clubs	1	1	2		536		352
Co-operative Junior Organizations ...			32*	550		475	
Youth Clubs			17		520		730
British Federation of Young Co-operators ...			7		85		65
Wayfarers' Club			1		25		25
Evening Institutes and Recreative Centres Juvenile Evening Institutes with Recreative Evenings			21		397		400
Recreative Centres ...	1	1	4		314		418
Gross Total Clubs of all kinds	**166** plus 14*	**82** plus 13*	**427** plus 71*	**4,169**	**14,189**	**5,667**	**23,028**
Less Deductions for duplicate affiliations	36	9	52	428	2,422	941	3,288
Net Total Clubs of all kinds	**130** plus 14*	**73** plus 13*	**375** plus 71*	**3,741**	**11,767**	**4,726**	**19,740**

* Units catering for members under fourteen only.

TABLE XLIX

DISTRIBUTION OF YOUTH POPULATION AND OF YOUTH ORGANIZATIONS IN THE PARLIAMENTARY WARDS OF THE CITY

Municipal Wards	Approx. area in sq. miles	Number of Youth Organizations plotted					Approx. population age 14-20
		Total	Youth Clubs	Unif. Voluntary	Pre-Service Units	Others	
Acocks Green	3	63	24 .	31	4	4	2,768
All Saints	1	22	10	9	—	3	1,856
Aston	1	29	10	16	1	2	2,081
Balsall Heath	1	41	18	17	2	4	2,194
Bromford	4	39	14	18	4	3	2,237
Duddeston and Nechells ...	1	39	22	15	—	2	1,849
Edgbaston	4	50	14	29	4	3	2,288
Erdington	2	53	28	19	3	3	2,670
Gravelly Hill	3	43	16	21	—	6	2,440
Hall Green	3	47	19	21	2	5	3,678
Handsworth	2	41	14	22	1	4	2,168
Harborne	3	45	14	22	4	5	2,720
King's Norton	5	33	11	19	1	2	2,895
Ladywood	1	20	7	9	—	4	1,700
Lozells	1	34	12	18	2	2	1,965
Market Hall	1	23	9	4	2	8	950
Moseley and King's Heath	3	49	17	22	3	7	3,625
Northfield	9	67	26	29	2	10	3,700
Perry Barr	5	53	26	19	3	5	5,960
Rotton Park	1	27	13	12	—	2	2,115
St. Bartholomews	1	26	11	12	—	3	1,270
St. Martin's and Deritend ..	1	35	17	14	1	3	1,445
St. Mary's	1	21	11	9	1	3	1,195
St. Paul's	1	21	10	8	—	3	1,490
Saltley	2	25	12	9	—	4	1,850
Sandwell	2	32	9	21	1	1	1,668
Selly Oak	3	43	21	14	1	7	2,420
Small Heath	1	25	9	14	—	2	2,088
Soho	2	31	8	19	1	3	1,842
Sparkbrook	1	29	13	12	2	2	2,128
Sparkhill	2	35	13	17	2	3	2,556
Stechford	7	67	25	33	4	5	4,844
Washwood Heath	2	38	13	23	1	1	2,481
Yardley	2	34	15	14	1	4	2,840
TOTAL ...	82	1,280	511	591	53	128	81,976

CHAPTER VI

THE CONTENT OF THE LOCAL YOUTH SERVICE

IN THIS CHAPTER we propose to describe the various activities in which young people engage when they attend youth organizations in the city, and to describe what we have seen in connexion with such determining factors as leadership, finance, premises, and the availability of playing fields.

The programmes offered by different movements are of an almost bewildering variety, but it may be convenient to classify the various youth organizations in three main groups:

(A) Non-uniformed organizations whose members are brought together by a particular common interest and who engage in fairly specific activities.

(B) The Uniformed organizations.

(C) The Clubs.

(A) NON-UNIFORMED ORGANIZATIONS OTHER THAN CLUBS

It is impossible to generalize about the activities of the organizations which fall into this group, because they are so very varied. They include the political youth movements, the Youth Service Corps, and such interesting groups as the Young Farmers' Clubs, the Welsh League of Youth, the Habonim (a Jewish Zionist Youth Movement) and the (Roman Catholic) Young Christian Workers. The Youth Hostels Association should be included, together with other Rambling and Cycling Organizations. It is difficult, indeed, to know where to draw the line. To give a complete picture of all the societies in which Birmingham young people come together for some organized activity, it would be necessary to include such varied groups as Harriers, Pigeon Clubs, Works Football teams, Bible Classes, Model Aero Clubs, Bands of Hope, a Bird Watching Society, a British Railway Association, and even a Weight-Lifting Club, and a Frank Sinatra Fan Club! Except for the political Youth Movements, the Welsh League of Youth, the Habonim and the Young Christian Workers, we have not included in our list of 1,384 youth units or in our membership statistics any of the other groups mentioned above.

The Rambling and Cycling Organizations, however, deserve more than this passing reference. The Youth Hostels Association was founded in 1930 to provide hostels where its members, either on walking or cycling tours, could find food, shelter and companionship at small cost. An undoubted contribution is being made to the health of young people, many of whom are being helped to discover the beauties of the countryside. The Association owns something like 300 hostels in England and Wales. Members fall into three groups: Juveniles, age 9-16, Juniors, age 16-21, and Seniors, 21 and upwards. It is estimated that members resident within the City of Birmingham include 1,900 Juveniles and 3,225 Juniors. We might assume, therefore, that there are 3,500 members between the ages of 14 and 20, or, in other words, one in twenty-three of the city's adolescent population. It is thought, too, that about 1,000 young people are members of the Cyclists' Touring Club. These two organizations unite with the Ramblers' Association to promote 'The Wayfarers' Club', where members of the three bodies meet socially once a week for a programme of talks, discussions, or films on subjects of common interest. On the occasion of our visit we estimated that about a quarter of the two hundred people present were under twenty years of age.

During the last few years, as we have seen, each of the political parties has made great efforts to attract young people into its youth organizations. It cannot be said, speaking generally, that the effort has met with much success. We very much doubt whether more than 2 per cent of our 80,000 adolescents are in touch with any political youth movement. In our city, the Young Unionists, who have an organizing secretary and a central headquarters, are by far the largest of these groups. These movements are outside the Youth Service, and therefore they are not grant-aided in any way. They cannot obtain a canteen licence, nor are they allowed the use of school premises at a nominal charge as are other youth organizations. The problem of premises is often their greatest difficulty, as church halls also are denied them. Membership of these groups runs up to 25 years of age in the case of the Labour League of Youth, and up to 30 in the case of the Young Unionists and the Young Communists. Some branches appear to have few members under the age of 20. There are those who deplore the attempt to indoctrinate young people with party creeds, but it cannot be denied that valuable political education is being given in these groups. In some cases, it is true, social and recreational activities are more evident than are more serious pursuits—we visited one Young Unionist branch where the young people present were very restless during a political talk and were obviously itching to be at the table tennis and darts which were to follow. We had the feeling that they would have been equally happy—or equally bored—had the group been of a different political complexion. On the other hand, the various political youth groups have attracted many of the more serious-minded and more public-spirited young people, and a typical programme includes ar more talks, discussions and debates than does that of the average youth club. The Young Communists are few in number, but we have been impressed by their genuine passion for social justice. The Young Unionists offer in their programmes Discussion Groups, Debates, Topical Talks, Brains Trusts, Quizzes and Mock Parliaments. A typical Labour League of Youth syllabus is illustrated by the following programme of one group during a period of six weeks in February and March 1949:

> Informal Discussion (Nationalization of the land)
> American Supper
> Speaker (Subject—'Education')
> Theatre Visit
> League of Youth Birthday Party
> Business Meeting

These young people are often very one-sided in their thinking, but they are receiving political education, they are learning to formulate and to express their own convictions, and they do engage in political activity. Occasionally debates take place between a branch of one party and a branch of another. We suggest that a debate of this kind between groups of two different political parties, 'staged' on the premises of an ordinary non-political youth club, might be an excellent stimulus to the members of the 'home' club.

The Welsh League of Youth and the Young Farmers' Clubs are each represented in Birmingham by one small unit only, so that we ought not, perhaps, to discuss their activities further, important as these organizations are in other parts of the country.

The Youth Service Corps, of which at one time there were a number of branches in the city, is now represented by two units, one of which is a school society, while the activities of the other resemble those of a very good open youth club.

Some of the other movements which are included in this first group, though relatively small in membership, present features of special interest. This is particularly true of the Young Christian Workers and of the Habonim, both of which organizations have succeeded in inspiring young people with a sense of purpose, the noticeable absence of which, in so many organizations, gives rise to our greatest concern as we think about the Youth Service in this country as a whole. ★ The Young Christian Workers are organized in small 'cells' of about half a dozen young fellows or girls, who meet together to discuss ways in which a Christian witness may be made effective in industrial life, whether in factories, in Trade Unions, or in Local and National Government. Their activities can be summed up in their own slogan: 'See, Judge, Act'. Habonim is a Hebrew word which means 'The Builders' and in this organization young Jews—some of them workers

★The final chapter of this Report is devoted to a discussion of Purpose in the Youth Service.

in industry and some of them students and members of one or other of the professions, meet together to train and prepare themselves for the day when, as they hope, they will be able to go to Palestine, where by working on the land they will help in the building of the State of Israel.

(B) THE UNIFORMED ORGANIZATIONS

Most uniformed organizations would probably share the belief that 'the attainment of the fullest possible development is best achieved within the framework of a uniformed, disciplined corps; uniformed because only by this can class distinction be abolished and a real pride in personal appearance be encouraged; disciplined because only by the experience of wise discipline can we learn that self-discipline and self-control without which our efforts are of no avail'.*

The uniformed organizations are distinguished from all other youth movements, not only by the distinctive dress of their members, but also because they are all single-sex units, and because they all follow a prescribed curriculum of training and activity which is drawn up in London. The Regional Commanding Officer of one of these organizations who told us 'when you have seen one of my units, you have seen them all' was perhaps a little unfair to his own movement, but there was a measure of truth in his remark. These organizations fall into several groups— Brigades, Boy Scouts and Girl Guides, Red Cross Units, Boys' Pre-Service organizations and the National Association of Training Corps for Girls.

(i) *The Brigades*

The oldest of the uniformed voluntary organizations is the Boys' Brigade, which was founded by Sir William Smith in Glasgow in 1883. One unit we visited was established as long ago as 1891. The object of the Boys' Brigade is 'The advancement of Christ's Kingdom among boys, and the promotion of habits of Obedience, Reverence, Discipline, Self-Respect, and all that tends towards a true Christian manliness'. In the belief that 'Religion and Discipline are the primary needs of youth' the activities of a company centre round a compulsory Bible Class and a compulsory drill parade. Most companies, however, meet several nights a week and provide all the typical boys' club activities. Several companies turn out two or three football teams every Saturday. If Sunday Bible Class and Saturday football be included, the fourteen units we visited were open on an average of over five days a week. A number of boys seem to attend every day. In one case, it is true, very little could be seen but drill, but most companies offer ambulance, physical training, first aid, band, signalling and swimming. Quite the best L.E.A. woodwork class we have seen was that attached to one Boys' Brigade Company—a unit which, incidentally, possesses its own excellent club rooms. During the summer about half the boys attached to companies in the Birmingham Battalion attend camp. Boys between the ages of nine and twelve belong to Life Boy teams, and we were able to visit nine of the forty-six teams in the city. Unless they become officers, boys must leave the movement at the age of eighteen, when in any event many of them are called up for military service. All companies must be attached to a church and most meet in church halls, though a number find additional accommodation in local schools.

We visited twelve of the city's fifty-eight Girls' Life Brigade Companies. This organization can be regarded as in many respects the sister to the Boys' Brigade, its object being 'to help and encourage girls to become self-reliant and useful Christian women'. Girls can join when they are 6, becoming Juniors at 10, Seniors at 13 and Pioneers at 16. Units are generally small, the average membership in the 14-20 age-range being less than 10. Most companies usually meet one evening a week only, when a carefully planned programme usually includes drill, physical training, games, and perhaps first aid, hand-work, or singing, with a devotional introduction and dismissal. Proficiency badges may be won. The leaders of many of these companies are women inspired by great devotion, but we feel that programmes tend to be too rigid. If the half-hour allowed for handcrafts, for instance, expires at eight o'clock, the girl who is absorbed in the leather glove she is making is exhorted to 'Come along now. Put that down: it's time for games'.

* From a publication of the Women's Junior Air Corps.

A BOYS' BRIGADE PARADE: *Semi-military uniform and discipline are distinguishing features of the Boys' Brigade and Church Lads' Brigade and the corresponding organizations for girls.*

GIRLS' LIFE BRIGADE. *A Birmingham Company gives a display of National Dancing at a Royal Albert Hall Rally.*

There is no leisure in which to do what one likes or to talk to one's friends. One leader reported trouble caused by the fact that boys would hang about outside the premises on the night of the Company meeting. She had asked the police to keep an eye on the place. It would apparently have been quite impossible to have invited the boys in at a certain time during the evening for some joint activity.

The Church Lads' Brigade and the Church Girls' Brigade are Anglican organizations and are represented in Birmingham by seven and two companies respectively. Military drill seems to be the main item in most programmes, but the week's activities of one boys' unit also included games, a film show, band practice, first aid, signalling, a study of the Highway Code, and Saturday afternoon football.

(ii) Boy Scouts

In the whole history of youth work in this country, and perhaps in the world, no other name stands out as prominently as does that of Robert Baden-Powell. With a brilliant insight into the boy's mind he invented the greatest of all open-air games and directed the gang impulse into creative channels. Baden-Powell did not believe in military drill, preferring that boys should be helped to become self-disciplined and self-reliant. The difference between the Brigade and the Scout approach is seen by a comparison of their camping methods: the typical Brigade camp is large and highly organized, with all the tents pitched with military precision, while the typical Scout camp is an expedition in which a patrol of half a dozen boys adventure forth on their own. Scouts tend, even more than the Brigades, to lose their members at school-leaving age, and it is hoped that the raising of this age to fifteen and the recent inauguration of Senior Scouts for boys age 15-17 will reduce this leakage. Of the 170 Scout groups in the city, we visited thirty-four. These included one Sea Scout Troop, one for deaf boys, one for blind boys and one attached to an orphanage. The nature of Scouting is such that it permits of greater variations of success or failure than does an organization with a more stereotyped programme (it is probably easier to find a good Brigade Captain than a good Scoutmaster), and it is inevitable that these variations should have become apparent in the course of our visitation. We met many enthusiastic and imaginative leaders whose keenness was matched by that of their boys; but we also found one troop where neither the Scoutmaster nor any of the boys were in uniform, and where the whole time of the weekly meeting was devoted to table tennis. Many Scout groups are attached to churches, but the link is much looser than is that of the Brigades, and is sometimes quite nominal. We have always thought of Scouting as an outdoor rather than as an indoor movement, and were surprised to find, therefore, how few outdoor activities took place during the week of our visit as compared with those found in other organizations. Our visits took place in October and November, but among the thirty-four Scout groups visited, cycling, rambling, youth hostelling, boating and camping were mentioned once each only.

(iii) Girl Guides

There are in Birmingham about two hundred Girl Guide and about fifty Ranger companies. The movement consists of a large number of small units which normally meet once a week only. We attended the weekly meeting of forty-two Guide and of nine Ranger companies. The average attendance at meetings of Guide Companies was rather less than twenty, the great majority of those present being under the age of fourteen. The usual evening's programme was made up of roll-call and inspection, a few general games or country dancing, badge work under the direction of patrol leaders and a final 'camp fire' or 'sing-song'. Other activities included six church parades, one swimming party and three Saturday evening socials. Only three units reported any Saturday outdoor activities, these being a nature ramble, a ten-mile hike and a hip-picking expedition. The movement as a whole is concerned about its failure to retain the older girl in membership. We wonder how far this failure is due to the fact that the normal programme of the Ranger company differs very little from that of the younger section of the movement. The nine Ranger companies we visited included one Sea Ranger Company and one Air Ranger

Flight, and it is significant that 23·3 per cent of the members were still at school, 66·7 per cent engaged in clerical occupations and only 10 per cent in manual occupations. Does the Ranger movement appeal, in the main, to the more intelligent type of girl?

(iv) *The British Red Cross Society and The St. John Ambulance Brigade*

These two organizations only muster about four hundred girls and one hundred and fifty boys in the 14-20 age range, though they have a larger membership in the younger age groups. In one instance, where the membership had fallen from fifty to about a dozen, the leader attributed its decline to the fact that 'fathers and brothers who have come out of the Forces sneer at any kind of uniformed voluntary service'. Though small in numbers, however, these organizations provide many recruits for the nursing and medical services. Activities usually include first aid, nursing and hygiene, and periodical examinations take place in these subjects. As always, the secret of success is in inspired and inspiring leadership. In one instance we found a small group of rather listless boys sullenly taking part in drill of poor standard, while another unit, where a schoolmaster had gathered together a group of his own schoolboys, was one of the happiest and friendliest companies we discovered in any of our visits to any organization. Many members give service in hospitals or nurseries, or assist adult members on first-aid duty in cinemas and theatres.

(v) *Boys' Pre-Service Organizations*

It is perhaps surprising to discover four units of the Sea Cadets in our midland city so far from the sea. We were able to visit three of these units, each of which had the use of several boats on one or other of the city's reservoirs or lakes. Typical training includes seamanship, signals, physical training and swimming. One unit had a band. Each of the three units met on Saturday afternoon and on one week evening, while two met also on Sunday morning. One Commanding Officer was trying to give his boys a club night once a week, free of Service training, but was badly handicapped by the condition of the building he had to use, with its concrete floor, bad roof and total absence of heating.

The training offered by the Army Cadets links up with the primary training of the Army recruit and so provides a real preparation for military service. Units normally meet on Sunday mornings and on one or two evenings a week, but we visited one large unit which offered a programme on Sunday morning and on four evenings. Activities include football, weapon training, map reading and open air military manœuvres, but some units add boxing, table tennis, billiards, football and basket ball. Companies usually meet in spacious drill-halls where all the required equipment is available, so that they are not troubled by the difficulty in obtaining premises, which is a problem to so many youth organizations. Opinions, however, will differ about the desirability of bringing fourteen-year-old boys four evenings a week into a building where, to quote our visitor 'there is a strong armoury of rifles, machine-guns and live ammunition on the premises'.

We were only permitted to visit three units of the Air Training Corps, all of which met on Sunday mornings and on four evenings during the week. All members are taught Morse, mathematics, drill, physical training, aircraft recognition and rifle shooting. Other subjects offered include training in navigation, guns and bombs, while technical trades taught include wireless operator, wireless mechanic, engine mechanic and aircraft mechanic. In two instances one evening was of a recreational character, and in two cases football was played on Saturday afternoon. All officers and instructors are appointed by the Air Ministry and give their services voluntarily. Many of them are teachers who prefer to give their evenings to voluntary instruction in the A.T.C. rather than to take classes in Evening Institutes where they would receive payment. One of the most impressive·features of A.T.C. training is the lavish provision of equipment supplied by the Air Ministry. Some units have the use of aero engines and wireless transmitters, the value of which must be very great. The girls in the W.J.A.C., meeting perhaps in the same building, must themselves raise the money for any equipment they require and provide their own uniform. Members of Boys' Pre-Service organizations pay no subscriptions and if they have to travel any considerable distance to attend the unit, may even have their 'bus fares provided!

(vi) *National Association of Training Corps for Girls*

The N.A.T.C.G. co-ordinates the activities of the Girls' Training Corps, the Women's Junior Air Corps and the Girls' Nautical Training Corps. The last organization is not represented in Birmingham, but there are twenty-four units of the W.J.A.C. and eighteen of the G.T.C. The aim of the National Association is to provide girls with a general training for National Service, this training to be given within a disciplined framework, with an accepted code of behaviour and etiquette. Compulsory subjects are first aid, hygiene, physical training and drill, but other social and recreative activities may be added. Most of the units visited by us met only one evening a week, though one company was open on four days. Units differ even more widely than do those of other organizations. The Company with a four-day programme offered aircraft modelling, physical training, gym, band practice, domestic science, 'air-training', handcrafts, ballroom dancing, visits to places of interest and service to local hospitals on Sunday evenings. On the other hand, the only activity of another unit was a weekly band practice with an occasional game of netball. The leader of this particular unit complained that membership was falling because their boy friends objected to the girls wearing uniform. In another unit, the greater part of the weekly meeting was taken up by a physical training class with an L.E.A. instructor. In some units there is a strict military discipline, the girls being required, if they wish to speak to an officer, to salute and stand to attention, with their jackets buttoned and their hats on. In another unit, where most of the evening was taken up by a lecture on 'Mothercraft' (in which the girls were very interested) there was a much more informal atmosphere.

(C) CLUBS

Clubs are of many kinds. They may be Boys', Girls' or Mixed societies; they may be attached to a school, a factory, a co-operative society, a community centre, a Y.M.C.A. or Y.W.C.A., a church, or they may be completely independent. If sponsored by a church they may be 'closed' clubs (i.e. with membership restricted to young people of the church) but usually they are open to 'all-comers'. One Anglican club reserves 'full' membership to communicants, and another stipulates that committee members must be communicants. Free Church clubs, in the main, do not make the stipulation that members must be associated with the church to which the club is attached.

A great majority of the clubs appear to have come into existence during the last few years. Only one-third of the clubs visited by us have a history which goes back to 1942. It is interesting also to discover the many varied ways in which clubs came into being. In one instance, eleven boys formed themselves into a football team and met together from time to time in a shed on an allotment. A few adults became interested and this original group has now grown into a large and flourishing club, meeting in the local school. In another case, a group of young people approached a church asking if they might have the use of a hall one evening a week. Permission was granted and the young people approached the Birmingham Association of Girls' Clubs and Mixed Clubs, who were able to find them a leader. Club activities also are very varied. There are youth clubs whose members appear to do nothing but dance, there are boys' clubs whose activities seem not to extend beyond billiards and table tennis, but there are clubs where the range of interests includes indoor games and socials, physical training, outdoor activities, craftsmanship, drama, educational classes, committee work, the production of a club magazine, the organization of special events (parents' nights, the Christmas pantomime, the annual dinner or the summer camp), service to the community, prayer and worship. The programmes offered by the Weoley Castle Boys' and Girls' Club and by the Warstock Y.M.C.A.-Y.W.C.A. for the first week of March 1949, were as follows:

95

	WEOLEY CASTLE BOYS' AND GIRLS' CLUB		WARSTOCK Y.M.C.A. AND Y.W.C.A.	
MONDAY 5.30 p.m. – 7 p.m. 7 p.m. – 10 p.m.	*Girls age 11-14:* Games, Felt Work, Raffia, Magazine *Boys and Girls age 14-18:* Table Games with classes in Boys' Woodwork and Girls' P.T. Dancing the last hour	6.30 p.m. 8.0 p.m. 8.0 p.m. 9.0 p.m.	Table Games Badminton Puppet Group Girls' Dancing Class Violin Lesson
TUESDAY: 7 p.m. – 10 p.m.	*Senior Club for Members age 16 and over:* Table Games with classes in Girls' Woodwork, and Boys' P.T. Boys' Football Training	6.0 p.m. 7.30 p.m. 8.0 p.m. 9.0 p.m.	Junior Drama Boys' P.T. Boys' Choir Girls' Choir Table Games
WEDNESDAY: 5.30 p.m. – 7 p.m. 7.30 p.m.–10 p.m. 7.30 p.m. 9.30 p.m.	*Boys age 10-14:* Games, Gym, Handwork, Drama, Junior Boys' Committee *Over Eighteen Club* Badminton, Football Training General Club Committee Over Eighteen Club Committee	7.30 p.m. 8.30 p.m.	Puppets Boys' and Girls' Drama Table Games
THURSDAY: 5.30 p.m. – 7 p.m. 7 p.m. – 10 p.m.	*Girls age 11-14:* Games, Puppets, Drama, Cookery *Intermediate Club for Boys and Girls aged 14-16:* Games, Football Training, Girls' Dressmaking, Boys' P.T. Drama, Dancing		Boys' Night Puppets, Boxing, House and Football meetings Inter-house competitions Darts League Table Games
FRIDAY: 5.30 p.m. – 7 p.m. 7 p.m. – 10 p.m.	'Boys only' night. *Boys age 10-14:* Model-Making, Gym, Handwork, Drama, Games *Boys age 14 and over:* Games, P.T., Basket Ball Football Training Football Committee	6.0 p.m. 7.30 p.m.	Girls' Night: Junior Dancing Class Health and Beauty
SATURDAY:	Under 17, Under 19, Under 21 and over 21 Football Teams. Two Girls' Netball Teams	Afternoon Evening	3 Football Teams Badminton Dance, Music Practice (Instrumental)
SUNDAY: 7.45p.m.–10 p.m.	'Mixed Bag' Programme for members aged 14-16. Discussion Group for members 16 and over	3.45 p.m. 8.15 p.m.	Boys' Leadership Training Club Service

ONE WEEK'S PROGRAMMES
in two Clubs catering for both sexes

In so far as it is possible to classify various types of club, they may perhaps be described as follows:

(i) *Y.M.C.A. and Y.W.C.A. Clubs.* Usually owning their own premises, and staffed by full-time professional club leaders, these clubs are comparatively few in number, but they usually have a fairly large membership and they offer a comprehensive programme of activities. Sometimes the unit is primarily a youth club, but elsewhere, youth work is subordinate to work among older age groups.

(ii) *Independent Clubs.* With their own buildings and with professional leaders, this type of club, which is found in large numbers in London and Liverpool, is a comparative rarity in Birmingham, but is represented in the clubs attached to the Birmingham Boys' and Girls' Union, and by the Weoley Castle Boys' and Girls' Club and by the Stonehouse Gang.

(iii) *Industrial Clubs.* The largest of these has its full-time leaders and its own premises and appears to offer a wider range of activity than does any other youth unit in the city. An interesting feature of the Co-operative Clubs, which fall into this category, is that they normally open on two evenings a week only, one evening for recreational activities and one for cultural activities. It is normally a condition of membership of these clubs that members must take part in at least one cultural activity.

(iv) *Clubs attached to other adult bodies.* We have included in our Survey those Community Centres which devote certain evenings or rooms to youth activities, and Citizens' Clubs which include adolescents in their membership. These activities (so far as young people are concerned, at any rate) appear to be almost exclusively social and recreational. There are successful youth clubs attached to the two branches of the Birmingham Settlement and to the Burlington Hall Neighbourhood Centre.

(v) *L.E.A. Clubs.* The Birmingham L.E.A., as we have seen, does not normally promote its own youth centres. There are a few Old Scholars' Clubs attached to certain schools, and a number of Junior Evening Institutes offer recreational evenings.

TABLE L

PHYSICAL AND RECREATIONAL ACTIVITIES
PROVIDED BY 141 CLUBS IN ONE WEEK

Outdoor	No. of Clubs	Indoor	No. of Clubs
Football	54 (75 teams)	Canteen	123
Netball	11	Table Tennis and other Indoor Games...	121
Swimming	6	Dancing	61
Week-end Camp	2	Gym, Keep-Fit, or Physical Training	37
Cycle Run	2	Socials	31
Hike or Ramble...	2	Boxing	13
Street Running	2	Badminton	7
Cross-Country Running ...	1	Dancing Instruction	'7
Youth Hostel week-end ...	1	Whist Drive	4
		Basket Ball	4
		American Supper	1

(vi) *Church Clubs*. Nearly half the clubs in Birmingham are attached to churches. These clubs vary in size from that associated with the Hall Green Parish Church, with its 750 members, to little groups of ten or a dozen young people meeting in a small vestry one evening a week. Generally, however, church clubs can be divided into two categories—they are either clubs proper—sometimes 'open' and sometimes 'closed'—with a more or less balanced programme of activities, or they are recreational societies where young people who are engaged in other church activities come together for social purposes one evening a week. There is, we feel, a real place for the one-night-a-week recreational club for young people who are engaged in other more purposeful activities on other evenings.

We propose, in a later chapter, to attempt the very difficult task of assessing the quality and value of the work that is done in clubs but at the moment we are merely listing the various activities which are included in club programmes.

Table L (page 97) shows the number of clubs, out of 141 visited by us, which offered the activities indicated during the week in which our visits fell.

Of the clubs affiliated to the Birmingham Federation of Boys' Clubs, the following activities are said to form part of the programme in the number of clubs specified:

TABLE LI

PHYSICAL AND RECREATIONAL ACTIVITIES
PROVIDED BY BOYS' CLUBS IN THE BIRMINGHAM FEDERATION

Activity	No. of Clubs	Activity	No. of Clubs	Activity	No. of Clubs
Football	75	Hiking	27	Wrestling ...	6
Cricket	69	Tennis	24	Gardening ...	6
Athletics... ...	49	Basket Ball ...	14	Hockey ...	4
Boxing	49	Badminton ...	11	Rowing	3
Cycling	48	Street Running ...	11	Fencing	2
Physical Training	44	Country Dancing	8	Rugby Football	2

It cannot be claimed, we think, that all these activities are organized on the extensive scale that these figures might suggest, or that the standard achieved is always very high, but they are at least indicative of the major pre-occupation of clubs in physical activities of all kinds. One largely attended club offers a Ballroom Dancing class on Monday, a Boys' Physical Training class on Tuesday, a Social on Wednesday, Table Tennis on Thursday, Swimming on Friday and Football matches on Saturday.

CULTURAL ACTIVITIES

In the 141 clubs visited the cultural activities shown in Table LII were included in the programme of the current week.

Nine of the clubs visited possessed a library of sorts. These figures indicate the number of clubs in which, during the week of our visit, the activities specified formed part of the programme. The number of actual group activities would be a little higher, as some of the larger clubs have a number of craft activities or have several Physical Training classes. At the same time, the number of cultural activities was something less than an average of two per club. Twenty-two of the clubs visited seemed to offer nothing at all except table tennis, a cup of tea, and a little casual dancing to a tinny gramophone or a hard-used piano.

TABLE LII

CULTURAL ACTIVITIES IN 141 CLUBS

Activities	No. of Clubs
Talks, Discussions, Debates, etc. ...	58
Handwork (Woodwork, Plastics, Leather-work, Toy-making, etc.)	51
Drama or Play Reading	42
Music (Community singing, Gramophone, Choir, Musical appreciation, 1 Orchestra 2 Dance Bands, 1 Operetta, 1 Opera)...	28
Concert Party Groups	8
Films	7
First Aid	6
Health Talks or Sex Education	4
Cookery	4
Art	3
Inter-club Visit	2
Theatre Party	2
Photography	1
Leadership Training Class	1

DEVOTIONAL AND RELIGIOUS

Of the 141 clubs visited by us, 68 were attached to churches and 73 were not. 17 of the non-church clubs—including the Y.M.C.A. and Y.W.C.A. units—offer 'epilogues' or club services in their programme. The remaining 56 clubs in this group provided no religious activities. Among these are the co-operative and industrial clubs. Of the 68 church clubs, 15 do not include any religious activity in the club programme as such. In some, this is because the club is intended to be merely a recreational society for young people who are engaged in other church activities, and in others it is because, though the club meets on church premises, the actual association is very slight.

Sunday activities were as follows:

TABLE LIII

SUNDAY ACTIVITIES IN 141 CLUBS

	73 Non-Church Clubs	68 Church Clubs
Not open on Sundays	45	35
Devotional Activities only	3	9
Devotional and General Activities	9	16
Social and Recreational Activities only and/or hikes, football	16	8

It is to be borne in mind that our visitation took place in October and November. Typical summer activities therefore scarcely appear in the above lists but in the programme of activities submitted to us by club leaders they figure very largely. The following list indicates the extent of outdoor activities included in the full programme of the 141 clubs visited:

TABLE LIV

SUMMER OUTDOOR ACTIVITIES PROVIDED BY 141 CLUBS

	No. of Clubs
Outdoor Sports and Athletics	110
Cycling	74
Swimming	68
Participation in Sports Leagues	66
Camping	65
Youth Hostelling	43
Foreign Travel	28
Hiking or Rambling	18

In their annual returns to the Birmingham Federation of Boys' Clubs a number of leaders report the existence in their clubs of groups engaged in radio listening, lino-cutting, clay-modelling, model-making, printing and weaving, but we saw none of these activities in any club visited.

MEMBERS' PREFERENCES

In our *Twenty Question* inquiry we asked: 'Do you belong to any club or youth organization? If so, what?' and 'When you go, what do you most enjoy doing?' We obtained many more completed questionnaires than the thousand which we selected as representing a sample of the youth population, and in this way we were able to compare the members' attitude to the activities of their various units with the programmes planned by their leaders.

It is, we think, particularly significant that in answer to the question: 'When you go, what do you most enjoy doing?' thirty young people answer 'talking', 'talking with friends', 'meeting friends', 'getting together', 'making new friends', 'mixing with other people', 'talking to the other lads', 'talking about football', 'together activities' and so on. One boy answered 'talking to the club leader' and another 'conversing with intelligent people'. Four boys were honest enough to write 'talking to girls' and one girl said 'talking to boys', and one other, 'flirting'. It is quite clear that whatever be the motives of the leader in promoting his organization, its chief value in the eyes of many of its members is that it gives them a chance to find themselves in a society of their contemporaries. Perhaps this, after all, is one of its chief functions.

It cannot be said that the results of this particular inquiry are very encouraging, at any rate as far as club members are concerned. In clubs, dancing and table tennis are easily the most popular activities, but while dancing is mentioned by 96 girls and table tennis by 45, the proportions are reversed with boys, table tennis being the favourite activity of 95 boys and dancing of only 24.

Among boy members, next in order of popularity come billiards or snooker 23, darts 11, gymnastics or physical training 10, and cycling 8. Six boys merely answer 'games' and three boys reply 'sports'. Badminton, reading, drama, boxing, chess, scrimmage and playing the piano are mentioned by three boys; while the following appear twice: woodwork, cards, organized games, debates, entertainment groups, socials; and the following once each: musical activities, watching 'variety', rugger, playing gramophone records, organizing cycle runs, basket ball, quoits, cookery (a sixteen-year-old clerk), singing hymns, ball games, educational subjects, and draughts. One boy answers 'supervising', another 'helping others', another 'helping the secretary', and one fifteen-year-old boy admits that what he most enjoys is 'eating the refreshments'. It is surely disappointing that only three boys mention drama, and only six any kind of musical activity. Only three or four boys mention football, although for vast numbers of them it is certainly their favourite activity—the question was evidently interpreted as referring only to indoor activities.

Answers given by girl members give evidence of a greater variety of interest and present, on the whole, a rather more encouraging picture. Physical activities rank very high. Ninety-six girls, as we have seen, mention dancing, five country dancing, but tap dancing, dance instruction, and American square dancing are each mentioned only once. Thirteen girls most enjoy physical training or keep-fit, three girls netball, two badminton, while the following physical activities each appear once: basket ball, vaulting, roller skating, and javelin. Fifteen girls answer 'games'. Outdoor activities are mentioned occasionally in the girls' lists; sports and gardening appearing twice and each of the following once: swimming, cycling, hockey, rambling, tennis, seeing the countryside, and horse-riding. Cultural activities are mentioned by more girls than boys. Twelve girls most enjoy discussions, while other answers are religious meetings 5, singing 4, lectures 3, music 3, playing the piano 2, and the following by one girl each: debates, films, crafts, reading, competitions, and 'putting records on'. Sewing is the most popular activity of five girls and each of the following crafts of one: knitting, raffia-work, leatherwork and cookery. One girl answers 'learning something new'.

Answers given by young people who belong to the uniformed organizations present generally a more balanced picture. Twenty-six boys belonging to Scouts or Brigades told us what they most enjoyed doing, and their answers were: table tennis 4, physical training 3, general Scout work 3, general Brigade work 2, football 2, games 2, 'everything' 2, training others 2, and each of the following once: reading, cricket, patrol work, first aid, cycling, and 'attaining higher standards'.

Of girls who were Guides or Rangers, seven girls answered 'games', two outdoor activities, country dancing and camping, while the following were mentioned once each: gymnasium, dancing, signalling, hiking, physical training, knots, handwork, Guide work, first aid, cycling, swimming, teaching new recruits, and teaching games. Similar answers were given by members of the Girls' Life Brigade. Four girls most enjoyed country dancing, two girls games, and two physical training, while the following were mentioned once each: skipping, first aid, sports, lectures, films, helping to organize, and teaching younger members.

In the Red Cross and St. John Ambulance organizations six girls preferred home nursing, three helping with cadets, while two members mentioned bandaging, first aid, and 'everything' while the following appear once: physical training, drama, games, discussions, lectures, teaching home nursing, and 'learning'.

Of members of boys' Pre-Service organizations, aircraft recognition and playing in the band are each mentioned by four boys, A.T.C. instruction, boxing, navigation and football by two, and the following by one each: running, physical training, manœuvres, flying, rifle drill, map reading, snooker, athletics and sport. One sixteen-year-old clerk most enjoyed 'cooking in the galley' and a G.P.O. messenger of the same age 'learning about the sea'. It is evident that one reason for the popularity of these organizations is that they can introduce members to a new range of experience. Girls who belong to the G.T.C. or the W.J.A.C. mentioned gym. or physical training 7, playing in the band 6, netball 2, and drill, drama and aero-modelling once each.

Half the members of political organizations who answered this question mentioned debates or discussions, the others mentioning table tennis, dancing, and games.

In these last few paragraphs we have, as it were, put the members of various youth organizations in the witness box, to speak for themselves. Their testimony has certainly been interesting, but not such, we think, as to afford club leaders any great satisfaction.

OTHER EDUCATIONAL SERVICES

No factual account of the activities and programmes which we have seen in operation would be complete without some reference to the services which are offered to youth organizations of all kinds by the Health Education Department of the Public Health Department and by the Economic League.

(a) *The Public Health Department*

The Public Health Department has a staff of lecturers who are prepared, without any charge to the organization concerned, to address any youth or adult audience on subjects concerned with health and hygiene, and an increasing number of units are availing themselves of this service. One question which we addressed to the leaders of all the organizations we visited was: 'Do you, from time to time, make any effective provision for sex education?' We were amused by the shocked answer of one leader who replied: 'Oh, no, we're a church club', but fortunately not all leaders of church organizations are so inhibited, though only forty-one of the leaders to whom this question was addressed gave us an affirmative answer. Only in four instances did any form of sex education take place in a unit during the week of our visit, and in each case this education was being given—and well given—by a lecturer from the Birmingham Public Health Department. We do not know how many organizations are served in this way during the course of a year, but a very valuable contribution is being made to the Youth Service in the city, a contribution all the more valuable because the sex education given always falls naturally in the larger context of the impartation of knowledge about health and hygiene generally.

(b) *The Economic League*

The Economic League is a voluntary organization the object of which is stated to be 'To give the public the facts which influence our national economic welfare'. The League is devoting a great deal of attention to youth and has recently appointed a full-time organizer whose time is exclusively devoted to activities among young people, and who is prepared, without charge to the unit, to send a speaker to any kind of organization to talk about almost any kind of subject. 140 youth audiences were addressed by invitation during a recent year. The League also sponsors an educational film service and is prepared to supply a programme of films to any unit on request. Perhaps the most interesting of the League's activities, however, is its annual speakers' competition. Youth organizations are invited to enter a team of four members (a chairman, a speaker, a proposer and seconder of a vote of thanks), all of whom must be between the ages of fourteen and twenty. We were present at the final contest of the sixth annual competition, held in March, 1949, when four teams addressed themselves to the rather difficult subject: 'Would a Federation of English-speaking nations guarantee World Peace?' All four teams acquitted themselves very well indeed, the winners being the Kings Norton Youth Service Corps, while the second place was taken by the Streetly Junior Conservatives, and the third by the Birmingham Settlement (Kingstanding). The League claims to be a purely educational organization, with no concern with party politics. We are not completely satisfied that this claim can be substantiated, and certainly the publications of the League have a very definite political bias. The Birmingham Co-operative Society refuses to allow its youth clubs to avail themselves of the service offered by the Economic League, and, as both organizations insist that they are entirely non-political, the explanation of this ban presents a nice problem. The services offered by the League, however, are undoubtedly so excellent that it seems a pity that the same kind of service cannot be provided either by the L.E.A. or by some other body about whose motives there can be no possible doubt. The National Association of Girls' and Mixed Clubs does indeed arrange a speech contest for youth clubs, and a team from Birmingham Settlement (Kingstanding) was one of seven teams chosen from all parts of the British Isles to compete in the final competition held in London in June, 1949.

PREMISES

One of the clearest facts to emerge from our Survey is that the Youth Service in Birmingham, as in so many places, is most inadequately housed. Of the 321 units visited by us only 51 had the exclusive use of the premises they occupied, and in 44 places we were told that the work of the organization was inconvenienced because their premises were often wanted for other purposes.

The various types of premises used by these organizations were distributed as follows:

TABLE LV

PREMISES USED BY YOUTH UNITS VISITED

Church Halls	157
School Premises	78
Premises owned by the Organization ...	41
Industrial Premises	13
Other rented premises or building ...	32

These proportions, we think, represent not inaccurately the situation in Birmingham as a whole. Approximately half the youth units in the city meet in church halls, a quarter in school premises, and the remainder elsewhere. Actually some 500 youth organizations use school premises but this number includes many Brownies, Cubs, Play Centres, etc., which do not fall into the age-range with which this Survey is primarily concerned, and also many football clubs

FIGURE 15

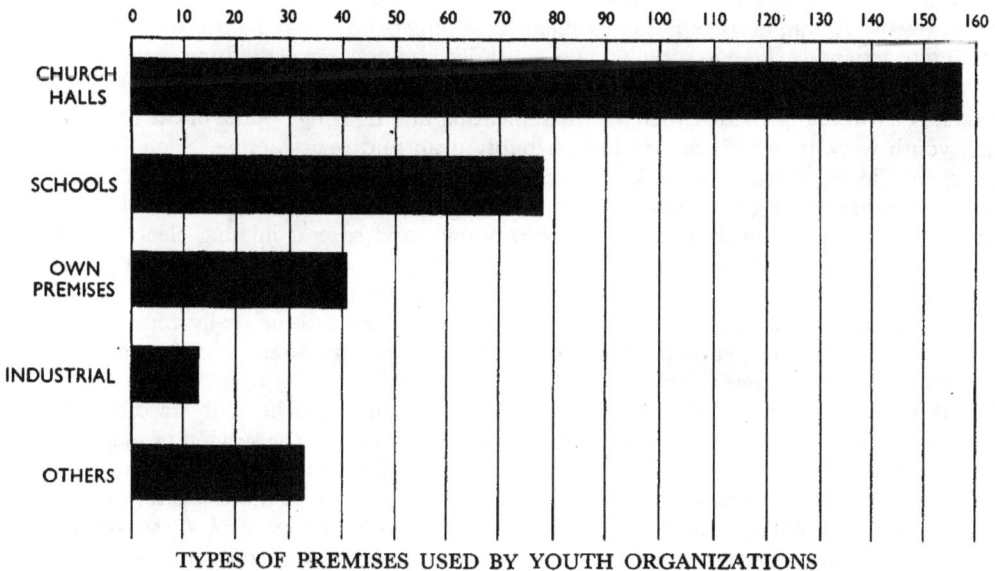

TYPES OF PREMISES USED BY YOUTH ORGANIZATIONS

The relative proportions shown, based on the units visited, represent not unfairly the situation in the city as a whole.

103

which have not been included in our list of 1,384 youth units. Units which own their own premises are few in number, but include most branches of the Y.M.C.A. and of the Y.W.C.A., a few of the larger clubs and several Scout troops which own their huts. Premises which have been specially built for youth work are very few indeed. Five of the units visited by us were found to be meeting in converted public houses, several in private houses, a number in office premises, one in a garage, one in a disused school, and many in various types of temporary building. The home of one uniformed organization was an old building, literally falling to pieces, where the only illumination was provided by candles and hurricane lamps. A Church Girls' Brigade met in a hall which was used as a factory canteen during the day, and was indescribably filthy. The heating apparatus in one church hall had been out of action for over a year, but throughout that time a club had succeeded in maintaining its weekly meeting which, on the occasion of our visit included games, dancing, and canteen for everybody, while three group activities offered a concert party, discussion and first aid. In one Red Cross unit we found twenty-two girls cramped in a small infant classroom which was filled with heavy desks, and in one St. John Ambulance Brigade over fifty boys were taking part in drill, first aid and band practice in the basement of a social club, the atmosphere of which was not improved by the fact that the place was stacked with potatoes.

It is interesting to compare the types of building in which our own students do their practical work. Those who are taking the Froebel teacher training course do part of their school practice in some of the magnificent school buildings which have been erected in recent years, while those who are taking the Youth Leadership course go into all kinds of 'make do and mend' buildings, where at times the physical difficulties to be surmounted make any constructive work almost impossible. Yet surely one form of education is as essential as the other. We vividly remember watching one of our students taking a play-reading circle in an open club on a large housing estate one Sunday night. This club was meeting in what can only be described as a dilapidated shed, with holes in the floor, inadequate heating, and walls that threatened to collapse every time the table tennis enthusiasts on the other side suddenly pushed against them. Despite a great deal of noise from the other rooms, the play went on, and a few young people caught a glimpse, perhaps for the first time in their lives, of the magic of words. Another of our students led a Sunday night discussion group for several weeks in the dingiest of church halls in one of the most depressing parts of the city. The one gas-fire was broken, the lighting was inadequate, the place was dirty, and there were chairs (mostly broken) for only about one-third of the young people present. Again, in spite of these difficulties, young people were helped to clarify their own ideas and to articulate them in speech. The Youth Service deserves something better.

School classrooms provide by no means an ideal setting for youth activity, but at least they are usually clean and provided with adequate heating and lighting. Some of the church halls in which youth work is carried on are indescribably drab and unattractive. Sometimes the only pictures on the walls are those of bewhiskered worthies of the past, while small rooms which would be invaluable for group activities are piled high with lumber and rubbish. Plaster falling from the ceiling, a few broken panes in the windows, and several missing electric light bulbs complete the sorry picture. Is it any wonder that young people prefer the Odeon or the palais de danse? Not all church halls, of course, are like this. Occasionally—but very occasionally—one goes into a club-room to find a few choice pictures on the walls, some really comfortable chairs around an open fire, a carpet on the floor, the room not without flowers, and the walls decorated by someone who had an eye to colour. But how rare this is!

The canteen, which might be the most attractive spot in the club, is often the most depressing. Few clubs have a room set apart for canteen. Where the serving of meals has been planned as part of the use of the building, a counter and hatch is the usual arrangement, and members buy their refreshments and eat them where they choose. A more sociable arrangement is often achieved in other premises by displaying the goods on a table. A nicely set-out table can greatly increase the attractiveness of the room. A table across a kitchen doorway often serves as a hatch and counter. One club has a canteen attractively planned with the premises. A counter separates the kitchen from the customers, and a service hatch connects with the next room, which has small tables, an attractive fire and fireplace and so on, so that members may either buy and eat their refreshments at a counter, or take them to a small table. Unfortunately, very little originality about the type of food sold was shown, and here—as in the majority of clubs—canteen was synonymous with 'Interval'. Several clubs sell home-made cakes. These are made either by an adult committee member (who often is responsible for the canteen) or by girls in a cookery group. In another club, buttered toast (*sic*) and tea are the only things sold. The time at which the canteen is opened considerably affects sales. Many Birmingham boys, particularly, have a heavy meal between 6 and 7 p.m. and are not ready for even a snack before 9 p.m. More support for the canteen is given when it is opened later in the evening. One club had an attractive American-cloth table cover on which the refreshments were displayed, but rarely are such refinements enjoyed. Cold soft drinks are rarely seen except at socials.

Several churches in our city have been able to build premises specially designed for their youth activities—we found three churches which had acquired an adjoining private house which had been adapted for this purpose—but usually church youth work has to be carried on in halls which were designed for other purposes and which have to be used by several societies. Even in these circumstances the rooms could be made attractive. They could at least be clean, and wonders could be worked with a few yards of curtain, a few rolls of wallpaper, a tin or two of paint—and one good bonfire.

Grants towards capital expenditure are paid, not by the L.E.A., but by the Ministry of Education. During the year 1947-48, the sum of £110,560 was given by the Ministry to individual units for capital expenditure. Only £900 of this money came to Birmingham, this sum being shared by three units. The need for better housing for the Youth Service is so clamant that this amount seems to be ludicrously small, though it may represent all that is possible at the moment, while other types of building must have priority. Indeed, very often the need is not of more money, but rather of more imaginative leadership. There are few things more conducive to the creation of club spirit than the decoration of the premises in which the club meets. To the leader who knows his job the existence of a dreary building is an opportunity to launch his members upon a project which may not only improve the surroundings in which his work is done, but bind his members in closer loyalty and attachment to the club. One church club wanted its own premise and was determined to get them. An ex-Army hut standing in a Staffordshire aerodrome was bought for £50. On the first Saturday of April, 1948, fifteen boys and one girl of the club went to Stafford and spent the day dismantling the 60 ft. by 20 ft. hut. The girl member, of course, was there to provide the drinks for the lunch-time break. The hut was dismantled, mounted on to waiting lorries and sent to Birmingham where other club members were waiting to unload. Normal club activities were suspended while the work of building went on and the twenty-five members of this club are quite convinced that theirs is the finest unit in the city. When we visited one Scout troop we found the boys actively engaged in the building of their own brick hut Dissatisfied with the partial use of an inadequate church hall they had obtained the necessary permits, and with the help of parents and friends had raised sufficient money to pay for the materials for the building which will eventually be used for the Scout and Guide activities of the Church.

PLAYING FIELDS

There is no doubt that one of the most urgent needs of the Youth Service is that of additional playing-fields. Ninety-four of the organizations visited by us claimed to experience difficulty in obtaining the use of grounds

The City's playing-fields fall into three main groups:
(a)   Those controlled by the Parks Department
(b)   Those belonging to the L.E.A.
(c)   Privately owned grounds.
The Parks Department is able to offer 126 football and 56 cricket pitches. Before the war

FIGURE 16

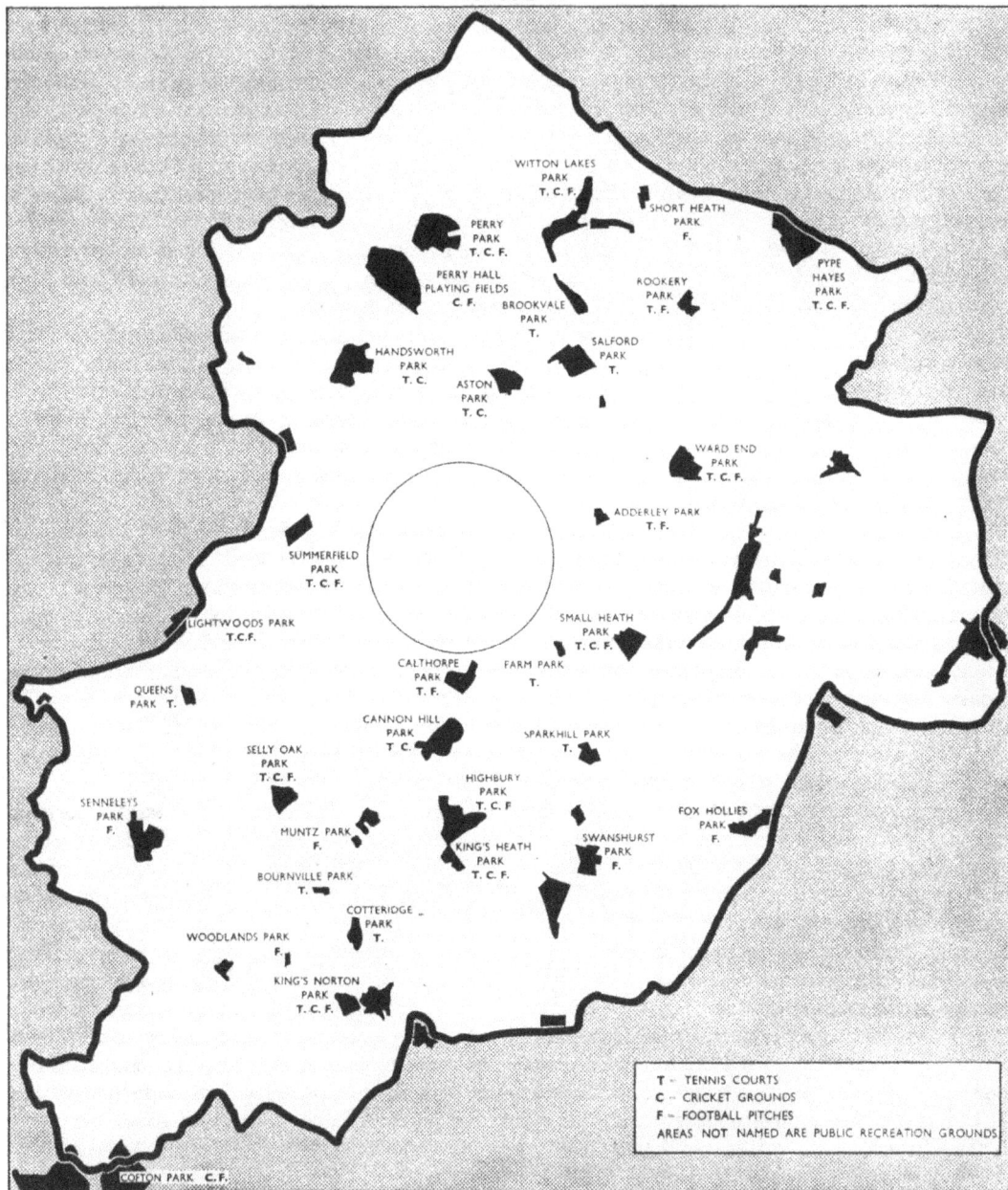

WITTON LAKES
PARK
T. C. F.

SHORT HEATH
PARK
F.

PERRY
PARK
T. C. F.

PYPE
HAYES
PARK
T. C. F.

PERRY HALL
PLAYING FIELDS
C. F.

ROOKERY
PARK
T. F.

BROOKVALE
PARK
T.

HANDSWORTH
PARK
T. C.

SALFORD
PARK
T.

ASTON
PARK
T. C.

WARD END
PARK
T. C. F.

ADDERLEY PARK
T. F.

SUMMERFIELD
PARK
T. C. F.

LIGHTWOODS PARK
T.C.F.

SMALL HEATH
PARK
T. C. F.

CALTHORPE
PARK
T. F.

FARM PARK
T.

QUEENS
PARK T.

CANNON HILL
PARK
T C.

SPARKHILL PARK
T.

SELLY OAK
PARK
T. C. F.

HIGHBURY
PARK
T. C. F

FOX HOLLIES
PARK
F.

SENNELEYS
PARK
F.

MUNTZ PARK
F.

KING'S HEATH
PARK
T. C. F.

SWANSHURST
PARK
F.

BOURNVILLE PARK
T.

COTTERIDGE
PARK
T.

WOODLANDS PARK
F.

KING'S NORTON
PARK
T. C. F.

COFTON PARK C.F.

T - TENNIS COURTS
C - CRICKET GROUNDS
F - FOOTBALL PITCHES
AREAS NOT NAMED ARE PUBLIC RECREATION GROUNDS

PUBLIC PARKS AND RECREATION GROUNDS IN BIRMINGHAM

The absence of sports facilities in the older, closely built-up parts of the city is emphasized by the circle which is drawn with a radius of one mile from the centre.

the corresponding figures were 198 and 117, but many of the pitches which were turned over to food production have not yet become available again. One result of this shortage is that the pitches which are available are subject to very heavy use, being played on in some cases, three or four times each week-end. We understand that it is proposed to extend the provision of concrete wickets for cricket. Some cricketers will no doubt raise their hands in horror at this suggestion, but such wickets are not unknown in other countries and have the advantage that they can be used in all weathers. Dressing room accommodation is available in most parks, but showers are seldom provided. The National Playing Fields Association recommends that as a minimum requirement there should be six acres of playing fields for each 1,000 of the population in addition to school and private grounds. To reach this standard, the Birmingham Parks Department would need to double its present park acreage. The difficulties attendant upon any attempt to attain this standard would be still further complicated by the fact that the L.E.A. also wishes to increase its playing fields from the present acreage of 500 to an ultimate 2,000 acres.

The Local Education Authority controls 46 grounds, but only 13 of these are in full use, 14 are still partly used for food production, 9 are for the exclusive use of Grammar or Technical Schools, and 10 are either newly acquired and undeveloped or are still held entirely by the County Agricultural Committee. These fields make available for use 42 football, 39 cricket, and 22 hockey pitches. School children naturally have priority, but pitches may be used by youth organizations when possible. These pitches are not available for Sunday play and are usually kept in much better condition than are those in the public parks. A temporary alleviation of the situation will be brought about by the decision of the L.E.A. to use a number of sites which have been acquired for future school buildings as 'playing spaces'. It may be some years before building is possible in some cases so that in the meantime games can be played on these sites.

The Parks Department and the L.E.A. between them provide enough football pitches for 168 matches (336 teams) to be played each Saturday afternoon. It is to be remembered, however, that this provision has to be shared among school children, members of youth organizations and adult teams. Facilities available for girls are very much fewer than those for boys The Parks Department is only able to offer eight netball pitches, but 51 youth organizations in the city enjoy the use of school playgrounds for girls' netball matches

Most of the privately-owned grounds belong to industrial undertakings and are only available of course to the employees (adult and junior) of the firm to which they belong. A few of these grounds are very extensive and have been professionally laid out. The Y.M.C.A. would appear to be the only youth organization (if the industrial units be excluded) which owns its own playing fields in the city, though several of them have their own camping sites in the country.

FINANCE

We have been allowed to examine the annual balance sheets of a large number of organizations, and it has been interesting to note the very different methods by which they are financed. The Boys' Pre-Service units are supported in the main by grants from the respective Service Ministries, the boys paying no subscriptions, though funds may be raised by concerts, dances or sports events for social and welfare purposes. The Co-operative organizations, as we have seen, derive their income from the Education Departments of the Society concerned, though grants towards the salaries of part-time leaders are received from the L.E.A. All the uniformed voluntary organizations including the N.A.T.C.G. and the Red Cross and St. John Ambulance Cadets are financed almost exclusively by the subscriptions and special efforts of their members. The Girl Guide County Commissioner says of L.E.A. grant-aid that while units are not actually forbidden to apply for such financial assistance, they are not encouraged to do so, while the secretary of the Birmingham Association of Boy Scouts says 'we do not normally encourage application for grants'. By contrast, the Regional Commissioner of the W.J.A.C., while saying that none of her units receives L.E.A. grant aid, suggests that this is 'perhaps because the application form is too complicated', and adds 'more money spent on youth work would mean less spent on Juvenile Courts'. Most church youth clubs are also financed in the main by the subscriptions and efforts of their own members, but it is to be remembered that as in the case of most of the uniformed voluntary organizations, their premises are usually supplied by the church with which the unit is associated, there are no leaders to pay, and their expenses in consequence are small.

Our Survey does not lead us to feel that the Youth Service generally is handicapped by the lack of adequate finance, or that except in the case of the large open club, the quality of work done would necessarily be improved if public money were available on a more generous scale. Of the 321 units visited by us, only 51 claimed to be financially embarrassed. Many units, as we have seen, are receiving a great deal of indirect financial assistance in the form of L.E.A. instructors or in the provision of school premises. The only youth organizations which appeared to us to be seriously handicapped by lack of money are the large units which are staffed by professional leaders and which are responsible for the maintenance of their own premises. There are few units of this kind in our city, but these few do appear to us to deserve more generous L.E.A. help than they are receiving. We imagine that few headmasters are distracted from the work of teaching by the necessity of organizing schemes for raising money, or are often unable to obtain the equipment they think to be necessary because of scruples about its cost. Professional youth leaders are frustrated in this way, and some of them have to resort to quasi-business methods of raising money for their own salaries by offering a duplicating or printing service, or by hiring out camp equipment, and so on. One Birmingham club incurred a gross expenditure in the year 1947-48 of some £1,700, towards which amount no less than £550 was raised by the club members. The year's working resulted in a deficit of £300, but the total grant received was less than £200, which seems a very small amount. Of the 321 units visited by us only 24 were in receipt of direct L.E.A. financial help (16 for the payment of leaders, 9 for the upkeep of premises, and 11 for equipment), and the total amount of such help given in our city in the financial year 1947-48 was only £2,810 which was distributed among 38 units. This, as we have already remarked, is a very small sum when one compares it with figures from other cities, though a partial explanation of this fact may be that there are fewer large independent professionally staffed youth clubs in Birmingham than in many other places. The refusal of the Birmingham Education Committee to grant-aid the Headquarters of voluntary organizations is discussed later in this Report.

Some leaders appear even now not to know that grant-aid is available towards the cost of equipment, and few people appear to realize that play-centre grants can be obtained towards the cost of work that is done among young people under the age of fourteen. Other leaders seem determined at all costs to maintain a financial independence, lest the receipt of aid should lead to interference and control by the State; a fear and suspicion which is, of course, quite groundless.

One of the conditions laid down by the Birmingham Education Committee is that 'Grant-aid will not be given for the rent of premises which are owned by the organization or its parent body'. The effect of this restriction is that if a church sponsors a youth centre on its own premises no grant can be obtained towards any contribution paid by the centre to the trustees of the church. Presumably if two neighbouring churches organized their youth work on each other's premises, they would both be eligible for grant-aid! No church, of course, can expect to receive public money for the prosecution of its religious activities, but there are churches, especially in the more crowded quarters of the city, which are virtually Youth Centres catering for hundreds of young people in their play centres, uniformed organizations and youth clubs. A number of clergy, ministers and deaconesses are giving practically all their time to youth work. The wealthy people who made this work possible in the past no longer exist, and in recent years a number of churches in the poorer parts of the city have been compelled to close. In some cases a modest grant would make the continuance of their work secure, and we suggest that as it would be far more economical to give a small grant to such an existing organization than to establish a new Youth Centre, the Birmingham Education Committee might re-examine this particular restrictive condition.

We do not wish to suggest, however, that grant-aid should take the place of voluntary effort. It is not good for young people that all they need should be provided for them without some effort on their own part. Much more care will be taken of a radiogram if the members have themselves raised at least part of the necessary funds than if it is supplied by a benevolent authority. Nor are young people today without money. Among the 280 attached boys who answered our *Twenty Questions* the 87 who smoke spend an average of 5s. 6½d. weekly on tobacco, the 220 who attend the cinema regularly spent 2s. 9d., and the 95 who dance spent an average of 2s. 10d. on dances. One of these boys spends 25s. weekly on cigarettes, and another, 22s. 6d. The 'attached' girls spend an overall average of 1s. 6½d. on dances, and 1s. 7½d. on cinemas. A weekly subscription of sixpence for a club which is open several evenings a week seems a very small amount. Very few clubs, however, ask their members for more than this amount, while many organizations ask for less. Most of the uniformed voluntary organizations still only ask for a penny or twopence a week. Often, of course, money is raised by members by other methods than by subscription. Organizations of all kinds promote concerts, displays, dances or sales of work: while Brigades and Scouts arrange annual 'Job Weeks', when members earn money both for the local unit and for the National Headquarters. An Annual Flag Day provides a substantial revenue for the local units and the area administration of the club organizations.

LEADERSHIP

Of all the factors which determine the quality of work done in youth organizations by far the most important is leadership. A club can meet in magnificent premises and it may have no financial worries, but without good leadership, it will accomplish little. On the other hand we recall that one of the most effective pieces of work we have seen is being carried on in a building which the members themselves have constructed out of hen-houses and sheds.

Most of the youth organizations in Birmingham are led by men and women who are giving voluntary services. The number of professional youth leaders is not large. It is surprisingly difficult to say how many people there are who are fully engaged in the Youth Service, as a number of Y.M.C.A. or Y.W.C.A. leaders, Community Centre or Settlement Wardens, Church Lay-workers, and Factory Welfare Officers or Personnel Managers are in fact giving part of their time to youth leadership, though they may have other duties as well. We doubt whether there are more than five men and five women full-time leaders in our city, though to this number should be added at least eight Community or Settlement Wardens, seven Church Lay-workers, ten Y.M.C.A. and eight Y.W.C.A. Secretaries, who give a proportion of their time to youth leadership. In some cases they are giving almost all their time. This gives us a total of fifty-one people mainly or wholly engaged in youth leadership. We have included no ministers or clergy though there are some ordained men who are almost exclusively occupied in youth work.

We have not included in this figure those people who are better described as organizers rather than as leaders. A number of the youth organizations in the city have full-time secretaries and we estimate the number of regional secretaries or organizers to be fourteen. Nor have we included in these figures members of the staff of the L.E.A. There are in fact fourteen area organizers whose work tends to be more concerned with Youth Employment than with Youth Leadership. A very large contribution to the Youth Service is being made of course by L.E.A. Instructors. We have seen that during the year 1947-48, 263 classes in clubs were supplied with such instructors. At one time the L.E.A. had a panel of 24 assistant leaders whose services were offered to clubs which needed them. Some of these assistant leaders are still at work. A feature of the Co-operative Youth Clubs is that they are staffed by part-time paid leaders and assistant leaders, of whom there are 23. The whole subject of youth leadership is so important that we propose to discuss it at length in a later chapter of this Report, but at the moment we merely wish to point out that all the uniformed voluntary organizations, the boys' Pre-Service organizations, the Red Cross and St. John units, and the great majority of the clubs in our city are staffed by unpaid leaders. In the 321 units visited by us we met no less than 995 voluntary leaders and helpers. Even so, the chief complaint of nearly every leader in every type of youth organization is the lack of voluntary helpers. Four or five times during the course of our Survey we wanted to pay a return visit to a unit with which we had made earlier contact only to find that owing to the departure or resignation of the leader, the unit had ceased to meet altogether. Many more voluntary leaders and helpers are needed.

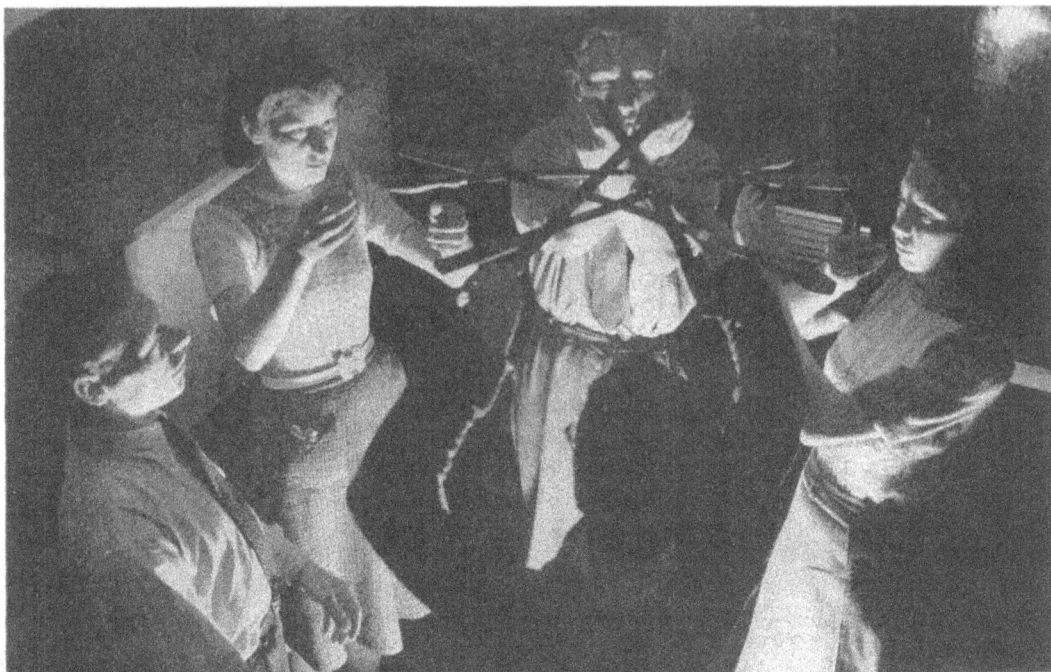

SWORD DANCING AT A Y.W.C.A. CLUB: *Both the Y.M.C.A. and Y.W.C.A.*
cater for adolescents through Club activities, some of which are open to both sexes.

HANDICRAFTS **IN THE CLUB:** *The youths in this photograph are employed in the factory and*
offices of a Birmingham industrial concern.   The voluntary supervisor is a foreman carpenter.

CHAPTER VII

THE QUALITY OF THE LOCAL YOUTH SERVICE

THE DIFFICULTY OF ASSESSMENT

OUR DISCUSSION SO FAR has been quite straightforward, having been concerned in the main with facts and statistics. We have summarized our discoveries about the number, distribution, membership, frequency of meeting and activities of youth organizations of all kinds. The most important questions, however, still remain. What can be said in appraisement of the *quality* of the local Youth Service? To what conclusions have we been led after nearly three years' close observation of the work of units of many types? Is the Youth Service producing results which justify the money and effort that is being expended upon it? What kind of contribution is it making to the development of its members? Is it possible to compare the achievements of one organization with those of another?

Such questions are more easily asked than answered. It is comparatively easy to discover how many members belong to a particular unit, how old they are, how often they meet, and in what activities they take part. Even the leader of the unit himself, however, may not discover until years have gone by how much membership of the unit has meant to a particular boy or girl; he may, indeed, never know. How much less, therefore, is an occasional visitor able to assess the contribution the organization is making to any of its members? There is, indeed, something almost presumptuous and impertinent in attempting to appraise the work of any unit, unless one is familiar both with its history and with many factors in the local and immediate situation. One leader, moreover, may be superficially brilliant and apparently successful, and yet fail to produce the lasting results that may be achieved by another leader whose work is much less spectacular.

The task of assessment is one, nevertheless, that must be attempted. In order to put ourselves in a position where we could discover more about the work of a unit than could be learned from questionnaires or from occasional visits, we obtained permission from a number of leaders to associate ourselves with the total life and activity of their particular unit for a period of several months. The seventeen organizations with which this arrangement was carried out comprised one large and one small Y.W.C.A. club, a Girl Guide group, an independent boys' club, a Scout group, a Boys' and a Girls' Life Brigade Company, one large and one small unattached mixed club, a Sea Cadet Corps, a Youth Service Corps, three Church Youth Clubs of different sizes and denominations, a Women's Junior Air Corps and a political youth organization. At the end of our association we wrote a report (which has been seen by no one but ourselves) in which we endeavoured to assess the degree in which the unit was achieving its own aims, to characterize the personal relationships among members of the unit, and to assess the extent to which the unit was helping its members in any way in their physical, intellectual, emotional and religious development. To guide us in the compilation of these reports we drew up a questionnaire (designed solely for our own use and never produced in any of the organizations) which included inquiries under such headings as atmosphere, relationships, health and fitness, further education, etc. The questions listed under the heading of 'Further Education' for example, were as follows:

Can this unit be said to be making a real contribution to further education, either formally or informally?
Do the activities suggest a balanced and progressive programme?
Are members discovering how to use their leisure in creative ways?
Are they acquiring any skills?
Is there any evidence that any permanent interest in any cultural activity is aroused?

Is there any evidence of achievement in projects, performances, displays or magazines?
Are members encouraged to take an interest in politics or current affairs?
Is there a regular place for discussion?
Does the unit make use of the specialist contribution which can be given by the occasional visitor of personality or eminence?
Does the unit make available to its members opportunities of travel in this country or overseas?

AIMS IN YOUTH SERVICE

In this task of assessment the first difficulty we encountered arose from the fact that there is no agreement among organizations of different kinds about aims and purpose. It is obviously only possible to characterize a unit's success in achieving its aims in the light of a knowledge of those aims. If a particular unit has no aims it does not find it difficult to achieve them! It is interesting to note that whereas most of the uniformed organizations have definite aims precisely formulated, it is quite otherwise with the clubs, few individual units of which seem ever to have addressed themselves to the task of clarifying their purpose. Club leaders, when asked the aims of their organization, offered an extraordinary wide range of answers, of which the following are examples:

To promote the physical, mental and spiritual well-being of members.
To provide opportunities for useful employment in leisure.
To keep young people off the streets and to give them a good time.
To promote Christian citizenship.
To provide social activities for young people.
To attract young people to the Church.
To make members Co-op conscious.
To promote the welfare of children and young people in the poorer quarters of Birmingham.
To cater for and promote cultural and recreational activities on a strictly Catholic basis.
To meet the social needs of members, excluding politics and religion.
To foster friendly, neighbourly relationships throughout the community in recreational, social and informal educational pursuits.

In these statements of aims we can trace the continuing influence of the two motives which were at work in the early days of the club movement in the last century—the philanthropic desire to provide unprivileged boys with an alternative to the street, and the propagandist desire to communicate a religious (or, in some cases, a political) faith. These two aims only find their justification in a larger purpose which is concerned with the total all-round development of young people, both as individuals and as members of society. It is the widespread failure to envisage this larger purpose on the part of so many youth organizations that gives rise to our greatest concern as we think of the Youth Service as a whole—a concern we discuss with our readers in the final chapter of this Report.

Meanwhile, if it be true, as has been asserted, that the chief business of the adolescent is to stop being one, we imagine that most people would agree that it is a primary function of the Youth Service to facilitate the development of the adolescent towards full maturity. Mr. L. J. Barnes, discussing 'the expanding outlook' in Youth Service, has said:

The emphasis is less on goodness . . . . and more on maturity . . . . morality is not, indeed, belittled, but maturity is seen as the more comprehensive conception. To be a satisfactory person, it is hardly enough to be good, one must also grow up. One can practise all the proper loyalties from the cradle to the grave, and still, as one totters into senility, discover that one has by-passed maturity on the journey.*

In a more recent Report Mr. Barnes has suggested that all youth organizations fall into one or other of two categories: those which are concerned with the inculcation of dogma, and those which are concerned with the facilitation of the development of the individual. This antithesis, so sharply put by Mr. Barnes, has been a stimulating one. It is a salutary reminder of how easily any of us who have strong opinions, whether religious or political, may be disposed to press them upon young people. It is probably difficult for any organization which is committed to a way of

* *Youth Service in an English County*, p. 80

thought to avoid the belief that deliberate inculcation should be part of its policy. But, we think, it may be just as hard for those who are the product of modern educational thinking and who see so clearly the need for all growth in young people to be from within themselves to recognize how necessary it is for them to encounter some strongly held standards of faith and conduct. For ourselves, we fear as greatly the consequences of 'uncharted freedom' as we do the oppressions of authoritarian beliefs. There cannot be sincere opinion unless it is freely held; no more can there be true opinion unless it be measured against the considered judgments of the past. We hold it to be a proper responsibility of all leaders of youth to be able and willing to embody the standards to which they have themselves arrived in their personal beliefs about life and conduct. We are more than a little troubled that so many seem to have no such definite guidance to give to young people whose freedom has brought them a facility which is enfeebling rather than enlightening. While therefore we are grateful for the sharp antithesis, and admit the special liability of religious organizations to put too much emphasis on inculcation, we much prefer to see these two terms offered as methods to be held in tension with each other. Prof. B. A. Fletcher has well described the mutuality of the two processes when he says:

> Education has always a dual role to fulfil. Its conservative function is to pass on from one generation to the next the knowledge, skills and values that represent the heritage of the past. If this function were not fulfilled, mankind would slowly revert from civilization to savagery. It has also a regenerative and revolutionary function to perform, which is to allow the fullest blossoming of those tendencies in the young which will introduce new creative life into the world.*

The quality of the Youth Service must be judged, therefore, in the last resort, by its achievements in the discharge of this dual educational task; by its success or failure in meeting the needs of young people in acquainting them with all that is of permanent value in their inheritance, and in giving them every opportunity to add to that inheritance by their own achievements.

The Service of Youth, in short, must be youth-centred. There are times when one suspects that in the direction of the Service—both at national and at local levels—a concern for administrative tidiness has taken precedence over a concern to meet the genuine needs of youth. No prior convictions about the relationship of voluntary body to statutory authority and no anxiety about the future of any particular organization must be allowed to colour our judgment as we seek to answer the simple question: 'Is the Youth Service playing its part in the total national system of educational provision for young people?' The question one would need to ask about the work of any particular unit is even more simple: 'Is this unit meeting the needs of its members?'

Human personality is a unity and it is of course quite arbitrary to discuss the physical, intellectual, emotional and religious needs of young people as though these were unrelated to one another. For purposes of convenience, however, it is useful to make these distinctions, and, if this is done, the first conclusion to which we have come in our endeavour to assess the quali y of the Youth Service is that there are very few organizations indeed which appear in practice to be aware of the needs of the growing boy or girl on all these levels. There are some organizations whose almost exclusive interest is in the physical development of their members, just as there are those which are concerned only with their religious needs. The Youth Service, of course, is not the only agency which is shaping the lives of young people: home, work, cinema, friends, radio, Sunday newspaper and in some cases church or Evening Institute all have their influences, far-reaching and often conflicting, on boy and girl. It would be a mistake for any youth organization to attempt to usurp the functions of home, of church, or of Evening Institute. At the same time the fact must be faced that many young people never go, either to church or Evening Institute, that many of them come from broken or unhappy homes, and that no youth organization which is concerned with the total lives of its members could be indifferent to their intellectual or spiritual needs. It is, we believe, a positive responsibility of some youth organizations to try to expand the service they are offering to their members, and it is a positive condemnation of them if they hinder their members from coming under the influence of agencies which could contribute to their development in other ways. Sometimes it is the duty of a club leader to

* *Education and Crisis*, p. 18

113

encourage a boy to spend fewer evenings in the club and to attend an Evening Institute. It should surely not have been possible, for instance, for one sixteen-year-old hairdresser in our city to go to her club five evenings in one week where apparently she did nothing but dance. In saying this, we would also like to say that we are equally concerned about quite a number of schoolchildren who appear to spend most of Saturday and Sunday and every evening from Monday to Friday doing their homework.

THE PHYSICAL NEEDS OF YOUNG PEOPLE

When young people come to a youth organization in the evening, some of them will be tired after a strenuous day at work and may need nothing more than rest and comfort; others who have been sitting down all day may need the opportunity of getting rid of superfluous energy in dancing or in a physical training class. If they come straight from work they may be in need of a balanced meal. The popularity of sports and games of all kinds, especially among boys, is sufficient evidence of the satisfactions they offer to the needs of body and of spirit. Some boys, indeed, tend to overstrain themselves physically, and leaders may need to exercise a restraining influence. High among the physical needs of the adolescent, too, we would put outdoor activities of every kind, from rambling to rock-climbing, from gardening to gliding; and, even more important, opportunities of enjoying outdoor sports, not as spectators, but as participants.

It is in connexion with its contribution to the physical needs of its members that the Youth Service in our city is making its most obvious contribution. Other factors, of course, have contributed in no small measure to the improvement in the nation's health, but we suggest that the Youth Service can claim its share of credit for the fact that in health, physique and appearance, young people today probably compare very favourably with their predecessors in an earlier generation.

There are few youth organizations which do not contribute in some measure to the health of their members. Physical activities of all kinds, as we made clear in the previous chapter, figure prominently in all club programmes. Many clubs in our city—particularly boys' clubs—are, in effect, sports clubs. Football and table tennis are the chief interests in boys' clubs, dancing sharing the popularity of these two activities in mixed clubs. Club membership makes it possible for boys to play football while many of their contemporaries are merely watching other people play. Every week-end about five hundred boys play football in leagues sponsored by the Birmingham Federation of Boys' Clubs and about a thousand in leagues sponsored by the Local Education Authority. We have already discussed the shortage of pitches, but there is also a lack of referees, and, even more, of men who are able and willing to coach boys in the finer points of the game. Participation in a football league can contribute, of course, not only to physical health but to growth in character. We heard of one club whose football team sustained defeat week after week, but which continued to turn out in full strength though it reached the end of the season without winning a point. The members gained something more valuable than cups or medals. By contrast, a girls' netball team withdrew from the league to which it belonged as soon as it sustained its first reverse.

In an earlier chapter we described how a club developed out of the spontaneous association of a group of boys in an allotment shed where they gathered to establish a football team. This interest in football can provide boys with an immediate purpose and a basis of association which, under wise leadership, can become the beginning of their social training. It cannot be said that such opportunities are always seized or even seen. Too many boys' clubs are football clubs and little more.

We have been impressed by the enthusiasm and ability of some of the Authority's physical training and keep-fit instructors whom we have seen at work in a number of clubs. In many cases they have succeeded in arousing and retaining the interest of boys by a judicious admixture of basket ball, football training and swimming with the more formal exercises and apparatus work.

Among girls of all ages and many older boys, dancing is one of the most popular club activities. Most adolescents want to learn how to dance and it can be said of many girls that dancing is the one skill in which they display any marked ability. Even 'jiving'—often condemned by adults—can have an extraordinary beauty and grace. Dancing can be an extremely healthy form of exercise and can provide real physical and emotional satisfactions, as well as considerable social education. When a shy or uncouth lad has learned to dance with a girl with grace and courtesy, some very valuable social training has been given. We have, however, seen a great deal of dancing of poor standard, and a few kissing dances which we thought quite undesirable. Few clubs have produced their own dance bands, and we are not impressed by some of the 'three-piece bands' which are often engaged for club dances. We have seen surprisingly little country dancing (except in the girls' uniformed organizations), national dancing or American square dancing.

The uniformed organizations, like the clubs, make a considerable contribution to physical education, but in a different way. Drill is a major activity with the pre-Service units and with the Brigades, and very high standards of smartness are attained. Brigades commonly devote a good deal of time to preparation for Physical Training displays, and some of the more outstanding companies occasionally contribute items at national displays in the Royal Albert Hall. Most Boys' Brigades and a number of the pre-Service units run their own football and cricket teams. The Boys' Brigade organizes a battalion swimming gala and a battalion cross-country competition, no less than thirty-four teams entering for this latter event in 1947.

The Scout movement is traditionally suspicious of leagues and of organization generally, and we have not found any football team or any formal physical training classes in connexion with any Scout Troop. Scouting, of course, is intended to be chiefly an outdoor movement, but apart from week-end and summer camping, we did not discover as much evidence of outdoor activity as we had expected.

The annual summer camp is the great event of the year for units of all kinds, and many leaders know that as much can sometimes be accomplished in a fortnight at camp as in six months' normal activity. Pre-Service units, Brigades, Scouts, Guides and clubs alike all make great efforts to get their members to camp. Of the total number of Guides, Rangers and Guiders in Birmingham, 42 per cent attended a camp during 1948. Birmingham Boy Scouts Association owns a large camp site of 53 acres, attendance at which during 1948 reached a figure of 3,300 camp-nights. Most of the larger movements and a few individual units have their own permanent camp sites, but increasing difficulty is being experienced in finding sites. Farmers who at one time allowed young people to camp in a corner of a field without charge are now waking up to the economic possibilities of camping, and are charging as much as 1s. 3d. a head per night, which is an almost prohibitive charge for some organizations. On the advice of the King George Jubilee Trust, some of the South African Aid-to-Britain Fund is being used to establish camping centres. Part of this money was entrusted to the National Association of Boys' Clubs which has acquired a centre near Ludlow in one of the most picturesque parts of the unspoiled western Midlands. Camping standards among Brigades and Scouts are very high, very different as are the conceptions of camping held by the two bodies. Club camps vary immensely both in kind and standards. Occasionally their purpose is to provide cheap accommodation near a popular seaside town rather than to introduce young people to the joy of camping for its own sake. Grant-aided camps are now inspected by H.M. Inspectors and we anticipate that this will lead to a raising of the standards of club camping. In May, 1946, the Minister of Education set up an advisory committee to advise him on the technique and organization of camping. The committee has prepared the excellent pamphlet, *Organized Camping*, designed to assist those concerned with running camps for young people. The work of the committee has been reinforced by training courses in camping which have been held both for H.M. Inspectors and for Youth Service leaders and organizers.

No account of the contribution of the Youth Service to physical education would be complete without a reference to the formal instruction in first aid, home nursing and hygiene, which is the major interest of the Red Cross and St. John organizations, and an activity of considerable importance in the Brigades, Scouts and Guides. The Junior Red Cross organization in Birmingham is comparatively small in numbers, but during the year 1947-48, over 250 certificates and proficiency badges were gained by members in first aid, home nursing, hygiene, mothercraft and life saving. Birmingham officers of the St. John Ambulance Cadets have taken special interest in the use of films and other visual aids in the teaching of first aid and home nursing.

One of the most important physical developments which takes place during adolescence is the achievement of sexual maturity, and both boys and girls need, not only to be given a knowledge of sex facts, but to be helped to achieve a wholesome attitude to the whole subject. When parents, on whom this responsibility should rest, so often fail their children, the duty of youth leaders is clear. We doubt, however, whether very much sex education is being given in the youth organizations apart from the service provided by the Public Health Department which we have already described. Many youth leaders fail their young people at this point, either because they are themselves embarrassed, or because they just do not know how to tackle the job, and more attention needs to be given to this subject in all training both for professional and for voluntary leaders.

THE INTELLECTUAL NEEDS OF YOUNG PEOPLE

It cannot be claimed that the Youth Service on the whole is making as clear a contribution to the intellectual development of its members as it is to their physical health. It may be argued, perhaps, that it is not the purpose of the Youth Service so to do. Those young people who want further academic education are already in the Evening Institutes, and if they go to a club it is for emotional and social satisfaction rather than for class instruction. Young people, it may be further argued, are like their elders in that at the end of the day they are tired and in need, not of study, but of relaxation and of recreation. On the other hand our own *Twenty Questions* investigation has furnished ample evidence, if proof were needed, of the fact that many of the fifteen- to eighteen-year-old members of our society are little more than barely literate. Most of them have no interest in current affairs, many of them read nothing but 'comics' and very trashy though harmless magazines. Few of them can play an instrument or exercise any skill, apart from football, table tennis, or ballroom dancing. Their manifold intellectual needs, therefore, are obvious and any and every opportunity should be taken of offering them further education both formally and informally. If only their interest could be aroused in hobbies, skills and crafts of all kinds or in the delights of music, literature and drama, fewer of them would spend so much of their leisure in passive and uncreative ways.

Of all youth organizations, the Air Training Corps is perhaps making the largest contribution to further education of a formal character. This, we think, is not only because it is so lavishly supplied by the Air Ministry with expensive equipment, but because the prospect of flying provides an immediate incentive to the boy, who is made to feel that he has left boyhood behind and is already learning to do adult things. He belongs, not to a children's organization, but to an admired adult group, and he is prepared to accept the many demands the group makes upon him. Other organizations may find food for thought in this fact.

Some club classes are provided with L.E.A. instructors in quite academic subjects. Among Birmingham's 31,000 club members, however, there are only some 3,400 enrolments in L.E.A. classes and this includes classes in ballroom dancing, physical training and keep-fit.

Comparatively few club leaders take much interest in crafts of any kind, and, apart from a few boys' wood-work classes and several girls' soft-toy making classes, such groups as we have seen have usually been poorly attended and unimaginatively led. Too often, instead of encouraging a boy to build a puppet theatre or helping a girl to cut out a frock, a member is asked to complete somebody else's half-finished article left over from last year. An Arts and Crafts Festival arranged by the Birmingham Federation of Boys' Clubs in the Spring of 1949 produced some excellent exhibits of drawings, paintings, metal work, modelling and photography, but our impression was that most of these exhibits came from boys who happened to be club members rather than from boys who had produced these articles in the course of a club activity. The most

116

ambitious and comprehensive exhibition of this kind seems to be that which takes place each year in connexion with the annual Festival of Youth organized by the Sunday Schools and youth organizations of the Belmont Row Methodist Circuit. The 1949 Festival included over a hundred 'events' with competitions in singing, instrumental music, musical composition, elocution, essay writing, folk dancing, drama, dressmaking, embroidery, applied art, poster work, map and mechanical drawing, toy making, leather work and photography. The number of competitors taking part totalled over twelve hundred.

It can be said that all the uniformed organizations introduce their members to crafts and skills of many kinds. During the year 1948 no less than 2,040 proficiency badges were awarded to Birmingham Girl Guides. Over 200 girls obtained a Cook or a Laundress badge; over 100 obtained each of the following: Child Nurse, Country Dancer, Gymnast, Home-maker, Hostess, and Needlewoman; while the range of interest is shown by the occasional award of such badges as Aircraft, Beekeeper, Cobbler, Interpreter, Rabbit-keeper and Skater. It may be that some of these badges are easily obtained and it may be that some young people go in for 'badge-hunting', dropping their interest in a subject as soon as the badge is won. This, it seems to us, matters less than that large numbers of young people do acquire some very useful accomplishments and are at least introduced to a variety of interests and hobbies, in one or other of which some of them may go on to find a lifetime's satisfaction and pleasure.

In the Women's Junior Air Corps three badges are awarded, for the first of which a cadet must

(a) Obtain 75 per cent of marks in two basic subjects (choice from First Aid, Physical Training, Public Affairs, Health, Education, etc.)

(b) Obtain 75 per cent of marks in a specialized subject, (e.g. Domestic Science, Map-reading, Aircraft Recognition, etc.)

(c) Obtain 75 per cent attendance, and pass a drill test.

For the second badge this standard must be maintained for a second year and for the third badge, the Air Ability badge, a special aviation paper must be passed. During 1948, fifty-six Ability badges and eighteen Air Ability badges were awarded to Birmingham girls. Air training for boys in Birmingham offers the possibility of actual flying, which is not quite so easily available to the girls, who must be content with occasional practical demonstrations in the W.J.A.C's own aircraft, which is shared on a national basis, and comes to the local airfield occasionally.

One small industrial club specializes in visits of observation and expeditions to places of interest, (a coal-mine, the University, the Central Fire Station, etc.) and the Youth Service often puts opportunities of travel in the way of many young people to whom they would not otherwise easily come. One Birmingham club leader, taking boys to camp in the summer of 1948, was surprised to discover that a seventeen-year-old boy printer's apprentice had never previously been in a train. A few clubs have arranged exchange visits with clubs in other parts of the country. Many units take parties of young people to holiday houses of the organization to which they belong or organize a week-end in London, and twenty-eight of the clubs visited by us have taken parties abroad at some time or other. During 1948 Birmingham Girl Guides were represented in camps in France, Switzerland, and Belgium. One large industrial youth club is raising a War Memorial Fund which is being used to send members of the club abroad and to entertain young people from overseas. The first visitors to be welcomed under this scheme have been groups of boys from France and Holland. One branch of the Y.W.C.A. in a neighbouring town promotes a 'Travellers' Club' within the club itself.

The educational value of these overseas contacts must be very high, but we have not discovered in Birmingham any scheme which resembles the exciting French 'Zellidja' travel scholarships, the holders of which are required to select a subject for original study and research, to keep their entire expenses within the small sum allowed to them (the equivalent of about £8) and to write a report on their investigations on their return. Subjects chosen by holders of these scholarships have included Celtic civilization in Wales, Basque folk-lore, and ship-building on the Tyne. One boy went to Corsica and another explored the Rhine by barge. Reports handed in have sometimes been illustrated with sketches, photographs, plans and maps, all of which must be the writer's own work. Prizes are awarded for the best report submitted.

(a) *Music and Drama*

The unreality of the distinction between provision for the intellectual and for the emotional needs of young people is nowhere more apparent than in any discussion of music and drama, activities which can not only lead to a widening of intellectual horizons, but at the same time can provide deep emotional satisfactions and training in emotional sensitivity.

The very definite programmes of the uniformed organizations seem to leave them little time to explore the great possibilities of music and drama. A boys' unit may put on an occasional 'show' with a money-raising object. The programme is as likely to consist of solo items and individual turns as to represent the culmination of any group activity. An evening's programme in a girls' unit may include some singing, and some companies make use of informal drama in the teaching of first aid by 'staging' accidents of various kinds. Usually, however, the only use made of music, apart from singing, is that which occurs in connexion with country dancing.

Members of church units of all kinds—whether clubs or uniformed organizations—may take part in musical and dramatic activities in connexion with the observance of the Christian Festivals. The church service on such occasions may include a Nativity Play, a Passion Play or an Easter Play, and we have seen a few such productions of quite high quality. Usually, however, these are church-sponsored productions in which young people share, rather than efforts promoted by any individual youth group itself. It cannot be said that either music or drama is a major interest among many youth clubs in our city,* although most clubs, at some time or other, 'have a go' at one or the other. Of the 141 clubs visited by us, 42 included drama or play reading, 28 some musical activity, and 8 a concert party group during the week of our visit. Mention should be made in this connexion of the Y.W.C.A. clubs, in the programmes of which drama usually does play an important part. Among junior groups (11-15) mime and little plays often make up at least part of a club meeting, and this forms, as it were, an 'appetizer' so that when these members move into young senior sections they are keen to take an interest in dramatic productions. Nearly every one of the ten clubs has a drama group during some part of the year, and several have drama societies which have recently given very creditable productions including *Yellow Sands, Night must fall, The Brontës, Murder in the Cathedral, Ladies in Retirement*, and selections from *Hassan*. In these productions young people in their teens are usually associated with people in the twenties.

It is quite impossible to make any generalization about the qualities of musical and dramatic activities in clubs, as achievements vary so widely. We visited one or two clubs where all or most of the members were caught up in genuine enthusiasm in connexion with a pantomime or operetta or play which was carried through to the point of successful production. In this nearly all members of the club shared, as actors, carpenters, artists, electricians, dressmakers or programme sellers. More often, however, we found the 'Drama Group' to consist of half-a-dozen young people who were dragged somewhat unwillingly from table tennis or dance to slog away at the dreary task of memorizing lines from an ill-chosen one-act play. After several changes in cast the project is abandoned and one is not surprised later when the club leader says (as more than one did): 'We did try drama once, but the youngsters were not interested, and we have not tried it since.'

We have been interested in a number of experiments in informal drama and in the work of some leaders who cleverly introduce a few musical items in the middle of a 'Mixed Bag' programme. A Programme Adviser from the Headquarters staff of the National Association of Girls' and Mixed Clubs has been at work in Birmingham during the last three years and has conducted a number of experiments in the informal approach to drama. He has been working in close association with the Educational Drama Association. The emphasis has been on free expression and movement rather than on formal play-production, though several clubs have

* Only four youth organizations in Birmingham are affiliated to the British Drama League.

eventually made their own short sketches. The subjects chosen usually had something to do with the problem of adolescence, which were certainly more thoroughly hammered out in this way than they would have been in normal discussion. Through games, dramatic exercises, and improvisations many a shy or retiring club member has 'loosened up', and the group nature of the activity has been of value, particularly to the 'tough' clubs in the city.

Many young people have a genuine interest in music even though it may only show itself in the popularity of 'jazz concerts' or in the continuous use (or misuse) of the clubroom piano or gramophone. A leader who knows his job can turn this interest to advantage. One of our own students, who is not herself particularly musical, held the attention of the members of a quite difficult club as she introduced them to a programme of gramophone records on 'Dance Music through the Ages'. The following week another student, with the aid of some excellent Bureau of Current Affairs posters, took the same group further with a talk on 'Instruments of the Orchestra', playing records of orchestral music and pointing to a picture of each instrument as it was heard. We visited another club where the members had suggested a series of evenings devoted to talks about various composers and had themselves arranged one evening on Purcell and another on Bach. If only the right leader had been available, this club might have been able to carry its interest much further.

(b) *Reading*

On one of our visits to the Peckham Health Centre we watched a twelve-year-old girl who for an hour was completely absorbed in a book she had taken from the Centre's library, apparently quite oblivious to the life that was going on around her. It was something one rarely sees in a youth organization, though a few clubs are able to offer a comfortable lounge or a 'quiet room' where magazines and periodicals are available. Such club libraries as we have seen have been almost universally ill-stocked and neglected, and we wish the Youth Service could do more to raise the standards of the reading habits of its members. We were interested in the method adopted by one Birmingham club leader who made arrangements with a local bookseller for each of his members to visit the shop and to choose any book which, after it had been read, was to be added to the club library. Most members chose 'thrillers', but one boy (on probation from the Juvenile Court) chose a book on puppetry, and some time later gave a solo puppet performance at one of the club's concerts. We wonder if the Library Committee could emulate the Evening Institute by taking education right into clubs, by using youth clubs as sub-branches, supplying them with regular selections of books which could be changed from time to time. This is done in some towns.

(c) *Discussion*

During recent years there has been a welcome increase of public interest in discussion. This interest has been stimulated both by the activities of the Bureau of Current Affairs and of the B.B.C. We cannot say that in our judgment the Youth Service is accomplishing as much as it might in this direction. It is interesting to note that the youth groups in which discussion of current affairs has a regular place are usually the political units and the church youth clubs—it is the very groups that have a concern with inculcation which are facilitating the development of their members in this direction. The uniformed organizations promote much less discussion than do the clubs, their programme of activities being usually so completely organized that little time is left for casual conversation. An exception to this statement is provided by those Boys' Brigades which promote club nights. In clubs, coversation is a major activity, though even there few leaders recognize its potential value, or use all the opportunities that it offers to them. Very few clubs in our area seem to use the excellent posters issued fortnightly by the Bureau of Current Affairs and we were interested to discover that one Local Education Authority nearby offers to refund half the cost of these posters to any club in its area which uses them.

BARNES CLOSE, CHADWICH,

a conference house, about ten miles from the city, belonging to the Birmingham Youth and Sunday School Union.

WINDMILL HOUSE, WEATHEROAK,

provides week-end and other holiday accommodation for members of clubs affiliated to the Birmingham Association of Girls' and Mixed Clubs.

WESTHILL, BIRMINGHAM,

one of the Selly Oak Colleges, founded in 1907, provides training for workers among young people and children, in club, in day school and in church.

(d) *Radio*

One fact which has emerged from our Survey is that very few youth organizations of any kind make any use of radio. Few, indeed, even possess a wireless set of their own, and where they do, the Light Programme usually provides a permanent background of noise against which the life of the club goes on. The only 'listening' appears to take place when members (girls and boys) follow the commentary on a big fight or tune in to a programme like *Take it from Here*. We have not come across any 'listening groups' though they may exist. Some church youth groups listen regularly, with the aid of a borrowed radio, to the monthly broadcast services for youth groups, but if this programme is to win the attention of the non-church youth club, we think a more informal approach is needed and that the B.B.C. could offer a real help to leaders who are worried about the problem of Sunday evening activities.

(e) *Film Appreciation*

There is astonishingly little attempt to introduce film appreciation as a club activity. Cinema going, as we have seen, is youths' major leisure-time occupation and many young people have a comprehensive knowledge of the domestic lives and professional careers of the 'stars'. On the 1st May, 1949, hundreds of Birmingham young people queued all night to obtain tickets for a performance in which an American actor was to appear in person. In our discussions with young people we found evidence of the extent to which they are influenced by what they see on the films, in speech, in dress, in thought and in behaviour. The cinema exercises a greater influence over young people than does evening institute, church, radio, or the printed word. Margaret Thorpe, in *America at the Movies*, writes:

> The story has been told so often that it must be true that the fashion of going without undervests began when Clark Gable undressed in the tourist camp in *It Happened One Night*. The sale of masculine underwear declined so sharply immediately afterwards that knitwear manufacturers and garment-makers' Unions sent delegations to the producers asking them to take out the scene.

Young people are at the same time so very likely to adopt the values and standards set before them on the screen, and so ready to 'talk film' at any time, that it would appear obvious that here is an urgent need and a ready-made opportunity for leaders to direct the thinking of their young people. Seldom, however, is the need recognized or the opportunity taken. One local attempt to establish a film club where films are shown centrally and afterwards discussed in individual clubs, has not met with any great success. It was hoped that leaders of youth organizations would recognize the value of this experiment and include it in their winter programmes. Few did so. Once more the need of more imaginative leadership becomes apparent.

(f) *Holiday and Conference Houses*

We would like to record our considered judgment that some of the most valuable youth work we have seen being done at all is that which takes place at Windmill House, the holiday house belonging to the Birmingham Association of Girls' and Mixed Clubs, and at Barnes Close, which belongs to the Birmingham Youth and Sunday School Union. Windmill House is primarily a holiday house and it is used by Birmingham club members every week-end. From time to time the Association has promoted Study Week-ends on such subjects as 'Getting Things Straight', 'Civic Life in Birmingham', and 'Religion and Everyday Life'. At the close of one such Conference one boy declared: 'I am going to say something which will make those of you who know me think that I have gone queer. Up to now I have been leading three different lives—one at work, one at club and one at home. The week-end has helped me to see why that has been so and in future I shall try to blend the three into one. I have been helped to find the solution to many things that have worried me in the past'. An interesting development at Windmill House has been its use by several firms during midweek periods to provide a rest-break for some of their young employees, and by secondary modern schools for the promotion of 'school journeys' for their fourteen-year-old scholars.

Barnes Close is a conference house, and during 1948 it was used for fifty conferences, which were attended by 1,500 people. Four of these conferences were summer schools of a week's duration, seven were week-end conferences promoted by the Birmingham Youth and Sunday School Union itself, and thirty-two were sponsored by various Free Church Sunday Schools or youth organizations in the city. Barnes Close makes possible a good deal of valuable training both for voluntary leaders and for senior members of youth organizations.

(g) *Programme Advice*

We have already referred, in our discussion of Music and Drama, to the work of the National Association of Girls' and Mixed Clubs' Programme Adviser, Mr. Maurice Elliott, B.A., who has been at work in the Birmingham area for three years. The appointment of a number of Programme Advisers arose out of the suggestion made by Mr. L. J. Barnes in his Report, *Youth Service in an English County*, which was prepared for the King George Jubilee Trust. The terms of reference given to the Advisers were that they should 'explore with club leaders the development and extension of their club programmes, encourage the use of facilities and services available in the area, and carry out experiments and inquiries into new methods of presentation'. Mr. Elliott has supplied us with the following summary of some of his own conclusions:

> (1) There is no doubt that valuable educational work of an informal kind can be done in clubs, provided that one has time and patience to discover the right activity and the right method for any one group. A great majority of leaders do not regard work of this kind as their responsibility. They think it should be done by their club helpers; and this simply poses the problem of finding (and training) voluntary helpers. Training for the voluntary leader, especially in methods of informal education and of stimulating interests among their members, is probably the only solution.

> (2) Good results are beginning to show from the short courses and week-end training for leaders and senior members, but the number of leaders who find time for these courses, or consider them worth attending, is very small. Fortunately, those who do attend are mostly young leaders or recruits from senior members. I think it is true to say that the great majority of voluntary club leaders will remain untouched by experiments of this kind.

> (3) Experience seems to show that some sort of Programme Adviser, operating permanently in an area, is necessary. Many leaders go away from week-end or evening training sessions fired with enthusiasm. Back in the club their enthusiasm wanes. They just don't feel confident that they can tackle the job on their own and this is where a little help to get them started could be of such immense value. The problem is 'How to start?' rather than 'What to do?' It is equally important to know how to sustain an interest, when it is once aroused.

THE EMOTIONAL NEEDS OF YOUNG PEOPLE

The rapid physical growth, the heightened awareness of self, the new interest in the opposite sex and the transition from school to work, all of which mark the period of adolescence, produce in the growing boy and girl a sense of insecurity which reveals itself in the moodiness, the instability and the intensely emotional life which is so characteristic of these years. Young people need outlets for the release of emotional conflict in games, in conversation, in singing, or in dramatic or creative activities of some kind. There is perhaps nothing the adolescent needs more than a background of emotional security—a familiar place from which he can go out to conduct his exploration of the wider world beyond. He can be helped immensely by a group to which he 'belongs', or a society in which he is an accepted member. He needs help, too, in learning how to appreciate what is good and beautiful in music and the arts, so that he will be able to distinguish between what is genuine and sincere and what is false and sentimental. A central problem for many an adolescent arises from the fact that though he is physically and intellectually mature, he is yet economically dependent, and still subject perhaps to the control of his parents. There may be arguments at home about smoking, late hours or latch keys. The adolescent needs increasing independence and real responsibility. If he cannot satisfy his desire for personal significance or make his presence felt in ways that are legitimate, he is quite likely to do so in ways that are socially undesirable. One of his major problems arises from his need to attain mature adult relationships with members of the opposite sex.

The Youth Service can legitimately be expected to make a particular contribution to the emotional needs of its members, but only youth leaders who are themselves emotionally mature can even see—let alone satisfy—the many needs of their members in this direction.

The degree to which any unit will be successful in meeting the many emotional needs of its members is so very dependent upon the total social environment in which the activities of the unit are carried on, that we propose to devote a subsequent chapter to a discussion of the nature of any society which can fulfil a truly educational function (see Chapter X). We shall, therefore, confine our present discussion to a consideration of one matter only—the extent to which movements of different kinds are contributing to their members' need for independence, personal significance and social recognition. These needs can indeed be supplied in various ways—by membership of an admired group (this being one reason for the popularity of pre-Service units during the war), by opportunities for the exercise of any skill, by the acceptance of responsibility in leadership, or by the discovery of that sense of personal worth which is one of the fruits of religious faith.

Some of these matters are dealt with elsewhere in this Report and we propose at this point to discuss only the extent to which members of youth organizations are entrusted with responsibility in leadership.

It is difficult to make generalizations about organizations of different kinds because a good Scouter will hand over considerable responsibility to his patrol leaders, a good Brigade captain to his n.c.o's, and a good club leader to his members' committee, while other leaders, in each type of organization, will hold the reins very tightly themselves. There are uniformed units whose success seems to be measured by the military precision with which the members obey the orders of those in authority: there are other units where, in Court of Honour or Officers' Meeting, very real responsibility is exercised by young people themselves. In the Scout movement every patrol of six or eight boys has its leader and its second, and by this means boys are given real opportunities for the exercise of leadership among their contemporaries. We do not feel on the whole that the n.c.o. in the Brigade or the pre-Service unit has quite the same opportunities for the exercise of initiative.

Clubs vary very considerably in the extent to which members are in fact entrusted with self-government. Only rarely have we been able to attend a club members' committee, but some leaders have assured us that such committees function with efficiency and success. More often, however, a members' committee, if it exists, flourishes and languishes in turns, and some leaders have said: 'I tried a committee but the members would not accept responsibility so I now run the club myself'. We were interested in the view of one leader, who said that it was asking too much of young people to expect them to serve on a club committee for twelve months. His practice was to get his members to elect numerous *ad hoc* committees—one to arrange next week's party, another to carry through the Sports Day, and another to arrange the Annual Dinner. In this way all his members obtain some experience of government from time to time and earn the satisfaction of a job carried through to completion. Whether this particular method be desirable or not, a wise leader will give his members as much responsibility as they are prepared to accept, and will not be too disappointed if they sometimes fail him. Few things are more important in club management than the education of members in committee procedure, and in some cases of failure we believe that more responsibility would have been accepted if more genuine responsibility had been given. Only rarely is a club committee given any share in the administration of discipline or in the control of finance. It is possible for a leader, if he is too assertive in his authority, to contribute unwittingly to the arrested development of his members towards emotional and social maturity. The task of the leader is not so much to implement his own ideas in the club programme as to inspire and train his members to carry through their own plans. The ultimate test of his success is in the ability of the club to function in his absence.

THE MORAL AND RELIGIOUS NEEDS OF YOUNG PEOPLE

Many moral standards once universally acknowledged, even if not always accepted, are now widely repudiated. When a boy leaves school he often finds that in his new environment in factory or office the moral standards of school no longer apply. Many young people who come to our youth organizations are desperately in need of help in their search for moral standards. More than one boy or girl has asked us in discussion: 'You talk about right and wrong, but how do you know that what you *say* is right *is* right?'

Adolescence is a time of religious and spiritual awakening, though the healthy development of the religious sentiment may be hindered or misdirected by the environment of secular materialism in which a boy grows up or by premature forcing on the part of unwise religious teachers. He needs, nevertheless, a sense of security, a standard of moral values, a sense of personal significance, an experience of moral empowerment, and the discovery of an adequate purpose in life. All these are religious needs.

In the task of moral and religious education we have seen something of what can be accomplished by direct formal teaching, and something of what can be achieved by informal discussion and casual conversation, but in the last resort nearly everything depends upon the moral standards which are accepted by the group itself and upon the religious faith of the leader. The most vital influences are personal ones. It is quite useless for a leader to talk to his members about honesty if it is known to them that he 'reduces' their ages when applying to the Railway Executive for tickets for the annual holiday: or that he 'fakes' the returns to the Food Office (a desperately hard thing not to do when allowances for the autumn depend upon summer sales!) We regret to say that there are some L.E.A. instructors who openly complete attendance registers incorrectly, and some club leaders whose own standards of honesty—as revealed for instance in any discussion about the black market—are not above reproach. Young people will respond to what is genuine wherever it is found; they are uncomfortably quick to recognize the least vestige of insincerity or unreality.

We propose, in our final chapter, to return to a discussion of the place of religion in youth work. We wish at this point to make three comments:

(1) Our observations lead us to the conclusion that all the uniformed organizations do encourage their members to recognize and to practise such socially desirable moral virtues as promptitude, responsibility, loyalty, courtesy, and respect for authority. We do not think that we could make this statement with the same conviction about some of the clubs and we are anxious to call attention to the value of the work of the uniformed organizations in this respect, because in other ways we believe clubs are making larger contributions than are the uniformed organizations in facilitating the development of their members towards social maturity.

If the average Scout or member of the Boys' Brigade is a more responsible person than the average club member, the reason, of course, may be that Scouts and Brigades are unconsciously more selective in their membership. The Scout movement says in effect: 'This is the Scout Law: if you are prepared to accept it, we are glad to welcome you; if not, we are sorry, but Scouting is not for you'. When a boy becomes a Scout he is self-committed to the Law and the Promise. In many cases when a boy joins a club no obligations are imposed upon him other than the payment of a weekly subscription. A boy can sit much more lightly to his position as a member of a club committee than ever he could to the position of leader of a patrol. The dilemma for the clubs is to keep their doors sufficiently open to serve the boy who would never accept the many demands of the uniformed organizations, and yet not to have them so widely open as to do a disservice to their members by making no demands, asking for no loyalties, and thus almost encouraging moral slackness and social irresponsibility. We think that clubs should pitch their standards higher than they do, and commend them to their members with greater clarity.

(2) In asserting the importance of such virtues as loyalty, obedience, punctuality and smartness, we feel that some of the uniformed organizations are in grave danger of equating the observance of these virtues with the discharge of religious obligations. Certain things are not done. Why not? Because presumably of one's duty to God. A boy is not to be blamed if he comes to believe that such duty means not turning up late for parade, washing the back of his neck, avoiding bad language, putting in a monthly church parade and marching to the parish church on Empire Youth Sunday.

We do not suggest, of course, that all officers in all uniformed organizations fail to relate religion to the lives of the young people or that they all equate religion with what has sometimes been called 'public school morality', and there is no doubt that many boys and girls have been helped by leaders in these organizations to a true religious development. The danger, however, is real. 'We are by no means indifferent to religion', one pre-Service officer said to us, 'we have a church parade every year'.

(3) Our third comment concerns clubs. We only know of one or two clubs in our city which have made any attempt to provide themselves with a club chapel. This, we think, is disappointing. We would not suggest, of course, that by the mere provision of a chapel a club becomes 'religious', any more than by the addition of an epilogue to an evening's programme. Religion is the spirit in which all the activities of a club are carried on, or it is nothing. 'God is not nearly as interested in religion as the parsons make out', said one boy—this being his way of asserting the truth that God is by no means solely concerned with devotional activities.

> Religion in a boys' club must be identified with the whole life of the club. It is not something tacked on to the club evening in the form of prayers at the close of club, nor is the performance of any specifically religious ceremony to be accounted as meritorious. Religion is the life of the club, and in so far as club life is real life in miniature, religion is the inspiration and basis of the whole life of the members of the club.*

We believe, nevertheless, that the provision of a chapel can contribute immensely to the enrichment of the spiritual life of a club community. The mere fact that worship is acknowledged to be as deserving of special accommodation as the physical training class or woodwork group is significant in itself. If members decorate and furnish the chapel, and have their share in the conduct of club epilogues, the value of the chapel is still further enhanced.

CONCLUSION

John, at twelve, was a member of the 'Canal Terrors'—a group of boys who had a hide-out near a Birmingham canal towpath. Nearby, they stretched a wire across the path to trip up folk who walked that way. On the end of the wire was a bottle. When the noise of the bottle proclaimed a victim the Terrors lay low in their hide-out until the coast was clear to lay the trap again. But activity was not confined to mischief of this kind. They discovered how to take the bungs from barges so that they sank in the canal. If they could not manage this, they threw the goods from the barges into the water. All this John told in a *To Start You Talking* broadcast a year or two ago, and went on to say how a newspaper man had made contact with the gang and had helped them to erect their own club headquarters out of an old tennis pavilion and a poultry house. What John did not tell his B.B.C. audience was that for a considerable time the Terrors' bedevilment was merely transferred from the canal bank to the club, and what fun it was, for instance, to mount the backs of other boys, and using billiard cues as lances, to tilt at the electric light bulbs. Time came, however, when John was appointed House Steward in charge of repairs to all property damaged by the members, and in 1948 he gave up quite a good job to undertake full-time social work.

Not every youth leader could tell quite such a dramatic story as this about his work but there are a great many who can recall with satisfaction the names of at least a few young people whose lives they know have been enriched in one way or another through their membership of a youth organization.

As we think of all the youth service it has been our privilege to see during the last three years, we feel led to the conclusion that the quality of leadership is far more decisive than is the type of organization. The great difficulty that has faced us as we have tried to assess the quality of the work done by various types of organization is that horizontal differences which run across all types of unit vary even more than vertical differences which distinguish one organization from another. There are good Clubs, Brigades, Scout Troops, Guide Companies and pre-Service units, and—it must be said—there are poor representatives of each type of movement.

* *Club Leadership* by Basil Henriques, p. 159

There are, of course, some generalizations which may be made. The Youth Service as a whole is making a real contribution to the physical development of its members. Boys and girls in the uniformed organizations are acquiring many skills and they do usually practise many socially desirable virtues. The programmes of the uniformed organizations, however, are inclined to be very stereotyped, and reveal some surprising gaps. They make no attempt to help their members to make adjustments in personal relationships with the opposite sex (the case for and against single-sex organizations is discussed in Chapter X), and—except in the pre-Service units—they lose three-quarters of their girls and nearly as many of their boys in early adolescence.

The majority of boys and a large minority of girls join a club in their early 'teens, but, if clubs in our city are typical of others, only half of them remain in membership more than twelve months. One reason, we think, is not far to seek—these lapsed members have themselves given it to us: 'There was nothing to do', 'It was a waste of time', 'I lost all interest'. (There is a further discussion of the question of leakage in Chapter VIII). There are clubs with excellently balanced programmes, but there are too many clubs in which there does seem nothing to do, where membership is far too loose, where no demands are made of members and no loyalties are given. Once more the lack of purpose in the Youth Service becomes apparent, and the need of trained leaders urgently evident.

Most of the uniformed organizations demand certain standards, and, if these standards are not maintained, the unit is closed. It is rather otherwise with the clubs. It is true that the club organizations demand certain requirements before a club can be affiliated, but it is not difficult for any club to obtain recognition, and once affiliated there seems to be little attempt to ensure that standards are maintained.

The ideals which inspire the club movement have never been precisely formulated in anything equivalent to, say, the Scout Law and Promise, and for this reason they are not always communicated to, or accepted by, the individual member.

We wonder if more might be done by the Local Education Authority to raise the standard of club activities. At present the Authority is prepared to provide facilities for almost any group of young people who come together for almost any activity whatever. There is merit in this catholicity, but we wonder if a contribution might not be made to the raising of standards by the promulgation of a 'Code' or a 'Charter' which units of an organization might be invited to accept. We conclude this already very long chapter with the reproduction of a Code of this kind which was adopted in 1946 by the Surrey Education Committee as a statement of aims, the acceptance of which was urged upon all youth clubs in the County. The seven clauses of the Code were as follows:

1. A Surrey Youth Club recognizes as the aim of its existence the all-round development of its members as individual personalities and as citizens.

2. It provides basically a social club for healthy recreation, physical and mental. But it also provides as an essential part of its activities facilities for the physical, mental and spiritual education of its members—where unable to meet any such needs through its own resources it puts its members in touch with other voluntary or statutory organizations that can do so.

3. The members of a Surrey Club take a pride in the reputation of the Club for good management and care of their premises and equipment and they recognize their responsibility to assist in the financial maintenance of the Club.

4. The members of a Surrey Club therefore take an active part in the management of the Club, but they recognize the necessity for adult guidance, through their leaders and the adult members of the Management Committee.

5. The members of a Surrey Club recognize their responsibility to their homes, are interested in the affairs and needs of their own locality, their country, and the world, and they express that interest not only by taking part in lectures and discussions but also by acts of service to the community.

6. A Surrey Club recognizes the different needs of age-groups between the years of 11 and 25 and where necessary provides separate activities for junior, intermediate and senior groups.

7. A Surrey Club cannot be associated with a political party and should aim, in so far as it can, at being a cross-section of the young people in the district where it is placed.

CHAPTER VIII

THE UNATTACHED BOY AND GIRL

WE HAVE SEEN THAT youth organizations of all kinds in our city number among their members about 55 per cent of the boys and 33 per cent of the girls in the 14-20 age-range. The percentage of those who are neither members of youth organizations nor engaged in full- or part-time education is approximately 35 per cent of the boys and 45 per cent of the girls.

Perhaps the first fact to be recalled in our discussion of these unattached young people is that they are concentrated in the later rather than in the earlier teens. *

One somewhat surprising conclusion to which our inquiries would seem to point is that a considerable majority of the boys do become members of one organization or another at some period during their career, and that a great many of the unattached boys are in fact lapsed members. We have seen that in 1943 it was found that 62 per cent of the boys who then registered had at some time been attached to an organization, but that 17 per cent of them had lapsed by the time they reached the age of sixteen or sixteen-and-a-half. Our investigations would suggest

TABLE LVI

REASONS GIVEN BY GIRLS FOR LEAVING A YOUTH ORGANIZATION TO WHICH THEY HAD ONCE BELONGED

Reason for Leaving	Present Age						Total
	14	15	16	17	18	19	
Lost interest; nothing to do; found other things to do; too many children ...	10	11	10	18	9	10	68
Bad leadership; bad organization ...	4	8	9	13	10	7	51
Homework or evening classes	1	1	4	1	4	2	13
Personal reasons; quarrelled with friend; my friend left; too many cliques ...	2	7	6	1	2	—	18
Unit closed..	3	4	1	3	1	2	14
Too far; moved away	4	6	2	4	4	1	21
Insufficient numbers, not enough people there	—	—	1	1	2	1	5
Other reasons	1	3	—	2	3	5	14

* See pages 75-78

that at the present time something like 70 per cent of the boys do in fact become members of some type of organization, but that many of them do not remain in membership for more than a few months. It is significant and startling that a quarter of the members of youth clubs in our city have been in membership less than six months. The situation is rather different in the case of the girls, half of whom never join any organization at all, while the proportion of those who are in membership declines steadily in each succeeding age group.

The young people who completed our *Twenty Questions* inquiry were invited to tell us if they had once belonged to a youth organization and if they had left, why they had done so. This question was answered, not only by those who were no longer in membership of a youth organization, but by many who were attached, this showing that they had left a previous unit to join the one with which they were then in association. An analysis of the answers given to this question is shown in Tables LVI and LVII; the age indicated is the age of the people when answering the question, and not necessarily the age at which they lapsed.

TABLE LVII

REASONS GIVEN BY BOYS FOR LEAVING A YOUTH ORGANIZATION TO WHICH THEY HAD ONCE BELONGED

Reason for Leaving	Present Age						Total
	14	15	16	17	18	19	
Lost interest; same thing every evening; not enough to do; did not like it; fed up; boring	11	6	5	7	4	3	36
Bad organization; too rough; poor leadership	—	3	1	5	4	8	21
Night school and homework	1	1	—	4	1	1	8
Unit closed...	—	1	2	3	2	—	8
Left the district, called up, etc.	2	2	2	2	2	11	21
Too many cliques; unsociable	—	1	2	—	1	1	5
Other reasons	3	4	2	1	3	4	17

It is a very depressing experience to read the answers given to this particular question, and to find how often a boy or girl says: 'People just sat round but did nothing', 'because it wasn't much of a success', 'because it was the same thing every evening', or 'because the leader didn't take any interest in activities', and 'because it was badly run'. Other answers reflect some of the material difficulties under which the Youth Service is carried on: 'Because the club closed when the lease expired', 'because there was never any heating', or 'because there wasn't enough equipment to go round'. A number of young people say that they left single-sex units because they wanted to join a mixed organization. Many say they left an organization 'because the leader couldn't keep order', 'because it was too noisy', 'because there was no discipline'. Very few young people appear to have left a unit because discipline was too strict, although a number say: 'Because I didn't like the leader'. Many young people leave uniformed organizations 'because I grew too old' or 'because there were too many children there'.

We also asked the question: 'If you don't belong to any club or youth organization, why don't you?' Answers given to this question are summarized in Tables LVIII and LIX.

TABLE LVIII

REASONS GIVEN BY GIRLS FOR NOT BELONGING TO ANY CLUB OR YOUTH ORGANIZATION

Reason	Present Age						Total
	14	15	16	17	18	19	
Not interested; don't like them; never thought about it; they don't do anything; they're badly run	11	13	11	19	19	18	91
Other interests; too busy; no time ...	6	6	8	12	11	24	67
Don't know one; none near; no good one near	3	13	7	10	5	4	42
Homework or evening classes	3	—	6	4	—	—	13
No one to go with	6	2	5	2	—	2	17
Parental objection	4	2	1	—	—	—	7
Bad mixer; too self-conscious; prefer my own company	1	2	2	3	1	6	15
Not yet old enough	4	—	—	—	—	—	4
Other reasons	—	5	3	3	4	1	16

A number of young people say that they prefer to be at home or to spend their time with a few friends, and the time of others is occupied with homework or other interests, but youth leaders generally cannot feel complacent when they read the answer of the sixteen-year-old girl who says, 'because I am not the rowdy type', or the replies of a great many young people who say: 'they (the Clubs) don't do anything', 'they're rarely successful', or 'they're badly run'. Many of these young people believe, rightly or wrongly, that uniformed organizations cater primarily for children and that clubs on the whole are badly organized, that they 'don't do anything' and that attendance is 'a waste of time'. These young people have 'better things to do'.

What are these 'better things'? Readers will find on pages 31 and 33 a tabulated record of the way in which one week's leisure was employed by 337 girls and 220 boys who do not belong to youth organizations.

One cannot fail to be impressed by the fact that the great majority of these young people are spending their leisure in perfectly harmless, if rather uncreative occupations. One is gratified to discover how much time they spend at home—an average of about two-and-a-half evenings a week in the case of the boys and slightly more than three evenings a week in the case of the girls. Cinema attendances average about one-and-a-half a week, and dancing about once a fortnight.

129

Where a boy or girl said he 'walked around' or 'went out', we have entered this information under the heading of 'walk', but even so the total number of evenings employed in this way is very small indeed. Some of the fourteen-year-old boys and girls occasionally spend their evenings 'playing' and in these cases we have entered the information under the heading 'at home'

TABLE LIX

REASONS GIVEN BY BOYS FOR NOT BELONGING TO ANY CLUB OR YOUTH ORGANIZATION

Reason	Present Age						Total
	14	15	16	17	18	19	
Don't like them, they're not interesting; too boring	14	6	2	—	—	—	22
Not interested; never thought about it	2	7	2	5	4	4	24
No time; better things to do	2	8	8	3	4	11	36
I'm not a good mixer; too self-conscious...	2	—	1	—	—	1	4
Odd jobs prevent; Service reasons; etc.	3	2	—	—	2	2	9
Quite happy as I am	3	—	—	—	1	1	5
No club near	3	1	—	—	2	2	8
Too old to join	—	—	—	—	—	1	1
Intend to join	—	—	1	1	—	—	2
Night School, homework	—	1	4	—	—	—	5

though it is of course probable that some of these youngsters were in fact out in the streets on these occasions. Many of the girls told us how they were employed during those evenings which they spent at home. There appears to be a great deal of visiting of relations and prospective 'in-laws'. One sixteen-year-old factory worker went dancing with 'John' on Saturday, went to the pictures with him on Sunday and Monday, went to his house on Tuesday, Thursday and Friday, while 'John came to our house' on Wednesday. Many girls say of several evenings indeed, that they 'stoped (sic) in with boy friend'.

Apart from Sunday morning, which 232 of these 337 girls spent at home, mostly doing housework (though 25 of them said 'in bed') few evenings appear to be entirely taken up with domestic responsibilities at home. One evening a week appears to be required for washing the hair and having a bath, and other employments included knitting (mentioned 114 times), listening to the radio (93), reading (76), sewing (5), homework (50), writing letters (34), and music practice (22). These figures represent the number of evenings occupied in these ways—not the number of individual girls who mentioned each activity. One nineteen-year-old girl knits every evening.

The boys tend on the whole to have more interests than the girls. Many of the boys, even if officially outside the Youth Service, do belong to cycling clubs, works social clubs, or works football clubs, while a few claim to be members of snooker clubs, jazz clubs, Butlin's clubs, harriers or pigeon clubs. On Saturday afternoon, while 40 per cent of the girls are shopping and another 25 per cent are at home, about half the boys are either watching or playing football or taking part in some physical activity.

It is in our judgment quite erroneous to suppose that there are large numbers of unattached adolescents roaming the streets or going to the cinema every evening or spending their leisure in vicious or anti-social ways. What one does feel about the lives of many of these young people, however, is that they are very barren and restricted. Most of them left school at fourteen, many of them have not read a book since they left school, and they are little more than barely literate. Only 23 per cent of these unattached boys and girls appear to be in any real association with a church; they have few hobbies (one girl mentioned rug-making and another, drawing) a negligible percentage of the girls take part in any outdoor sports, precisely half the girls and about 40 per cent of the boys have never been to London, while 3 or 4 per cent say that they have never been to the sea-side. One twenty-year-old girl has never been either to London or to the sea-side and the last 'book' she read (six months ago) was *True Stories*. About 7 per cent of the girls and more of the boys, some of whom, of course, are in the Forces, claim to have been abroad, but we discovered in some cases that 'abroad' meant the Isle of Wight or the Isle of Man.

In a few years' time these young people will have the vote and many of them will have children of their own (three or four of them are indeed already married). To bring these young people under the effective influence of any kind of educational provision would be a valuable service indeed. They themselves are not convinced, however, that clubs have anything to give them.

We wonder to what extent there *is* a problem of the 'unattached'. That there are many eleven-, twelve- and thirteen-year-old children playing in the streets, breaking street lamps and generally getting into trouble we do not doubt. (5,219 street lamps in Birmingham are put out of action in one year by stone-throwing.) How far is there a similar adolescent problem? It may be, of course, that the tables on pages 28-33 suggest that the leisure habits of young people are more balanced than is in fact the case, because these tables conceal the fact that the interests of some young people are in fact very unbalanced. One nineteen-year-old chocolate machine operator went to a dance hall on Saturday, Sunday, Monday, Wednesday and Friday, and to the pictures on Tuesday and Thursday; a seventeen-year-old laboratory assistant managed five visits to the cinema; a fifteen-year-old boy salesman spent Sunday, Monday, Tuesday and Thursday evening 'courting', Wednesday evening dancing and Saturday evening at a revue. A sixteen-year-old 'stripper' actually went to the cinema every evening of the week. A nineteen-year-old electrician's mate spent all day Sunday, every evening from Monday to Friday, and Saturday afternoon cycling, only varying this programme by attending a dance on Saturday evening. A sixteen-year-old 'body-builder' went dancing on Saturday and Sunday and roller-skating every evening from Monday to Friday. A fifteen-year-old junior postman spent three evenings in a billiards hall and two at the pictures. An eighteen-year-old box-maker managed four dances, two visits to the cinema, and one to a skating rink, and complained that her pocket money was 'not enough'. A seventeen-year-old store-keeper visited a dance hall on Saturday, Sunday, Wednesday and Friday, varying this programme with a visit to the cinema on Thursday, spending Saturday morning and Sunday morning in bed and giving as his reason for non-membership of any youth organization that he had 'no time'. Equally unbalanced is the programme of the eighteen-year-old girl who spends every evening of the week at church. She never goes to a cinema, a dance or a youth organization. The last book she read (six months ago) was *Rebecca*. She is a 'games assembler', but she herself neither plays nor watches games. She has never been to London. A sixteen-year-old schoolboy spends Saturday afternoon and evening, all day Sunday and every evening from Monday to Friday doing his homework. We must confess sympathy with the eighteen-year-old 'bus conductress who works on Saturday evening, but says about each of the remaining evenings of the week that she 'stoped in'.

The above examples, however, are exceptional rather than typical. We are ready to believe

131

that there may be a larger 'unattached problem' than the evidence of our *Twenty Questions* inquiry would suggest. The most irresponsible young people of course are the very ones who will seldom complete a questionnaire at all, and while we report a large percentage of attachment in certain age groups it is to be remembered that many boys who become club members at fifteen or sixteen do not remain in membership for more than a few months.

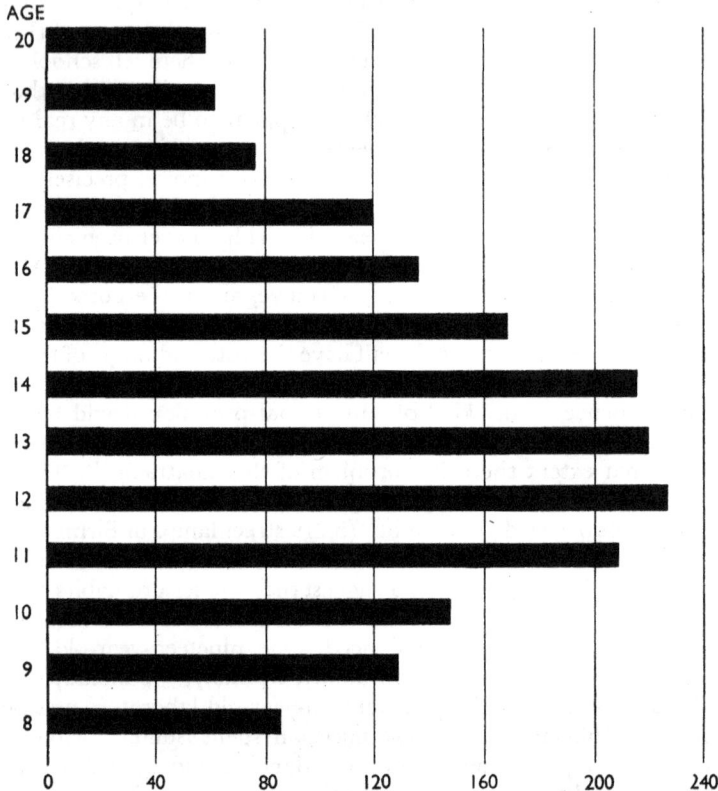

FIGURE 17

PERSONS UNDER 21 PROCEEDED AGAINST FOR INDICTABLE OFFENCES, 1948
The Chief Constable of Birmingham reported that children in the 12-year age group headed the list for indictable offences as a whole. 11-year-olds were responsible for the greatest number of breaking-in offences.

During 1948 the number of Juveniles dealt with in Birmingham Courts for indictable offences was 1,531—an increase of 188 on the previous year, and the number of offences they were proved to have committed totalled 1,290—an increase of 206 over 1947. The main offences in which they were concerned were larcenies of all types (878), breaking-in offences (350), and indecency (30). The total number of Young Persons brought before the Courts for indictable and non-indictable offences was 2,840 (2,452 boys and 388 girls), these figures including 443 charges of playing games in the street; 121 persons between the ages of 16 and 21 were convicted of drunkenness in 1948, compared with 48 in the previous year. There were several cases in which girls of fourteen or fifteen had taken a considerable quantity of alcohol in licensed premises. The number of children and young persons brought before the Court for being in need of care or protection or exposed to moral danger was 60 boys and 61 girls, an increase of 18 boys and 25 girls, compared with the previous year.

It is to be remembered, however, that the great majority of Juveniles who appear before the Courts were under the age of fourteen. The peak age for Juvenile Delinquency in our city in 1948 was twelve, while children in the eleven-year age group were responsible for the greatest

Dancing is not confined to the dance hall.

Lounging at the street corner is a favourite Sunday afternoon occupation.

IN THE STREET
For many adolescents in Birmingham and other large cities, the street is the only recreation ground.

133

number of breaking-in offences. Many cases of violence to property occur at week-ends and during holiday periods. On page 132 will be found a diagram showing the distribution in age groups of persons proceeded against in 1948 for indictable offences.

It is not, we think, part of our business in this Report to enter upon any general discussion of Juvenile Delinquency, its causes or its cure. We wish to say, however, that the heavy incidence of delinquency among boys of eleven and twelve certainly underlines the need both of the rapid implementation of the Report *Out of School** and of the speedy redevelopment of some of the crowded areas. One eleven-year-old boy who came before the Courts in 1948 lived with his father who was separated from his wife. The father was living with a woman who also had children and she was separated from her husband. This mixed family with a total of eight children actually lived in one room.

Birmingham Probation Officers were good enough to assist us by keeping a record of the attachment or otherwise of all the children and young persons who came before the Juvenile Court over a period of three months. It was found that 18 per cent of them were attached to youth organizations. This was a higher figure than the Principal Probation Officer expected, but, even so, it does show that a child who is attached to a youth organization is less likely to become delinquent than one who is not attached. Local Probation Officers complain that owing to the raising of the school-leaving age there is a tendency on the part of some clubs to raise to fifteen the age at which boys and girls can join the club, and that the most urgent need is of more organizations and play centres for children under the age of fourteen.† They also complain that so many youth organizations are only open one evening a week. The Youth Service has an important part to play in the anti-delinquency campaign. The late Chairman of the Birmingham Juvenile Court says that

> It is pitiable that week by week there appear before this Court juveniles who, it is obvious have no idea how to use their leisure time. There never was a time when it was more necessary for boys and girls to join appropriate youth organizations.

The most interesting attempt to make contact with the unattached is undoubtedly that associated with the Sherbourne Road Centre in the Balsall Heath District of the city, an experiment which was described in the pamphlet *Youth in a City* published by the (then) Board of Education in 1943. This Centre was opened in May, 1941, on the premises of a redundant school in an attempt to provide for the recreative needs of young people who were not attracted to the more formal activities of the Evening Institutes. The most interesting feature of the experiment is that it is a strict condition of membership that young people may be admitted only if they have never before been members of any kind of youth organization. If it is found that a would-be member was once attached the note shown on page 135 is sent to the leader of the unit from which he lapsed suggesting that contact be made with him again.

When the Centre was first opened invitations were extended to members of street gangs in the neighbourhood and 135 young people enrolled in the first week:

> By the fourth week—street contacts being made all the time—the roll had increased to 223 (97 girls and 126 boys) but the Centre lost forty-seven members who came in once or twice only. These were lost for one of three reasons—they did not find what they wanted in the Centre, or they could not have absolute freedom to wreck the place, or they found the very rough element too much for them. Twenty-two of those who left came back to the Centre after it had been working six months.‡

When the Centre first opened most of the members were dirty, untidy and ill-mannered, but the turning-point came after the boys' table tennis team had visited and played a club in another district. When the time came for a return match, the members of the Sherbourne team attended clean and in their best clothes, and from this time there was a general improvement in the appearance of the whole of the Centre membership. This meant, however, that the club was

* See below, p.156

† A National Under-Fourteen Council has been established to encourage the formation of junior clubs throughout the country.

‡ *Youth in a City*, p. 2

gradually becoming too respectable for the prospective new members for whom it really existed. To overcome this difficulty the names of prospective members were added to a waiting list, and when the list reached twenty or twenty-five these boys and girls were invited to come on a stated date. As there was then a number of similar type together, they tended to stay in the club.

A casual visitor to Sherbourne would find it difficult to say in what ways members were unlike those in any other club, and he would be still more impressed with the value of the work being done if he could learn something about the appalling home conditions from which some of the young people come. In April, 1949, the Centre had on its books 194 boys and 160 girls, of whom 160 boys and 131 girls were in regular attendance. A recent development has been the establishment of a separate Centre, in adjacent premises, for those members who are under

---

'Sherbourne Centre'

Sherbourne Road

BALSALL HEATH

Dear Sir (Madam),

The boy or girl named on the accompanying Card has applied to us for admission as a member of the 'Sherbourne Centre'.

Our Rules do not allow us to admit anyone who is or who has been a member of any other organization.

May I respectfully suggest that you make contact with the person named with a view to his or her re-instatement in your organization?

I remain,
Yours faithfully,

---

sixteen, so that work among the under- and over-sixteens is now carried on separately to the advantage of both. The success of the Sherbourne experiment is due in the first place to excellent leadership, but also, in our judgment, to the rule that members must take part in at least one activity other than games. Many club leaders excuse the poverty of their club programme by saying that 'members don't want anything but games', but the fact is that no club can live for long on table tennis and dancing. The reason why so many members lapse after a few weeks or months is, as we have seen, because 'there was nothing to do' or because 'it was not interesting'. It is significant that at Sherbourne, which caters for the toughest of the tough, young people have accepted this stipulation, many of them indeed voluntarily taking part in more than one activity. Sections at Sherbourne have included physical training, drama, crafts, ballroom dancing, concert party, woodwork, first aid, dressmaking, and even mathematics. Some of the best soft toys we have seen produced by club members were made by girls in this Centre. The club has its library, its outdoor sports and its summer camp.

An experiment of a very different kind is the opening of a number of Civic Restaurants for use by young people for recreational purposes during the evenings. About fifty Civic Restaurants in the city are managed by the Catering and Entertainments Sub-Committee of the City Council. This Committee has given consideration to the question whether or not it would be desirable for certain restaurants to be open in the evenings, either for the use of young people generally as an alternative to the public house, or for the use of one or more youth organizations in the area for which additional accommodation and catering provision could thus be offered. A further question under consideration is whether, when new premises are built, provision should be made for young people during evening hours. One suggestion for example is that a Civic Restaurant should be on the ground floor, but that there should be first-floor accommodation for young people.

We paid several evening visits to Civic Restaurants where provision is made for the leisure-time needs of young people, and we discovered that they were being used by quite young children. The Local Education Authority supplies a supervisor who gives out games (and sometimes gets them back), but who does not otherwise exercise any leadership. Many of the young children present ought, we thought, to have been in bed, but had the Restaurant not been open they would not have been in bed or even at home, but playing in the streets, as indeed were many of their local contemporaries. The problem is really one of adult education. Some parents at present find it convenient to send their children round the corner to the Civic Restaurant with threepence with which to buy a chip supper while they themselves sit quietly at home or spend the evening at 'the local'. Not many adolescents appear to use these Restaurants though some of those who come do so because there are no rules or regulations, no conditions of membership and no membership fee.

If any real service is to be offered to unattached young people by these means, it seems to us that the Restaurant should provide an introduction to genuine club membership. We could imagine that if a well-run club were associated with a Restaurant—the latter being open to all-comers but the activities of the club restricted only to members—it might be that young people hitherto unattached might find their way via the Restaurant into the club itself. At the present time little real service is being rendered to young people, and one supervisor to whom we spoke suggested that if too many activities were offered in the Restaurant it might happen that young people would be drawn away from the units to which they were already attached.

A somewhat similar attempt to provide a meeting place for unattached young people is the recent opening of the 'Penguin' in the Washwood Heath district of the city. The Penguin is sponsored by the National Commercial Temperance League and is intended to provide a counter-attraction to the public house. It was opened by Lord Ammon and the Rt. Hon. Isaac Foot in November, 1948, and is being well used by young people. The criticism we have offered of the Civic Restaurant applies, however, to the Penguin: that while an alternative is being provided to other less desirable meeting places no attempt is being made to lead young people into the membership of any true community.

SCHOOL AND CLUB

A schoolboy or girl who does not belong to a youth organization is not properly to be regarded as being unattached. At the same time, this would appear to be a convenient point at which to make a few comments on the relation of the Youth Service to the boy or girl who is still at school. It is strongly contended by some that many boys and girls who ought to be doing their homework are in fact wasting their time at youth organizations to the detriment of their future careers. It is argued by others with equal conviction that youth organizations can make a valuable contribution to the social and emotional development of the schoolboy whose growth in these directions is often retarded by the very fact that he is still at school.

Any discussion of this question must be informed by a factual knowledge of the extent to which boys and girls at school do spend their time at youth organizations. Our own information on this subject has been derived from two main sources:
(a) Our *Twenty Questions* inquiry has furnished us with information about the employment of one week's leisure by 119 boys and 60 girls who are attached to youth organizations and who are still at school.*
(b) The Headmaster of a large Boys' Grammar School and the Headmistress of a large Girls' Grammar School allowed us to make inquiries about the attachment or otherwise of all their pupils aged fourteen and over.

* We did not of course include all these questionnaires in our 1,000 'sample'.

The analysis of the *Twenty Questions* inquiry produced the following information: During one week the 119 schoolboys spent 299 evenings at home, this being an average of 2·3 evenings per boy. The same boys spent 218 evenings at youth organizations (an average of 1·8) and 161 evenings at cinemas, dances, billiards halls and skating rinks (an average of 1·3). The 60 girls spent 181 evenings at home (an average of 3), 73 evenings at youth organizations (an average of 1·2), and 62 evenings at public entertainments.

Of the 256 girls aged fourteen and over in attendance at the Grammar School, 142 were attached, a percentage of attachment of 55 as compared with 33 for the city's girl population as a whole. Of 211 boys, 123, or 58 per cent, were attached, as compared with 55 per cent for the city as a whole. The following table shows how often those who are attached attended youth organizations during the week before our inquiry.

TABLE LX

FREQUENCY OF ATTENDANCE AT YOUTH ORGANIZATIONS BY SECONDARY SCHOOL CHILDREN

	Once	Twice	Three times	Four times	Five times	Eight times	Average Weekly Attendance
123 Boys	90	21	8	1	2	1	1·4
142 Girls	96	37	8	—	1	1	1·4

The units to which these Grammar School boys and girls belong are as follows, some of them belonging to more than one unit:

TABLE LXI

ATTACHMENT OF GRAMMAR SCHOOL CHILDREN TO YOUTH ORGANIZATIONS

	Church Clubs	Other Clubs	Scouts Guides Brigades	Pre-Service Units
Boys ...	82	22	31	4
Girls ...	82	25	49	—

It is interesting to note that these same boys paid 134 visits to cinemas, theatres, dance halls and skating rinks during the week, while the corresponding figure for the girls was 159, this latter figure being swollen by an organized theatre party.

The conclusive evidence derived from these two sources would appear to be that there are very few boys and girls engaged in full-time education who are in fact spending many evenings a week at youth organizations. There are, of course, a few exceptional cases. One sixteen-year-old

137

boy put in eight attendances at his Boys' Brigade in one week. Another boy of the same age belongs to the Scouts, a church youth club, a dramatic club, a table tennis club and a harriers club, at each of which he put in one attendance during the week. One fourteen-year-old girl belongs to three organizations and puts in five attendances. These cases, however, are unusual. The average attendance at youth organizations would appear to be less than three evenings a fortnight, only slightly in excess of the amount of time these same young people spend in cinema, dance hall or skating rink. If, as we believe, a youth organization has a contribution to make to the training of the schoolboy, particularly as regards his emotional and social development, and if he on his part has a contribution to make to the youth organization, three attendances a fortnight would not seem to be excessive.

A SUNDAY NIGHT 'SWING' CLUB
This particular Club has seven hundred members.

CHAPTER IX

LOCAL AUTHORITY AND VOLUNTARY ORGANIZATION

IT HAS HAPPENED again and again in our history that a Social Service which began as a voluntary enterprise sponsored by a group of interested people has eventually been taken over by the State. Schools tend increasingly to pass from private into public control; the hospitals are now an integral part of the National Health Service; and we can see at the present time a public service for old people and for deprived children developing out of pioneer voluntary effort.

It is not within the province of this Report to enter into any general discussion of the many controversial issues which arise from these recent developments, but we can see reasons why the general movement is to be welcomed. Voluntary services are usually handicapped both by lack of finance and by lack of staff, and cannot meet all the needs in the field in which they are at work. It may happen that a voluntary society which has for long discharged a particular kind of social service resents and resists the provision of a more effective and universal public service by the State, and may actually hinder progress in the very field in which it is interested.

At the same time the fact that so much public service is discharged by men and women who give their time without payment or reward is a feature of our national life of which we may be justly proud. The paid official may occasionally be impatient of the unpaid magistrate, the town councillor, or the committee member, but it is good that it is still possible for the private citizen to be able to play some effective part in public life. When the voluntary worker is replaced by the paid official there is loss as well as gain. We hope that there will long be a place for the voluntary organization, both in the exploration of new territory and in partnership with statutory authority in those fields where at present responsibilities are shared.

In the realm of the Youth Service the Ministry of Education has repeatedly and consistently emphasized the importance of associating voluntary effort with the public system. In the 1944 Education Act, Local Authorities are urged to 'have regard to the expediency of co-operating with any voluntary societies or bodies whose objects include the provision of facilities or the organization of activities of a similar character'.* The Ministry itself implements this policy of partnership to the full by the grant-aid it offers to the voluntary bodies for their national administrative expenses.

Local Education Authorities, however, differ very widely in the way in which they implement or fail to implement this policy of partnership. In Birmingham, as we have seen, the Authority initiates little youth work of its own, but is ready to assist any and every type of youth organization. Some Authorities, however, appear to assume that the day of the voluntary organization is done, and seem determined to establish their own Youth Centres in every district under their jurisdiction regardless of any existing provision on the part of the voluntary bodies. In one small town in which an Authority had stationed a club leader, the leader discovered that there were very few 'unattached' young people, but reported to the Authority that recruits for the new Youth Centre could probably be drawn from the existing organizations in the town! One large Authority, on the other hand, has even refrained from setting up its own Youth Committee, preferring to work through the local Standing Conference of Voluntary Youth Organizations—a Conference which in that particular city has its own full-time secretariat.

The voluntary organizations are concerned about the unwillingness of certain Local Authorities to contribute to their local administrative costs—the expense, for example, of the

* Section 53.

139

salaries of one or more organizers where they are employed. Policy in this matter appears to vary in different parts of the country. The N.A.G.C. & M.C. reports, for instance, that of their 30 Associations in England which have full-time paid secretaries, all but four (one of which is Birmingham) receive grant-aid from their authorities. The N.A.B.C. reports, on the other hand, that of their 34 local Associations with salaried officials, precisely half are grant-aided. The general tendency, however, would seem to be in the direction of the reduction or cessation of this type of grant. The question was discussed in the Ministry publication *Further Education*, where the conclusion is drawn that:

> It is not the responsibility of the Authority to pay the salaries of the organizing staff of the voluntary organizations. But where, as a result of the enterprise and convictions of a particular organization, funds are raised and staff is appointed, the Authority should be ready to contribute in relation to the responsibilities and justifiable expenditure of the association in the area.

We have evidence that one or two L.E.A. officers—not in our city—have divorced the first sentence of the above quotation from its context, and have used it to support their own unwillingness to grant-aid the local administration of the voluntary bodies. If, however, the Ministry is prepared to grant-aid the National Headquarters of the voluntary bodies, it is difficult to see on what grounds a Local Authority, which is responsible for all Further Education in its own area, refuses to give similar aid to the local Associations. If it be argued that to assist one organization would commit an Authority to give similar financial assistance to all the others, it may be replied that the Authority should surely be competent to assess the needs of each of the organizations at work in its area. At the same time the voluntary organizations should be reasonable in their demands.

> For each voluntary association to seek to establish a substantial universal pattern of administration with organizing staff in every county would obviously cause a great deal of duplication and make collaboration with them by statutory authorities difficult, if that pattern implied grants-in-aid.*

It cannot be denied that there are places in which there is duplication of effort and wasteful use of man-power. In one Midland town the L.E.A. Youth Officer, and the local organizers both of the N.A.B.C. and of the N.A.G.C. & M.C. are all three providing the same kind of service to the same group of clubs, and we are informed that one evening they all three visited the same club! It might be argued that the needs of youth in that town would be better served if there were two organizers less and two club leaders more. On the other hand, the quality of the work accomplished in any youth unit is undoubtedly influenced by the vitality of the local organization with which it is associated. It has happened that the appointment of a first-class organizer has led to the improvement of the quality of club work done throughout a whole county. If, however, the club organizations claim that this is an argument for grant-aid towards the salaries of their local organizers, the uniformed organizations might retort that their local organizations are staffed, in the main, by voluntary workers.

Some district organizers to whom we have spoken prefer that their appointment should not be grant-aided, pointing out that partnership is much more real if they can meet the L.E.A. Youth Officer in an entirely independent capacity than if their own position is dependent upon his willingness to recommend a grant towards their salaries!

Our own judgment is that while public grant should never replace voluntary effort, and while L.E.A. assistance should not be used to keep alive an organization that has outlived its usefulness, there are occasions when some grant-aid to the local organizations of one or other of the voluntary bodies would be a real contribution to the Youth Service.

THE FUTURE OF THE VOLUNTARY BODIES

The question, however, whether or not the L.E.A. should grant-aid the local administration of the voluntary youth organizations presupposes that there is a place for them in the future pattern. This, however, is denied in certain quarters. The view has been expressed that the

* *Further Education*, 1947, p. 67.

voluntary bodies have no future in the field of Further Education. A more representative opinion is that expressed in the introduction to the Devon Further Education Scheme:

> The voluntary organizations still have a part to play, but it must be realized that there is a changed attitude on the part of the Local Education Authority . . . . the emphasis is switched; instead of the L.E.A. plugging leaks, the other agencies must consent to become part of a recognized whole.*

The voluntary bodies need to consider the situation that will be created by the advent of the County College, when every boy and girl will be engaged in whole-time education until he is sixteen, and thereafter will attend the County College one day a week until he is eighteen. It is quite evident that Authorities have ceased to limit their activities to the compulsory side of education, realizing that leisure-time occupations are an equally important part of the whole education field. We reproduce (page 142) a copy of a circular issued by one Birmingham Evening Institute, which is an example of the way in which the Authority is trying to 'sell' education.

It is almost certain that voluntary evening activities will grow up round the County Colleges. It has been stated in one Ministry publication that

> clearly the colleges will not fulfil their purpose if their students have no interest in them beyond the short hours of compulsory attendance. They must develop a corporate life among those who attend them, and through student clubs and societies take their place in a wider youth service. The colleges must be designed and equipped so as to realize these opportunities for corporate social activity.†

At the Rugby Day Continuation School, in March, 1949, about a third of the boys and about half the girls were returning to the school for voluntary evening classes. The actual figures were:

TABLE LXII

EVENING ACTIVITIES OF YOUNG PEOPLE ATTENDING RUGBY DAY CONTINUATION SCHOOL

Attending	130 Boys	128 Girls
Evening activities at the school	41	60
Other groups as well	37	24
Other groups only	60	15
No evening activities at all	29	53

When one reads *Youth's Opportunity*—the pamphlet in which the Ministry of Education describes the County Colleges of the future, with their gymnasia, workshops, laboratories and concert halls, one is inevitably driven to putt he question: 'What, with these developments, is the future of the small poorly equipped youth club?—Ought it, indeed, to have any future at all?'

There is a distinct tendency on the part of the representatives of some organizations to deplore the larger activity in the realm of further education which the Local Authorities are now contemplating. In conversation with us some of them have talked about 'the menace of the

---

* Quoted in the *Times Educational Supplement*, 11th December, 1948.
† *Further Education*, p. 64.

WHY NOT SPEND AN EVENING OR TWO IN PLEASANT COMPANY?

JOIN IN ONE OR MORE OF THE FOLLOWING ACTIVITIES

TEA AND BUNS AVAILABLE

Admission: Under 18, free Over 18, 5s. 0d. (January to July)

Class Hours: 7-0 p.m. or 7-30 p.m. to 9-0 p.m. or 9-30 p.m.

	ADULTS	**JUNIORS**
MONDAY	**Ballroom Dancing** (learners and dancers) **Dressmaking** (Knitting and Embroidery, 'Make-do and Mend') **Science**	**Shorthand** (Beginners and advanced) **Science** (Model drawing, Motor Engineering, Photography) **Woodwork**
TUESDAY	**Cookery** (All rations provided) A meal to take home!	**Book-keeping** **English** **Dance Orchestra** (learn to play) **P.T. Girls:** Eurhythmics **Boys:** Basket Ball
WEDNESDAY	**Record Club** Bring your records! **Woodwork** Make anything you've wood for!	**Homecrafts:** Leatherwork, etc.
THURSDAY	**String Orchestra** 'Play for Pleasure' **Homecrafts** — Leatherwork, Basketry, Gloves, Plaster-Casts, etc.	**Shorthand** **English**
FRIDAY	**Homecrafts**—Leatherwork, Soft Toys, Felt work, etc.	**Woodwork** **Ballroom Dancing** (Beginners and improvers) **Puppetry**—all the fun of the stage in miniature

ART CLASSES — Drawing, Design, Painting are proposed.
BADMINTON — Applications will be considered for any vacancies in present groups—Wednesday, Thursday and Friday.
CLUB CLASSES are held in which boys play Basket Ball, or do Football Training. Girls play Netball.

SUMMER ACTIVITIES

Cricket Practice Swimming and Life Saving Classes
Boys' Cycling Club Drama Group 'Plays in the Sun'

State' or 'the threat of the County College'. All this, of course, is foolish and regrettable. It is because the State did not recognize the needs of young people that the voluntary organizations came into being, and now that public opinion generally has recognized the value of the pioneer work done in the past and wishes to make the same kind of provision available for all, the voluntary organizations should be the first to rejoice. Are they more concerned with their own future than with the welfare of the adolescent?

While, however, we expect and hope that voluntary evening activities will grow up round the County Colleges, we think it most unlikely that the County College will render the voluntary organizations superfluous. Nor would many people in this country welcome a uniform 'nationalized' Youth Service. The whole emphasis in the past has been on variety, independence and freedom, and the Chairman of the N.A.B.C. is perfectly right when he says that 'no rigid prescription can provide for the diversity of young minds and personalities, whose growth to full self-disciplined maturity requires the equally diverse techniques that are employed by the voluntary organizations'.

The shape to be taken by the Youth Service in future will be determined, after all, not by Directors of Education, Research Commissions, or by the authors of Reports like this, but by the young people themselves; and there would be a natural resistance among many of them to any attempt at State regimentation. We do not regard the democratic State as an enemy to be feared, but at the same time we think there is still need for vigilance lest a passion for administrative efficiency or the increasing power of bureaucracy should lead to too much uniformity and regimentation.

We offer the following further additional considerations in support of our contention that it is neither likely nor desirable that the County College will supplant the voluntary organization altogether:

(1) The number of County Colleges required for the city has been calculated on a basis of 2,000 students a week in each College. It is proposed that all young people of County College age should attend the College both for general education and for any vocational courses they may wish to take. The Colleges will make available, therefore, not only evening activities of a social and recreational character, but evening classes in approved subjects. In other words, the College will eventually replace the Junior Evening Institute to a very large extent. It is quite obvious, therefore, that the accommodation available will be quite inadequate to supply all the recreational needs of 2,000 young people.

(2) Some young people will need to travel considerable distances to reach the County College, and some of them will prefer to join youth organizations which meet near their own homes. Many unattached girls have given us as the reason for their non-attachment that there is no unit near enough, and yet, as we have seen, Birmingham can offer them 481 girls' organizations, and 438 mixed units. Their needs are unlikely to be met by Birmingham's proposed twenty-one County Colleges.

(3) It is not unreasonable to expect that the Further Education which is to be provided in the future will stimulate a demand for more evening activities. Experience both at Rugby and at Bournville suggests that there are likely to be fewer 'unattached' young people among those who attend Day Continuation Classes than in the population as a whole.

(4) We believe that the most fruitful setting in which youth work can be done is one in which, while young people can go apart with a group of their contemporaries when they wish, they also have opportunities of association with those younger and with those older than themselves. (See Chapter X.) The County College will presumably be able to offer no such opportunities. Their members will be completely segregated from adult society; they will not be introduced to any continuing community.

(5) We believe, also, that there is a contribution which can be given to its members by a comparatively small unit which cannot be made by a vast Youth Centre. It would be very difficult to say what is the optimum size of a youth unit, and while we feel that most units in Birmingham are too small we also feel that a few are too large. Young people today are growing up in a very

FIGURE 18

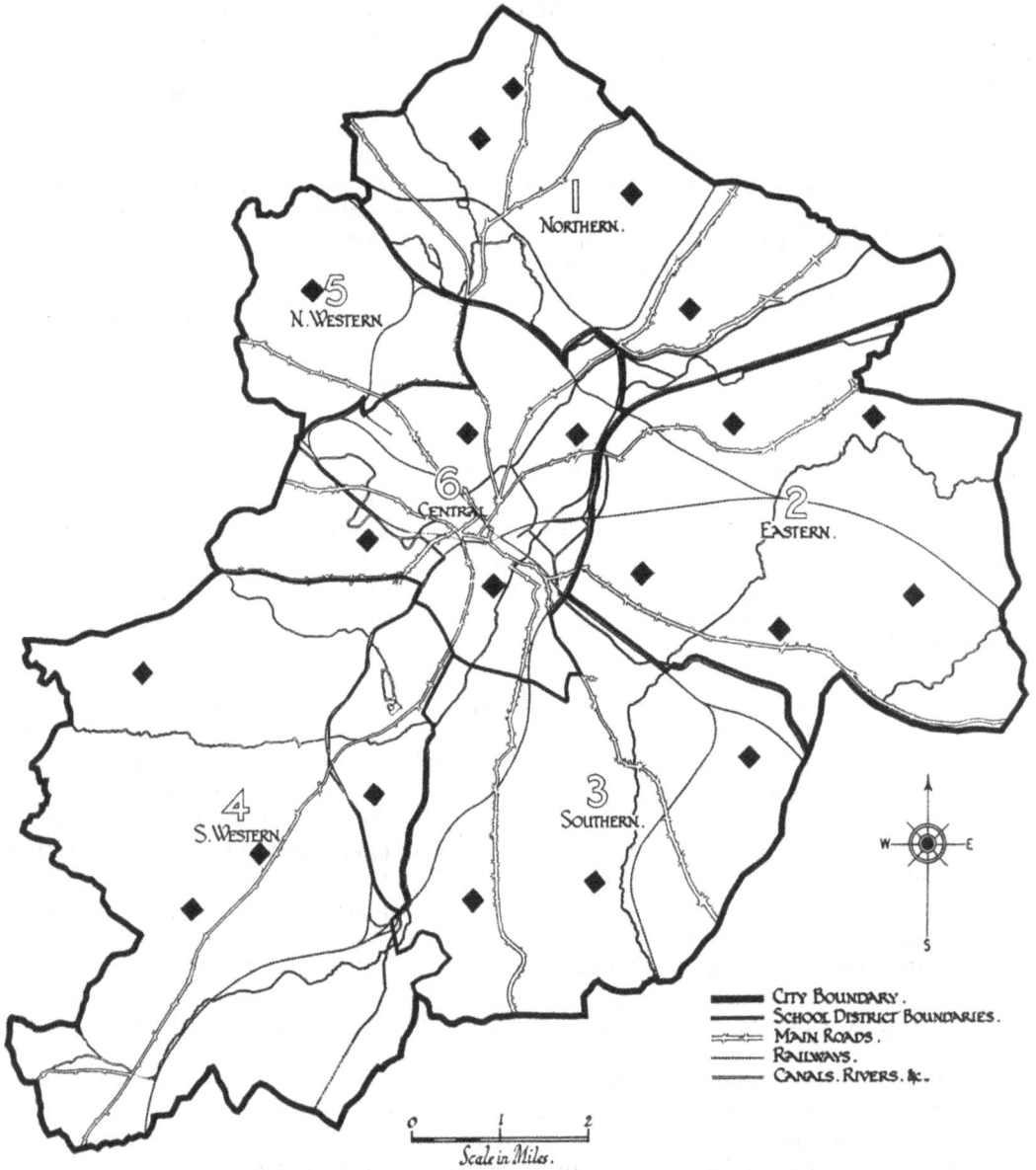

APPROXIMATE LOCATION OF 21 PROPOSED COUNTY COLLEGES IN BIRMINGHAM

impersonal world and know few true personal relationships. At work many believe themselves to be selfishly exploited by the remote 'boss' or the anonymous and distant management. Their leisure is largely spent in a seat at the local cinema or on the floor of the nearest dance hall. One's life, it appears, is largely ruled and controlled by a vague and unknown Authority ('they') which is to be outwitted as much as one can or dare. The inevitable resultant social irresponsibility is illustrated by a remark made by one boy—a member of a club committee—who explained his late arrival at club by saying that he had been working overtime, adding: 'We have reduced it to a fine art at our place—we go slow all day so that we have to work overtime at night'. How desirable it is, therefore, that they should become part of the life of some group which is small enough to be a true community, to introduce them to genuine personal relationships, and to give them the opportunity of discovering themselves and of making a contribution of their own in a society of their contemporaries. There are few things some of them need more than the security that is afforded by a place of their own, and a group to which they truly 'belong'. We question whether this particular need can be met by a very large organization. Dr. Marjorie Reeves has said:

> In expanding the Service of Youth we must not forget that its real significance lies, not in wonderful buildings, or lavish equipment, but in fostering societies of persons in which individuals can grow to full stature . . . . There will of course be many local patterns: what we must avoid at all costs are large Palaces of Youth where the young gather to be amused with little more effort than in commercial places of entertainment.*

In one large Birmingham club we have noticed a tendency for boys to stroll in, to become 'members', to play a game of table tennis, and to stroll out, without ever accepting responsibility or identifying themselves in any way with the life of the club. There comes, somewhere, a point at which a society becomes a crowd and community becomes gregariousness. What is more important, there is a limit to the number of members a club leader can really know if he is to take a genuine interest in each. A club leader is not merely an organizer of evening activities, he has a vocation which we think is most truly thought of in terms of a pastoral ministry.

(6) Perhaps the clearest difference between the voluntary organization and the L.E.A. Youth Centre or County College is that the former is staffed, in the main, by voluntary workers, and the latter, in the main, by paid teachers or leaders. This distinction is very generally true, in spite of the fact that a minority of voluntary organizations are professionally staffed and that a few voluntary workers assist in L.E.A. Youth Centres. We would not wish to suggest that a voluntary leader necessarily establishes a quality of personal relationship with his members which cannot be achieved by the paid leader, but at the same time one of the first questions a boy will put to a club leader is: 'Are you being paid for this job?' (as though to say: 'It's all right, but let's know just where we are'.) One of the most valuable contributions which membership of a voluntary organization can bring to a girl or boy is the introduction it gives them to men and women who are prepared to work hard and to give freely of their time without being paid for so doing. The complete replacement of the voluntary helper by the paid leader would be a major disaster in an acquisitive society where, to quote one observer's description of the effect of the environment of a large engineering firm upon the lad just entering its employment:

> everybody expects him to dodge as much work as possible; if he works steadily during the day he is regarded as an oddity, a despised 'master's man', toadying and sucking up to the bosses. It is unknown for anyone to work for one minute after the hooter has gone . . . †

(7) It may finally be suggested that the County College can never take the place of any organization which has a distinctive technique or purpose of its own. No one imagines that the County College will take the place of any of the uniformed organizations, though we can imagine that a college, like a school, might quite possibly promote its own Air Training Corps or its own Rover Scout crew. Similarly, churches and political parties will continue to work among young people, and we have no doubt but that there is a future for the church youth club, though its leaders will be wise to remember that in the future the church youth club, like all other organizations, will probably get the place it deserves. If it is a true community, offering its members a balanced programme, and communicating the Christian Faith to them not only in precept but through its own personal relationships and its own accepted standards, it will play its part in the future; if, on the other hand, it is merely a hall in which boys play table tennis and girls shuffle round the floor, it will perish and will deserve to do so. There are those who suggest that one cannot be quite as sure about the permanent future of the 'open club' which has provided in the past very much the same kind of service that, in future, the County College will offer to all.

* *Growing up in a Modern Society*, p. 116.

† *The Church and Youth.* Report of the Church of England Youth Council, 1947, p. 10.

PARTNERSHIP DEFINED

It would be useful to attempt to define the respective contributions which, in an ideal society, might be made by the Authority on the one hand and by the voluntary organization on the other, in order to eliminate the overlapping, competition and wastage of man-power which are not unknown in the Youth Service at the present time. This would be no easy task, partly because local circumstances vary in different parts of the country, and partly because no pattern can ever be final and permanent. The question is one which might be continually under review by groups like the Future Policy Sub-Committee of the Birmingham Youth Committee.

As a general policy, we think it preferable that in general, and apart from what is provided in the County College, the Authority should not normally promote its own Youth Clubs, but leave the actual conduct of clubs to the voluntary bodies. We realize, however, that this is not always a practical policy. It was pointed out to us by the Youth Organizer of one Authority in the north of England that in his city all the voluntary organizations, including the churches, have attracted only 23 per cent of the population of young people who are no longer in full-time attendance at school. In such a situation it is the inescapable duty of the Local Authority to make some provision for the 77 per cent who are not members of the voluntary organizations. We do feel, however, that where an Authority promotes its own clubs, grant-aid to these clubs should only be offered on the same scale and on the same terms as it is offered to the clubs promoted by the voluntary bodies. There are areas where clubs promoted by the Authority are lavishly grant-aided, and where other clubs are starved.

The following are examples of the services which might be offered by an Authority to the youth organizations in its area:

(1) Grants, use of premises, playing-fields, swimming baths, etc., the provision of instructors and specialist advisers in music, physical training, drama, etc.

(2) The promotion of training courses for voluntary workers in all types of organization. Basic needs, after all, are similar in all types of unit, and it would be to the mutual benefit of the Boys' Brigade Captain and of the Co-operative Youth Club leader to learn something, each from the other. There is at present a waste of man-power and opportunity when each of several voluntary bodies is sending training officers into a city to meet small groups. It would be a valuable contribution to the Youth Service, we think, if the Authority were to appoint a Recruitment and Training Officer, who would give his full time to the enlistment and training of voluntary leaders and helpers. It is extraordinary that in a city the size of Birmingham there should be so few training facilities for voluntary leaders and helpers in clubs.

(3) 'The establishment of "youth centres"—premises which can be used regularly or for special occasions by individual Clubs, Cadet Corps, Scouts, Guides and Brigades, according to their particular needs for accommodation. The emphasis in this use of the term "youth centre" is on the hospitality of a building given to different organizations rather than on a corporate organization specifically identified with the building.' Here we have quoted from a Ministry publication. *
The kind of 'youth centre' we ourselves would have in mind, however, would be one of the 'Conway' type described earlier in this Report, which can contribute greatly to the small unit, both by enabling it to enlarge the range of its activities, and also by introducing its members to young people of other youth organizations than their own. 'We see the County College as providing such physical facilities as accommodation, swimming baths, concert halls and playing fields which would be made available to all voluntary organizations in their neighbourhood as well as to any clubs and societies of their own.'†

(4) The promotion of all kinds of co-operative and competitive activities, such as Youth Weeks, Drama Festivals, Sports Days, Public-Speaking Contests, etc.

(5) The publication of a Youth Service Newsletter by means of which leaders in all types of youth organization may be informed of courses, special events, etc. An excellent newsletter of this kind is issued by the Youth Sub-Committee of the City of Leicester Education Committee.

* *Further Education*, p. 68.
† *Purpose and Content of the Youth Service*, p. 6.

(6) The establishment and maintenance of Conference Houses, to be used, not only by the Authority for its own courses, but by any voluntary organization or individual unit. Houses of this kind could make an immense contribution to the Youth Service, and, once established, should be financially self-supporting.

(7) The encouragement of Youth Parliaments or Youth Councils, composed of representative members of all types of youth unit in the area, where young people could meet, not only to make their voices heard, but to discover ways of corporate service to their own local community. We propose to discuss this suggestion further in our final chapter, where we suggest that the L.E.A. Youth Officer should be a man who is, in the truest sense, a Youth Leader—one who can capture the interest of young people and guide them in purposeful activity.

There are, similarly, functions which in our judgment are best discharged by the Voluntary Organization:

(1) We have already suggested that the actual provision and conduct of youth organizations is, in general, best undertaken by the voluntary organizations. This, of course, is the most important task of all. Where an area appears to be under-provided, the various bodies might agree among themselves as to which of them can best initiate development in that area. When, even then, there is under-provision, it is clear that the Authority must itself establish clubs.

(2) Where an organization has a specific technique or purpose, it must obviously be responsible for a certain proportion of the training of its own leaders. One hardly expects the L.E.A. to instruct would-be scouters in scouting, or church youth leaders in evangelism, though, as we have suggested, both might very profitably share the advantage of basic courses provided by the L.E.A.

(3) Voluntary organizations will continue to promote competitions, sports leagues, and an exchange of visits among units of their own body. It is good, we think, that there should be an annual Boys' Brigade Display, a Baptist Youth Rally, or a N.A.G.C. Drama Festival. (The winners of the Festival might well enter with finalists in Festivals promoted by other bodies in a Town Festival promoted by the Authority.) One is no less good an Englishman because one is proud to live in Birmingham, and pride in one's own organization is something to be valued. The voluntary organization, indeed, is able at this point to offer something which no Authority can provide. There are many desirable things which the L.E.A. Youth Officer can produce, as it were, out of his hat, but he cannot organize an International Scout Jamboree in France, a Catholic Pilgrimage to Rome, a G.L.B. Display in the Royal Albert Hall, a N.A.B.C. Training Week at Ford Castle, or find a Guide Camp site in Guernsey, or a Methodist Guild Holiday Home in Scotland.

(4) There are fields in which each of the voluntary organizations has made, and can continue to make, a specialist contribution. Scouts and Guides can teach us all something about camping, the N.A.G.C. and M.C. produces literature which is in a class by itself, the denominational Youth Departments have something to tell us about informal religious education. L.E.A.s would surely be advised, when arranging their training courses for leaders, to draw upon the services of the staff of these various bodies, just as they accept help from the Central Council of Physical Recreation, the Bureau of Current Affairs, or the Religious Drama Society.

The suggestion has been made that routine services should in future be provided by the Authority, the voluntary organization being free to engage in enterprise of an experimental or pioneering nature. In Birmingham, as we have seen, experimental work has been initiated, both by the Authority and by voluntary bodies. We wonder if it is possible to generalize on this question, because it is probable that the genesis of all genuine experiment is to be found, not in the resolutions of any committee, either statutory or voluntary, but in the vision of an inspired individual, who may find his opportunity in either field. We suggest, however, that there are certain considerations which point to the view that pioneering work can sometimes be initiated more easily by an Authority than by a voluntary organization. The real hard core of the youth problem is to be found in the 'bottom 10 per cent' of semi-literate young people who have not yet been attracted to any type of organization whatever. It might be possible to make a first

CITY OF BIRMINGHAM EDUCATION COMMITTEE
BIRMINGHAM YOUTH COMMITTEE

★

GRANT-AID TO YOUTH ORGANIZATIONS

1. The Education Committee is prepared to consider, through the Youth Committee, applications from approved youth organizations for grant-aid towards the purchase of equipment, maintenance or rent of premises, salaries of leaders.

2. This Scheme of grant-aid is not intended to act as a substitute for voluntary effort, but as a supplement to it.

3. Applications must be submitted on the appropriate form, and in the case of units affiliated to a central organization must be submitted through such organization.

4. As a general principle, the scheme is intended to apply to youth organizations catering for young people up to the age of 20 years, who are no longer subject to full-time compulsory attendance at school.

5. Youth organizations applying for grant-aid must have a responsible Management Committee, including at least three adults and must, except in special circumstances, meet for two or more sessions per week, with an average attendance of not less than 20 members at each session, and must keep an official attendance register.

6. Grants will not exceed 50 per cent of the total estimated cost of the items recognized for grant purposes.

7. When provision of equipment is the subject of the application, a detailed price list must be submitted.

8. When the payment of rent for premises is the subject of the application, it must be established that additional cost is caused as a result of the premises being used for youth activities, and grant-aid will not be given for the rent of premises which are owned by the organization or its parent body.

9. Youth organizations receiving direct grants from the Ministry of Education for the purchase of equipment will not be eligible to apply to the City of Birmingham Education Committee for further grants for the same purpose.

10. Admission to the premises of clubs applying for grant-aid shall be given at all reasonable times to the Chief Education Officer and to persons authorized by him.

11. Payment of any grant offered will be made in each case on submission of bills for the whole amount of the expenditure involved for that purpose, either fully receipted or partially receipted, to the extent of the organization's share of the cost. Payment upon partially receipted bills will be made only upon the understanding that the fully receipted bills will be submitted to the Education Committee for inspection.

12. The Education Committee reserves the right to make a proportionate reduction in grant' should the actual expenditure fall below the estimates on which the grant is based.

13. Grants will be made on the condition that:-

     (a) In the application of the grant the primary concern will be the needs of young people up to the age of 20 years, who are no longer subject to full-time compulsory attendance at school.

     (b) A certified statement of income and expenditure, signed by the Chairman and one other member of the Committee, must be submitted at the end of the financial year, together with a statement, similarly signed, certifying that the conditions under which the grant was made have been complied with.

     (c) In the event of the activities of the organization being discontinued, the Education Committee must be informed immediately.

     (d) The Education Committee is not committed to provide assistance towards the acquisition of goods which are in short supply, and every effort should be made to secure second-hand articles wherever possible.

     (e) The Education Committee reserves the right to require the removal of any equipment, in the event of the equipment ceasing, whether by discontinuance of the organization's activities or otherwise, to be used for the purpose for which its provision has been aided by grant.

E. L. RUSSELL,

Chief Education Officer.

CITY OF BIRMINGHAM EDUCATION COMMITTEE
BIRMINGHAM YOUTH COMMITTEE

★

GRANT-AID TO YOUTH ORGANIZATIONS

APPLICATION FORM

Name of Organization ....

Central Organization to which affiliated (if any)..

....

Name and address of Leader or responsible officer...

....

Boys, Girls, or Mixed ....

Live membership on date of application:

    under 14........................15-20........................... Over 20....................

Average attendance per meeting ....

Place of meetings ....

Days and times of meetings ....

Amount of member's subscription (state if paid weekly)....................................

Is attendance register marked regularly?..

Constitution, including numbers, of the Management Committee............................

....

Nature of the activities carried on or proposed by the applicant body ....

....

Specific object of this application, stating:

    (1) The nature of the facilities in respect of which grant is sought............................

    ....

    (2) The total estimated cost of the proposal (when the provision of equipment is the subject of the application, a detailed price list should be submitted)......................

    ....

Names and addresses of officers of the applicant body:

    (1) The Chairman ....

    (2) The Treasurer ....

    (3) The Secretary ....

General Statement supporting the application:

....

                    Date..

Signed on behalf of the applicant body...

This form, on completion, must be returned to the Chief Education Officer, the Education Office, Margaret Street, Birmingham 3.

In the event of the unit being affiliated to a central organization, the form must be submitted through such organization.

The form must be accompanied by a statement of accounts of the applicant body for the previous twelve months, and an estimate of income and expenditure during the next twelve months.

contact with them through a 'Youth Café', by means of an 'In-and-Out Club', or through a Civic Restaurant, but few voluntary organizations, we imagine, would be willing to take the risk of possible failure or financial loss or of the lowering of their standards which such an experiment might involve. An Authority could afford to take risks.

We conclude this chapter with the remark that it will be a number of years yet before the County Colleges are all built, and in the meantime there is abundant need that education, in the broadest sense of the word, should continue to flow down to young people through every possible channel.

AT A BIRMINGHAM REGION YOUTH HOSTEL

CHAPTER X

THE TRAINING OF YOUTH FOR LIFE IN COMMUNITY

In an earlier chapter, when we were attempting to characterize the success or failure of different organizations in meeting the emotional needs of their members, we pointed out that such success or failure was related in no small degree to the total social environment in which the activities of the group were carried on. In all education, indeed, the most potent influences are social. Young people are influenced far more by what is taken for granted in the groups to which they belong than they are by anything that is 'taught' them in words. There is tension in the minds of many young people just because the values and standards commended to them at school or church are often disregarded and even flatly contradicted in the assumptions that characterize the speech and conduct of so many of their associates in office or workshop.

It is not sufficient, therefore, to examine the provisions offered by various youth organizations to their individual members—account must be taken also of the total social setting in which such provision is offered. We suggest that if a youth organization is to fulfil a truly educative function and offer its members both emotional training and true social education it must (a) provide them with a background of law and order, (b) enable them to discover the meaning of true personal relationships, and (c) provide them with opportunities of making adjustment, both with those who are younger and older than themselves, and with members of the opposite sex. *

LAW AND ORDER

True freedom is only possible against a background of law and order. Just how much external law must be enforced to ensure personal freedom is the great political debate of our time. In some youth organizations discipline is imposed from above, while in others the aim is to encourage members to accept a self-discipline for themselves. The difference between these two conceptions is most clearly seen if Brigades and Scouts are compared. 'The Scout view is that discipline is an inner quality and that it is developed by encouraging efficiency and controlled independence in the individual. The other point of view is that only by drilling to the last degree of precision, until technique and exactitude of movement have become reflex habits, can true discipline be established.'†

The weight of opinion today in this matter would come down on the side of the Scouts rather than on the side of the Brigades, and much has been written in recent years about the social dangers and psychological limitations of military drill in education. It is to be remembered, nevertheless, that for boys and girls in late childhood and in the early teens drill can provide a sense of solidarity with the community and an experience of disciplined order which together give them that security which best facilitates all true personal development.

We do not suggest, of course, that it is only by the wearing of a uniform or by participation in military drill that this sense of community and this awareness of law and order can be communicated to young people. It is not impossible for membership of a team in a sports league to offer the same kind of experience. We recall the visit to a youth club where a similar contribution was being made to girls in a tap dancing class, where not only was exact precision of movement required, but it was also laid down that regularity and punctuality in attendance was essential if the privilege of participation in the final 'show' was to be enjoyed.

It is to be put to the credit of all the uniformed organizations that they do carry on their

* For a further discussion of this subject see *Growing up in a Modern Society*, by Dr. Marjorie Reeves.

† *The Needs of Youth*, by A. E. Morgan, page 309.

activities within the disciplined framework of accepted law and order. There are rules that must be obeyed and there are authorities that must be recognized. There are too many clubs in which 'membership' is far too loose—where it is possible for a boy to stroll in, to 'join', to play a game of billiards or table tennis and to drift away again after a few weeks without ever having been asked to accept any obligations or to offer any loyalties. We talked to one boy who 'belonged' to three youth clubs, but only attended any of them if the programme took the form of a dance. We have already suggested (Chapter VII) that those clubs which make no demands and ask for no standards may be doing a positive disservice to their members, some of whom need more help than they are being given to enable them to acquire self-discipline.

TRUE PERSONAL RELATIONSHIPS

In our discussion of the optimum size of a youth organization (Chapter IX) we made the point that one of the advantages of the comparatively small unit is that it can foster genuine personal relationships more easily than can a large organization.

Describing the breakdown of true societies in the last century Dr. Marjories Reeves has said that in place of neighbourhoods of fairly stable population we now have 'huge and shifting masses of people, gathered in vast housing estates to sleep, in vast factories to work, and in vast cinemas for their social life'.* This is a generalization which, we think, needs some qualification, because we have been surprised to discover what a large place the home still plays in the lives of most young people—especially of girls—and the visiting of friends and relations appears to be a major leisure-time occupation in our city. There would be much truth, nevertheless, in the contention that outside the home young people know few true personal relationships—relationships, that is, in which they really *meet* other people, not to use them or to exploit them, but to share thought and to work together. This kind of 'meeting' occurs, we are sure, in every type of youth organization, but in our judgment is more easily possible in a democratic than in a hierarchical society and in a unit which provides its members with sufficient time free from organized activity in which they can discover one another as personalities. In this latter respect the Brigades, we think, have an advantage over the Scouts, because a Scout troop usually meets once a week only, when the whole time-table is carefully prepared beforehand, while most Brigades have one or more club nights and there is abundant opportunity for general conversation and spontaneous activity. On the other hand, if a boy attends a Brigade four or five nights a week, as many do, he is thereby cut off from other possible social contacts.

To attain social maturity, a person must learn to live with other people in the ordinary relationships of life and to work with members of a group without trying either to dominate it or to withdraw from it. He must also achieve an attitude of tolerance towards people with whose opinions he may be in disagreement. Such maturity is not easily achieved by the adolescent. He is subject to strong upsurges of emotion and is a creature of moods and extremes. He is anxious both to conform to type and to assert his individuality. He (and she, even more) is swept by strong and even violent emotional attachments. He falls in love—and out of it. A capacity for stable personal relationships is one measure of emotional maturity.

How can the Youth Service help the adolescent to discover the meaning of true personal relationships? Chiefly, we think, by offering him respect, understanding, and tolerance, and by providing the setting in which right relationships become possible and wrong relationships can be dealt with. It is perhaps salutary that youth leaders should remind themselves that whatever be their own motives in running a youth organization, the chief reason why young people come (whatever the type of unit) is to meet their friends and to make new ones. Membership of a group of his contemporaries can satisfy some of the adolescent's most urgent needs. We think it important that in planning the activities of their various units, leaders should leave some time when young people can dally in conversation and be given opportunities to form friendships and to learn social behaviour. Quite apart from what the organization provides in its programme of activities, its *raison d'être* lies in the experience it gives of personal and social relationships.

* *Growing up in a Modern Society*, page 86.

SEGREGATED GROUP OR FAMILY SETTING?

We have suggested that if a society is to offer its members adequate social training, it must provide them with opportunities of meeting both those who are younger and older than themselves and members of the opposite sex.

We turn first to a discussion of the highly debated question whether the needs of young people are best met in mixed or single-sex societies.

MIXED OR SINGLE-SEX?

One feature of recent developments in the Youth Service in the last few years has been the astonishing growth of mixed youth clubs. Most of the clubs directly sponsored by Local Education Authorities are mixed. Before the war mixed youth organizations were comparatively few, and the National Association of Boys' Clubs still declares that 'it does not believe that it is in the boy's best interests to join a mixed club which has a common membership for boys and girls.' *
This contention is not without support from other quarters. In contrast, the National Association of Girls' Clubs added 'and Mixed Clubs' to its name in 1944, and now reports twice as many mixed clubs as girls' clubs, and in the age group 14-21 only 25,000 girls in girls' clubs as compared with 40,000 girls and 45,000 boys in mixed clubs. The Methodist Youth Department reports over 4,000 clubs (which are mostly mixed) and 90,000 members in the 14-20 age range.

The general consensus of opinion today is moving steadily in favour of mixed organizations for young people in their teens, but it is not to be forgotten that there are weighty considerations which can be advanced on the other side.

In favour of single-sex organizations it is contended that:

(a) Both physical and intellectual training are best given to each sex separately during those years when young people are not mature enough to have achieved controlled relationships with the opposite sex. It is easier, for example, to get boys to discuss current affairs or politics when they are by themselves than when they are in a mixed group.

(b) Boys in mixed clubs are less 'manly' or 'virile' than are boys in boys' clubs. The element of truth in this contention would appear to be that whereas in a single-sex unit boys have a healthy rivalry in ways which foster skill and courage, in a mixed society they tend to compete for the attention of the girls in ways which encourage vanity. The ground of competition is changed.

(c) The fact that girls develop physically and emotionally so much more rapidly than do boys makes it unwise to put them together. The girl of fourteen wants to meet with boys—the boy of fourteen is not eager to be with girls. He needs, therefore, to be protected from the girl.

(d) In the early teens at least it is better for boys and girls to find their interests in the activities which form part of the club programme rather than in one another. The presence of the other sex can be a distraction and leads to divided loyalties and waning interest in cultural activities.

(e) The best character-training is achieved if boys engage with boys and girls with girls in the pursuits appropriate to the respective sexes.

On the other hand, and in favour of the mixed organization, it may be said:

(a) The natural setting of all true growth and education is the family. All segregation is artificial. At every age we need what companionship with the opposite sex can give as an important element in training.

(b) It is much better for boys and girls to meet together for shared activities of all kinds than that they should only meet under 'romantic' associations at dance-halls or cinema. There is less likelihood of relationships of a sentimental character when association is taken for granted in frequent contacts of all kinds.

(c) A mixed organization, therefore, facilitates the development of mature adult relationships with members of the opposite sex, to attain which is one of the most urgent of the adolescent's needs. Segregation in any single-sex organization may positively retard this development. There are adults who have taken refuge from the effort of adjustment in single-sex societies.

* *The Contribution of Boys' Clubs to the Life of our Time*, 1948.

(*d*) Some very valuable activities—especially in connexion with music and drama—are only possible in mixed groups.

(*e*) Boys and girls will meet together in any case, and it is better that we should provide the place of meeting than that they should meet at street corner or in public dance-hall. In our *Twenty Questions* inquiry we asked whether young persons answering the questions thought there should be mixed clubs or separate clubs for boys and girls, and it is interesting to note that 75 per cent of the boys and 81 per cent of the girls came down on the side of the mixed club. The highest vote for single-sex clubs was among boys of fourteen years of age but even then it only amounted to 30 per cent. We were particularly surprised to discover that most members of single-sex organizations of all kinds expressed themselves as being in favour of mixed clubs.

Our own judgment is that the case for the mixed organization is stronger than that for the single-sex unit, although we are sure that in any mixed club there should be some opportunities for boys and girls—especially for the younger boys—to meet separately. We have found no evidence in support of the assertion that boys in mixed clubs are less 'manly' or 'virile' than boys in boys' clubs. The former appear to be just as keen on football or boxing or athletics as are boys in boys' clubs, and distinguish themselves as frequently in leagues and competitions. There are no doubt some boys and girls who go to a mixed club merely go because they want to be in each other's company, but it by no means follows that in a mixed club all activities are shared. Of the 126 mixed organizations we visited, twenty-eight offered one night a week for boys and nineteen one night a week for girls only. Sometimes, however, we found ourselves wishing that there were more mixed activities. It is surely desirable that boys and girls should meet together not only for half an hour's dance at the end of the club evening but for other activities as well. It is good that the boy should see how his girl friend behaves when she does not get her own way on the committee, and that the girl should see how the boy friend shapes when on canteen duty.

We do not feel that the charge that is sometimes made that mixed clubs promote a too free-and-easy relationship between boys and girls can be generally substantiated, though we do not think that all leaders know how to tackle problems of relationship when they arise, or how to use the opportunities of mixed activities to promote high standards. We return to a discussion of this matter in the chapter on *Leadership*.

The desirable policy, in our judgment, so far as clubs are concerned, would seem to be in the provision of some separate premises or some separate facilities for boys and girls in the setting of a mixed community. Uniformed organizations would be well advised, we believe, to promote more frequent mixed activities. We did discover one instance where members of an Air Training Corps and of a Women's Junior Air Corps share certain training together, but this must be almost unique among pre-Service units. Both the Boy Scout and Girl Guide organizations have officially accepted the principle of some combined activities, but the implementation of this principle is still only very occasional, though we learnt of one Birmingham Rover Crew which shared a camp on the Isle of Wight with members of a Ranger Company.

AGE-GROUPING

All youth movements find it necessary to sub-divide their members according to age, but there are wide diversities of practice concerning the ages at which divisions are made. Our own primary interest in this Survey has been in the 14-20 age-range, but we realize that this is a quite arbitrary age-grouping, and in fact we have encountered very great difficulties in all our attempts to compile comparative statistics just because actual sub-divisions in important organizations like the Brigades, Scouts and Guides do not correspond with this scheme at all. In these Movements the official age-divisions are as follows, though there is in practice some elasticity about them:

Boys' Brigade: Life Boys 9-12, Boys' Brigade 12-18.
G.L.B.: Cadets 6-9, Juniors 9-13, Seniors 13-16, Pioneers 16 plus.
Boy Scouts: Wolf Cubs 8-11, Junior Scouts 11-15, Senior Scouts 15-17½, Rovers 17½ plus.
Girl Guides: Brownies 7-11, Guides 11-16, Rangers and Cadets 16-21.

ST JOHN AMBULANCE: *Cadets receiving instruction in First Aid.*

JUNIOR RED CROSS: *Members of a Cadet Unit distributing parcels of materials for hand work, sent by the American Junior Red Cross to child patients at a Birmingham Hospital.*

155

Since the publication of *Circular* 1486 in 1939 the main interest of the Youth Service has been in the 14-20 age-range, and fourteen has been the age of entry to most of the clubs. At the present time, however, there is a growing awareness of the leisure-time needs of school-children—needs to which public attention was drawn, in 1948, by the publication of *Out of School*—a Report presented to the Minister of Education by the Central Advisory Council for Education (England). Among the recommendations of this Report were the following:

> The Minister should make an urgent appeal to Local Education Authorities to apply their powers under the Education Acts so as to increase and improve by every possible means facilities for the play and recreation of children out of school hours.*
>
> The Minister should be prepared to make grants towards the expenses of voluntary bodies that serve out-of-school interests of school-children on terms at least as favourable as those upon which he now makes grants to voluntary organizations taking part in the Youth Service.†

Just as there is a growing realization of the leisure-time needs of children under the age of fourteen, so also, at the other end of the age-range, there is increasing concern about the need of more adequate social and cultural provision for people in their early twenties.

Mr. L. J. Barnes, in a recent discussion of the question of age-grouping, has suggested that the present somewhat arbitrary concentration of interest in the 14-20 age-range should cease, and that it should be recognized that the Youth Service should concern itself with the total age range 7-25, but with one major division at or about the sixteenth birthday.

> The Youth Service sector divides naturally into two main sub-sectors. One is concerned with the anti-delinquency effort, with devising programmes and activities suited to young people still at school, and with influencing the home in ways calculated to raise the level of parentcraft. In the other sub-sector the responsibility is for easing the transition to full-time employment, for straddling the period of conscription so that club members do not disappear from the ken of their organization when they enter the forces, and for bridging the gulf between youth work and adult work.‡

Mr. Barnes believes that at the present time 'there are too many youth organizations trying to do much the same kind of thing in much the same kind of way', and his most startling suggestion is that each of the voluntary bodies and other Youth Service agencies should 'specialize within the field either of the 7-16 age-range or of the 16-25 and that normally *none should attempt to cover both.*'§

This suggestion has not been welcomed by any of the voluntary movements—the uniformed organizations being unwilling to 'hand over' their members at sixteen, and the clubs being unwilling to surrender their interest in members under that age. We ourselves would not be prepared to accept Mr. Barnes's suggestion without qualifications, but, in fact, a very strong case can be made in support of his proposal. The Youth Advisory Council, in a Report issued in 1943, declared that 'it is essential that the Youth Service should so operate as to lead young people onwards towards adult life and not keep them back unduly in the atmosphere and surroundings of adolescence.'‖ Two years later the Council reaffirmed this conviction:

> No youth organization must become an end in itself. It must always lead on to the wider adult life of the whole community. It ought to be the case that members of a youth organization, when they reach the age limit for it, naturally move on to adult societies and clubs of various kinds.¶

We do not deem that the Youth Service generally has discovered a way by which the progression of young people from youth to adult communities can be facilitated. What, in fact, does happen at the present time? The uniformed voluntary organizations, in the main, lose the greater part of their members at or before the age of sixteen. It would be a searching experience, we think, for leaders of the uniformed voluntary organizations to read through the completed

---

* Op. cit. page 19.
† Op. cit. page 21.
‡ *Outlook for Youth Work*, page 112
§ Op cit. page 113 (italics our own).
‖ *Youth Service after the War*, page 15.
¶ *The Purpose and Content of the Youth Service*, page 15.

Twenty Questions which have been answered by so many Birmingham young people and to discover how often their one-time members left these organizations because they 'lost interest', or 'grew out of it', 'got tired of it', or because 'there were too many kids about'. Our own inquiries underline the conclusion of Miss Pearl Jephcott that the girls who were the subject of her study:

> appear to have given up their societies mainly because at 13 or 14 they felt it was time to leave the company of children. One girl of 13½ who had recently abandoned the Girl Guides, referred to them contemptuously, and inaccurately, as 'a lot of kids about 8'.*

The chief reason why the uniformed voluntary organizations lose their members at the age of fourteen or fifteen or thereabouts is, in our judgment, as we have already said, because they fail to recognize the developing maturity of these young people. We have failed to discover very much difference, for instance, between the programme of a Girl Guide Company and of a Ranger Company. It has been remarked that 'for the older member over fourteen years a uniform must have some connexion with adult life. For the child at school it is sufficient in itself.' It is for this reason that many young people in their middle 'teens have been glad to join a pre-Service unit, while it is comparatively seldom that a boy or girl joins the Scouts, Guides or Brigades after school-leaving age. Is this because the Ranger and Rover movements, for example, as they exist at present, seem to suggest a prolonged adolescence rather than a step forward towards adult life? Some young people in these movements no doubt find real personal fulfilment in the units to which they belong, but we have sometimes felt about others that their emotional and social development is being arrested by a continued association with an adolescent movement.

We are aware, of course, that both in the Scout and in the Guide organizations there is concern about the failure to hold the older member, and publications like the *Senior Scout Handbook* and *Ranger Post-War Programme* represent attempts to offer expanding opportunities to the growing boy or girl. We do not feel, however, that these organizations will succeed in retaining their members unless they can offer them at, say, about the age of sixteen the opportunity of a much more definite promotion from a children's organization to one that is quite manifestly adult in its associations and in its purpose.

Nor has the problem been solved by the clubs. At the present time most boys leave the clubs at eighteen (if, indeed, they have not left before) when they are called up for military service, and few girls remain in membership after the eighteenth birthday. Miss Pearl Jephcott suggests that one reason why clubs fail to retain the older girls is because

> they do not, on the whole, tie up sufficiently with the interests of the older people of the girls' normal background . . . . Today's youth organization is in many respects external to . . . . the social activities in which the other people of her family take part.†

On the conclusion of their period of national service young men of twenty do not join community centres. Most of them do not join anything. Some who need organized social life may

> tend to hover ambiguously around their old club, an embarrassment to the leader, suspected by the under-twenties of a desire to dominate, and thus themselves come to form little more than an introverted clique devoid of any valid communal function.‡

We have seen one or two clubs in our city where leaders are faced with this problem.

Miss Margaret Allen says that:

> There is still too big a gap between the time young people leave the youth club from 18-21, and the average (minimum) age of the members of most community centres which seems to be round about 35-40. There is obviously a need for the provision of some common meeting place for fellowship and the sharing of common interests for young people between 20 and 30, other than a public house, the dance hall or the public restaurant.§

* *Rising Twenty*, pages 162-3.

† Op. cit. page 166.

‡ *Outlook for Youth Work*, by L. J. Barnes, page 111.

§ *A Survey of Mixed Clubs*, page 17.

157

It would appear, therefore, that neither the uniformed nor the club organizations have discovered how to facilitate the movement of their members from juvenile to adult societies. It is interesting to note that youth organizations which have a fairly high proportion of eighteen- and nineteen-year-old members are those with adult associations, such as political units, Y.W.C.A's, or groups which are very closely associated with the life of a church, such as some Church Fellowships, Guilds or 'Demob' Clubs. There is much to be said for Mr. Barnes's suggestion that at sixteen or thereabouts there should be a clean and definite promotion from a children's unit to a more adult group. The questions that arise, however, are: first, whether a complete segregation of youth and age is desirable; and secondly, whether such a promotion must necessarily involve a transfer from one Movement to another. We do not believe that any transfer from one Movement to another is either necessary or desirable, but rather that the need could be met by a much more definite demarcation of junior and senior sections at about the sixteenth birthday within each separate organization.

FAMILY CENTRES

We do not feel that the Youth Service generally has ever squarely faced the challenge offered by the Pioneer Health Centre at Peckham to its whole major pre-occupation with youth. * The promoters of the Peckham Health Centre believe that the family is the natural setting for all true growth and education, and that it is a disservice to young people to segregate them in strict age-groups or to separate them from members of the opposite sex and from contacts with young children and with adults. The unit of membership at Peckham is the family and not the individual.

The dilemma in which we are caught up arises from the difficulty of creating a social setting for youth work which will give full recognition to two conflicting facts—the fact that much can be given to adolescents through their association with children and with adults—and the fact that the younger adolescents desperately need a society of their own, where, away from parental influence, they can make their first explorations of the wider world.

There is little doubt, we think, that adolescents have much to gain both from the exercise of leadership among young children and from association with those who are older than them- selves. On one of our own visits to Peckham we watched a table-tennis foursome in which a boy was playing with his girl friend and her parents—something we have never seen in any youth club. After the game the boy exchanged some backchat with a younger sister who was disporting herself in the swimming bath, and then he went off to another part of the building with his girl friend and a group of adolescents. On the same evening we watched the finals of a billiards competition, the finalists being a boy of sixteen and a man of about sixty.

Very often in the course of our observations among youth organizations in Birmingham— particularly when visiting the larger units—we have felt the need of the presence of more adults. In an unpublished memorandum on *Voluntary Help in Clubs*, the Sheffield Association of Girls' and Mixed Clubs says of the club leader that:

> he must never be too busy, too harassed or too flurried to be 'bothered' with the individual member. Ideally, he should be able to discuss with individuals or with small groups whatever is agitating them at the moment or whatever is 'giving them to think', with genuine concentrated interest. To them it is vitally important. It may even be a turning point in life if it is properly handled, just as on the other, it may be an important opportunity lost. The most fruitful of 'heart-to-heart' or 'man-to-man' talks most frequently occur spontaneously and unexpectedly, arising out of some apparent triviality.

The average club leader, however, is too busy and too preoccupied with administrative responsibilities to be able to give his young people this kind of help (he should, of course, make every effort to allow himself freedom for the exercise of this kind of leadership), and he needs far more adult assistance. There is one boys' club in our city where, five nights a week, one man is the only adult among a hundred or more boys. It is not good for the man himself, nor is it good for the boys.

* *The Peckham Experiment*, by Innes H. Pearse and Lucy H. Crocker.

There are, however, weighty considerations on the other side. If young people are to achieve maturity, they must be 'weaned' from the family. Some parents—and particularly some mothers—find it very difficult to 'let go', but however good a home may be, there comes a moment in their development when young people need to get away from it into a society of their contemporaries. It is for this reason that any suggestion of a 'Parents' Night' is not usually greeted with enthusiasm by the younger members of a youth club. They may be quite fond of their parents, but they 'don't want them butting in here'.

The success of the Peckham Health Centre in resolving this dilemma is due in some degree to the nature of the building in which activities take place. Not only has it been planned with very great care to serve its own particular purpose, but it is large enough to provide facilities for young people to prosecute activities on their own, when they so wish, where they are not under the immediate observation of their parents. We believe, nevertheless, that if all our existing youth organizations were to be wound up and replaced by Centres with a family rather than an individual basis of membership, there would be very great loss as well as gain. We conclude, therefore, that whenever circumstances permit each youth organization should retain its separate identity (recognizing the increasing maturity of its older members by making a clear age division at about sixteen), but that its activities should be carried on in the setting of a larger Family or Community Centre.

This would also appear to be the general view of the Youth Advisory Council in saying:

> We believe that there is much to be said for having different parts of the same building, whether club, community centre or county college, available for adults and young people at the same time: but they would naturally have different interests and wish to avoid interruption and interference from each other. The principle should be insulation within the same whole rather than any isolation or segregation from the whole.*

COMMUNITY CENTRES

The earliest Community Centres were established in some of the poorer quarters of our cities, or were designed to ameliorate the social consequences of the industrial depression of twenty years ago. The present demand for Community Centres comes, however, from all types of neighbourhood. 'A Community Centre should be regarded as an essential amenity of a normal community living in normal circumstances'.† So said the Ministry of Education in 1944.

The Government has decided that the provision of Community Centres to promote the social and physical training of the community should be regarded as coming within the scope of the education service administered by Local Authorities, and in pursuance of this decision, the Report from which we have just quoted was published at the end of 1944. The point of view taken in this Report on the place of youth work in Community Centres was expressed in these terms:

> While youth activities proper should find a place in Community Centres, they should in general be kept quite separate from the adult activities either in time or place. If the building is large enough, a separate wing should be allowed to the young people; or, failing that, separate rooms at one end of the premises. If accommodation is restricted, a room or rooms might be set aside at certain times of the day for youth work . . . . We believe that indiscriminate mixing of youth and adult activities is likely to prejudice both.‡

In Birmingham any attempts to promote youth activities in Community Centres have not met with great success. In one instance one evening a week was set aside as 'Family Night' for all age-groups, but the older people gradually dropped off until the evening became nothing but a weekly dance for young people. In another centre we were told that 'experience has proved that youth work is not usually successful in a Community Centre because the noise of the young people tends to drive out the adults.' The Secretary of the Birmingham Council for Community Associations declares that 'youth work should be carried on, but in separate or adjoining build-

* *The Purpose and Content of the Youth Service*, page 15.
† *Community Centres*, page 5.
‡ Op. cit., page 13.

159

HELPING THEMSELVES

The 'Stonehouse Gang' builds its own headquarters.

Members of a club decorate their own premises.

HELPING OTHERS

Members of a Birmingham Youth Club run a club in the boys' ward of a local hospital.

ings.' He also says that 'most Community Centres are very badly housed and all available accommodation is needed for our adult activities and it is not anticipated that there will be any early change in this situation.'

If Community Centres are not over-eager to welcome youth organizations into their midst, it is equally true that few youth organizations are eager to be welcomed. The secretary of one of the uniformed voluntary organizations said to us: 'we find that it is quite impossible to promote one of our units in a Community Centre.' Club members, as we have seen, do not pass on easily into association with a Community Centre—there is too great an age-gap; and where a Community Centre runs its own 'Youth Night', few of the young people who are present associate themselves with any of the adult activities which take place in the Centre.

It would seem, therefore, that while on the one hand youth organizations generally fail to pass their members on into adult societies, the Community Centre, which should presumably provide the means for solving this problem, does not in fact offer a solution. The failure of the Community Centres to promote successful youth work is due in part we think to inadequate housing, in part to inadequate leadership, and in part to the simple fact that young people are not really wanted. Most of all, however, this failure is due to inability to recognize a simple but fundamental truth about family and community life: there can be no mutual understanding or healthy co-operation between youth and adult except through shared activity. Only so does each discover the need it has of the other. No planning of highly organized Community Centres, and no mere multiplication of Peckham Health Centres over the country is likely in itself to achieve this.

One suggestion that has been made to us is that in each 'Neighbourhood Unit' there should be a central block of buildings, comprising the County College, the Community Centre, and the Youth Centre. Certain premises, such as a library, a concert hall, a gymnasium and a swimming bath would be centrally situated and commonly shared, while other accommodation would be reserved for adults or for young people. This suggestion (inspired, we believe, by developments taking place in Russia) has many attractive features, and would overcome the difficulty that will often arise when an attempt is made to promote both youth and adult activities in the same building. At the same time this suggestion presupposes an organization of such a size that the continued life of the small unit—the importance of which we have stressed in this Report—would be ended. In many ways the best illustration of the association between the youth unit and the adult community is to be found in the club which is truly integrated in the life of a church community.

THE CHURCH AS A COMMUNITY CENTRE

In a recent P.E.P. publication it is said that:

> so much emphasis is put on the decline in Church attendance that it is sometimes forgotten how important a part is played in many areas by Church Guilds and Clubs or organizations such as the Mothers' Union. A Survey of organizations joined by housewives suggested that about one in four of these was associated with some religious body.*

This, we think, is a much-needed reminder. It is so frequently asserted that the church has lost the position it once had in the community generally, that it is easy to underestimate the influence it does still exercise. Half the youth organizations in our city do, in fact, meet on church premises, and we have seen some churches which are in fact Community Centres: that is, they provide the permanent corporate fellowship within the totality in which provision is made for the needs of each age-group. Thus a girl may attend, say, the Sunday School and the Girls' Life Brigade until she is fifteen, at which time she may transfer to the Youth Club and to the Sunday afternoon Youth Forum. Three years later she may join the Guild or the choir or the dramatic society and a year or two after that the Young Mothers' Club. If at any time she moves to another part of the country, there is, not far from her new home, a church within which is the same familiar pattern of organizations. We realize, of course, that this description is by no means

* *Can Communities be planned?* March, 1949.

161

applicable to all churches and that there are many churches where the organizations, far from being integrated in a larger fellowship, are uncompromisingly independent. At the same time the Church is a Community Centre for many thousands of families, and, at its best, can nourish the truest personal relationships.

CONCLUSION

In this chapter we have propounded many questions, and we have certainly not succeeded in discovering answers to them all. Some of the questions probably have no answer of universal applicability. The Youth Service in this country is like a kaleidoscope of ever-changing colour and pattern. This, perhaps, is its strength. Any regimentation or uniformity would be foreign to our whole national tradition. No two young people are alike, nor can their needs be met in the same way.

We would like to record our own conviction, nevertheless, that the danger that besets the Youth Service arises from the fact that it *is* the Youth Service. The needs of young people are often discussed without any apparent recognition of the fact that it should surely be a main purpose of the Youth Service to facilitate the entry of the adolescent into the life of the adult world. It is, we think, because so many youth organizations tend to hold young people back in the activities and associations of childhood that the maturing boy or girl leaves them in such numbers in the middle teens. But 'the chief business of the adolescent is to stop being one'. Adolescence is a bridge across which young people should be helped to take their place in the life of the larger community.

It is important, therefore, not so much that youth work should be carried on in the physical setting of a community organization, but that in the youth organization it should be possible for young people to enter into living relationships with adult people who are wise enough to give them their freedom, and understanding enough to give them security. The fact of community can be communicated to young people, not by the promotion of youth activities in the building of a Community Centre, but by shared activity in which differences of age are largely forgotten in the pursuit of common enterprise. We are concerned to recruit into the Youth Service the ordinary adult who can make any contribution to young people along the line of friendship or interest. Young people will feel that they are part of the community as a whole when that community can offer them opportunities of continued service and usefulness after they have left the 'teens behind them.

In this matter the Church has a supreme opportunity just because it is itself a total community within which youth activities can be promoted in a natural family setting. This unique opportunity—which we know to be the envy of other organizations—is not always taken. It is indeed often thrown away, when activities for young people and for adults are promoted in strict segregation. We have seen in our city churches where these opportunities have been missed: we have also seen churches in which young and old work closely together in the service of a common purpose.

CHAPTER XI

LEADERSHIP

IN THE SUMMER of 1945 the *Times Educational Supplement* published a letter from a correspondent in which he described his experiences during a day's camping by the side of a river:

> Moorhens and swans sailed by with day-old chicks, and cygnets, heron, woodpeckers, wood pigeon, bullfinches, kingfishers, goldfinches, jays and jackdaws were all on view. And—a sight I shall perhaps never see again—a pair of otters threaded their way porpoise-like in and out of the water. Within 300 yards of my camp site was a water mill, lock and floodgates, manor house and church. In short, as perfect a spot as could be wished.

Four times during the day this place was visited by youth. The first party consisted of twenty young people who (the writer went on) danced to the music of a piano accordion—played by their leader—in the middle of a field which provided the miller with his winter hay. The miller, of course, objected, but before he could persuade the young people to depart, their leader told him that he was 'a something capitalist', that these boys and girls belonged to the Local Education Authority, and that he would write to the then Board of Education about it. They went upstream and landed in another meadow, where after lunch, they threw paper bags, tins, bottles and half a loaf of bread into the river. The second party consisted of a select girls' club, who, with the leader's eye on the alert, undressed in strict decorum behind some bushes and bathed just where the effluent from the manor house's cesspool entered the river. They drank quantities of the effluent from the overfilled cesspit. Later in the afternoon two boys, two girls and a leader tied up their punt against and across the upstream side of the floodgates. On the down stream side was a drop of some four feet. The writer hesitatingly pointed out to the leader that perhaps this was a silly place to tie up. She said 'They're only out for the day, so let them enjoy themselves!' The fourth party was still to come:

> A benevolent dusk brought peace, silence and sanctuary for the birds. The tiny moorhen chicks squeaked and whisked as they hurried about the water. The swans brought out their three cygnets—then, the unmistakable plug and hiss of an air rifle. Drifting downstream in a canoe were two boys in pre-Service uniforms lying on their stomachs. With rifles standing out like cannon from a Spitfire, they were shooting, on such an evening, at sitting moorhen chicks, just two days old. Then, and only then, I rose in my wrath, and pre-Service uniforms or no, I had my say.

Not all youth leaders, of course, are so ignorant of the rudiments of countryside behaviour, but the experience of this correspondent may serve to remind us of the supreme importance, in all Youth Service, of the quality of the leadership by which it is directed. A good leader will succeed, however inadequate may be the premises in which his unit meets and however handicapped he may be by lack of finance; a poor leader will fail, however favourable may be the conditions under which his work is done. We have seen the size of club membership and the quality of club work rise and fall with astonishing rapidity with a change in club leadership. In the long run the Youth Service will stand or fall, not by the magnificence of the premises provided by church or Local Education Authority or by the generosity of the Ministry of Education, but by the degree to which men and women of ability and goodwill are prepared to give themselves in friendship to young people. We do not agree with those American psychologists of a past generation who asserted that adolescence is necessarily a time of intense unhappiness, but the rapid physical development and the emotional consequences of the adjustments which have to be made in so many personal relationships give rise to the insecurity and instability which is characteristic of the boy or girl in his or her 'teens. One of the chief needs of the adolescent is that of the understanding and affection of a trusted adult—an adult whose attitude to the boy or girl has been well expressed by Dr. W. D. Wall of Birmingham University, in the following passage, though the leader, of course, would never express his attitude in as many words:

> Whatever you do, we like you; we are willing and anxious to understand your point of view, to give you the chance to achieve independencè, to meet you on an equal footing, and to give you your share of attention. We prefer that you should act thus and thus; the result will be for the advantage of all of us; but whatever you choose to do, you are sure of our affection.*

There are a great many men and women in our city who are giving this kind of understanding friendship to young people. Many as there are, however, more are needed. When we have asked leaders to tell us their greatest need, the almost invariable reply has been 'more voluntary helpers'. It often happens that the removal or resignation of a leader means that the unit ceases to meet because of the difficulty of finding a successor. Regional officers of nearly all the voluntary organizations have told us that they could easily establish more units if more leaders were available. Leaders on the new working-class housing estates on the city outskirts find particular difficulty in securing adequate voluntary assistance.

We are impressed, not only by the necessity for more leaders, but by the fact that so many present leaders are but poorly equipped for the work to which they have put their hands. We have, of course, seen many excellent leaders at work, and we are reluctant to criticize men and women who freely and generously devote so much of their time and energy to the service of young people.

> A student of the work these dedicated public servants do among young people may strive to watch with critical eye and appraise with dispassionate judgment, as he visits the clubs and units evening by evening. But he will be less than human if he is not touched to deep humility and high admiration by what he sees. The best of faith and friendship are here, and before them a man can only bow the head in homage and thanksgiving. Neither the reward they seek, nor the reward they find, gleams in the light of common day.†

We are compelled to say, however, that often the zeal of youth leaders is not matched by their ability, and that their efforts would produce more results if only they could receive more training for their work. We would like to draw attention to five weaknesses in leadership which have become apparent to us:‡

(1) *Need for a wider Outlook*

The Youth Service suffers from too many leaders whose vision is limited to their own organization or even to their own unit; leaders who fail to realize that there is a place for every type of movement, and that their particular organization does not possess the sole monopoly of wisdom. Some of these leaders seem unwilling to trust their members out of their sight (one leader was unwilling to allow his boys' club to take advantage of the offer of a Head of an Evening Institute to give them a physical training class in the gymnasium of a nearby school), and do not encourage any form of co-operative activity. The 'Conway' Club, the Kingstanding Youth Parliament and the Digbeth Film Club experiments have all suffered from the fact that some leaders in the area have been uncooperative, and the comparative weakness of the city's Youth Advisory Committees is largely due to the fact that so many leaders neither attend them nor do they see that their unit is represented. This limitation of outlook becomes particularly disastrous when it is found within the community of a church, when the Brigade Captain, club leader and Sunday School Superintendent regard one another as rivals rather than as partners in a common task.

* *The Adolescent Child*, p. 90.
† *Youth Service in an English County*, p. 58.
‡ We are interested to note that Miss Margaret Allen makes some similar comments in her remarks on leadership in the recently published *A Survey of Mixed Clubs.*

(2) *Lack of Initiative*

The lack of initiative which characterizes so many leaders is particularly apparent, for example, in their failure to make the best of the premises in which their work is done. We have already drawn attention (page 103) to the shocking housing conditions under which much of the Youth Service has to be carried on. These conditions are sometimes unavoidable, but very often they are due to bad leadership. Club members can transform dirty, dingy church halls into attractively decorated and comfortably furnished club rooms, but all too often their leaders themselves seem lacking in initiative and imagination and are content with low standards.

(3) *Lack of Experience in Mixed Organizations*

Mixed youth organizations are a comparatively new development and there is no accumulated body of experience upon which leaders can draw in their approach to the peculiar problems and opportunities of mixed club work. Not all leaders, however, are able to deal with the problems or seize the opportunities with which a mixed organization presents them.

The charge is sometimes made that a major activity of mixed youth clubs is 'organized osculation'. This charge, we think, is quite unfounded, and on the whole the general standard of behaviour between boys and girls in mixed clubs is very good. At the same time we have found one or two clubs where the leaders themselves appear to have low personal standards of their own, and others where leaders seem quite unable to handle problems of personal relationship when they arise.

Young people are often desperately in need of help and guidance in their desire to find standards of conduct and personal relationships. They have no experience of life which would help them to criticize the false sentimentality of so many films, and the standard of conversation and behaviour of the adults they meet in their working environment is not always of the highest. The personal example of an unromantic friendship between the man and woman joint leaders of a mixed club can be of the greatest help to them in their own attainment of mature adult relationships with the opposite sex, and men and women who can lead their thinking on 'Boy meets Girl', 'Falling in Love', or 'Courtship and Marriage' are discharging a service of youth indeed.

(4) *Lack of Technique of Informal Education*

Some leaders of uniformed units seem unable or unwilling to introduce any activity which falls outside the curriculum offered by their headquarters, and some club leaders fail to create a demand for anything beyond table tennis and dancing. This latter task, we know, is far from easy. Many young people come to club tired after a hard day's work; having been under direction all day long they need the maximum of freedom in their choice of leisure activities; their main purpose in coming to club is not the pursuit of further education. The majority of them seem to think of education as being necessarily dull and uninteresting. It conveys little suggestion of joy or delight. Too many leaders appear to share this attitude. One voluntary leader who gives five nights every week to a boys' club in the centre of the city is unable to point to any activity except billiards and table tennis and explains apologetically that 'they don't want anything else'. Too often, when some activity group is established, it is because 'it keeps the members occupied', rather than because it meets a need or serves a larger purpose.

We do not feel that it falls within the province of this Report to catalogue a list of the desirable qualities that a youth leader should possess, but high among them should be the precious gift of vitality, and the ability to arouse and share enthusiasm. Happy is the boy or girl who, in club or uniformed unit, meets people who enjoy good music, read books, watch birds, handle tools or climb mountains—just because they truly enjoy these things. In such ways boys and girls can be led to new discoveries, and shown the view through unexpected and exciting windows. Something is happening in a club when a group of Sinatra fans listen in to Dobson and Young as they talk about Haydn's London Symphony, or a heated argument takes place in the canteen about Jews and Arabs in Palestine, or when a group of boys and girls decide that instead of their usual week in a Blackpool boarding house they will go youth hostelling in Snowdonia. Much education in the youth club must be informal and opportunist and the techniques and possibilities of informal education present a field that is, as yet, largely unexplored.*

There are far too few club libraries, insufficient use is made of people with hobbies and enthusiasms, little or no attempt seems to be made to promote film appreciation (surely one of the most obvious and fruitful of all our opportunities), and radio is hardly used at all.

(5) *Failure to take opportunities of Informal Religious Education*

However desirable it may be to offer systematic religious instruction in youth organizations, there are many units in which religious education, if it is to be given at all, must be occasional, spontaneous, and opportunist. Here again, not all leaders seem able to recognize or to use the opportunities that arise in general conversation or to give an answer to the direct question put by the young seeker after truth. In a world where young people are assailed by the claims of many competing ideologies leaders need to know more than they do, both of Christian doctrine and of the possibilities of informal religious education.

We hope that the above paragraphs will be interpreted, not as a condemnation of youth leaders generally, but as an indication of points at which some leaders are in need of additional help. Nor are these paragraphs to be read as though they applied only to voluntary leaders— some of our criticisms have been called forth by what we have seen of professional as well as of voluntary leadership. There are, we repeat, many excellent leaders and no praise is too high for many men and women who spend their time in the service of youth.

THE VOLUNTARY LEADER

By far the great majority of youth units, as we have seen, are staffed by voluntary leaders and helpers. The National Association of Boys' Clubs reports that of some 23,000 adults who help with boys' clubs as leaders, assistants, or instructors, only about 7 per cent receive any payment for their services. Just because his service is freely given, the voluntary leader has a unique contribution to make to the lives of adolescents, and we hope that he will always have a large place in the Youth Service. Several other kinds of voluntary service are needed in addition; the helper who can make himself generally useful and who can act as an assistant leader, the person with some particular skill or talent (the man who can play chess or make a wireless set and the woman who can cook pastries or play the piano), and the occasional visitor who can contribute to one evening's programme.

The uniformed organizations are staffed, almost exclusively, by voluntary leaders. This applies not only to the Brigades, Scouts and Guides, but also to the pre-Service organizations. This does not mean that their leaders are unqualified. On the contrary, some of these organizations have very comprehensive training schemes and demand high qualifications before leaders are given their commissions or warrants. No Scouter or Guider can take boys or girls to camp unless he himself possesses the necessary camping qualifications.

The latest annual report of the Birmingham Girl Guide Association, for example, records that 170 Guiders received pre-Warrant training during the year. For the more experienced Guiders there were special courses in drill and ceremonial, first-class test work and drama, while weekend courses were held for Brownie Guiders, Sea Ranger Guiders and Commissioners. Sixty-five Guiders attended the County Training Camp at Berkswell Grange, and during the year twelve Guiders successfully qualified as Camp Advisers, twelve obtained a Camper's Licence, and nine gained their Quartermaster's Certificate, and one a Camp First Aid Certificate. Three Rangers obtained Campcraft Certificates, and seventeen were awarded Ranger permits to enable them to run small camps by themselves.

The above account of the training programme of the Birmingham Girl Guide Association may be regarded as typical of the kind of thing that is done in all the uniformed organizations.

* Dr. Macalister Brew's *Informal Education* is as good a summary as has yet been given of what has been attempted and achieved in this realm.

Almost all officers receive training, and, in the case of the Brigades, Scouts and Guides, most of them are men and women who have themselves grown up in the movement. Such training as is given appears to be very thorough but an apparent weakness is in the rigidity of training which is concerned only with the methods and aims of one particular organization. Officers seem often to know little about the Youth Service as a whole, and they are sometimes more familiar with the history of their own movement than with the psychology or social environment of the adolescent; they may know how to drill recruits or to teach first aid, but not how to lead a discussion group on the subject of film appreciation or boy-and-girl friendships.

The Club organizations cannot claim that such training schemes as they have promoted have been attended by more than a small fraction of voluntary helpers in clubs. Miss Margaret Allen reports that 'there seems to be a prevailing idea among a great many paid leaders and others, that you cannot set any specific standards for voluntary workers in youth clubs or *expect* them to take any training to qualify for their positions—as, for instance is demanded of every Guider or Scouter'. *

In connexion with the National Association of Girls' Clubs and Mixed Clubs four full-time tutors in club leadership work in different areas under the guidance of a local committee. The courses arranged by these tutors are attended in each case by about twenty-four students who give two nights a week over a period of two years. The courses provide a range of practical experience and observation as well as lectures and tutorials on the principles of club leadership. As we go to press with this Report we learn that a tutor has been appointed to take charge of such a course under the auspices of the Birmingham Association. The National Association also promotes full-time courses which can vary in length from a fortnight to three months. Among students attending a recent three months course was an officer from a Birmingham industrial firm who was released for this training before taking up part-time leadership of the firm's Youth Club.

Through the generosity of the Carnegie United Kingdom Trust, the National Association of Boys' Clubs has been able to acquire a country house near Chepstow as a centre of training for leaders of boys' clubs. A number of one-month residential courses for voluntary leaders has been made possible by a large measure of financial aid from the King George V Jubilee Trust. Tuition and maintenance at these courses have been free, and compensation for loss of earnings has been paid where necessary to the students attending. Firms have released employees to attend these courses and students have included miners, engineers, transport workers, and clerks. The syllabus of the course has included general educational subjects as well as training in club management. Special courses in art, drama and music are promoted at Bakers Cross. A recent innovation has been the establishment by the N.A.B.C. of a Mobile Training Wing, which consists of a van equipped with audible and visual aids to training, carrying a staff of three. The function of the wing is to provide intensive training for groups of leaders in various parts of the country by taking training to their doors.

The recruitment of additional voluntary helpers is, as we have seen, one of the most urgent needs of all organizations. The most obvious field in which to look for leaders is, of course, among the senior members of the organization itself. The great strength of the Guide and Scout movements is in the patrol system under which each group of six or seven boys or girls meets under the leadership of a patrol leader and of a patrol second. By this system these movements are continually training their own leaders. The N.C.O. in the Brigade does not exercise quite as direct or personal a leadership as does the patrol leader, but the Brigades, too, can claim that they are training their own officers of the future.

There is a great need in all the Club organizations for more concentration on senior member training. In saying this we have in mind the desirability of delegating a measure of responsibility to promising senior members for the organization of programmes and the leadership of activities, and also of promoting many more residential conferences for the study of general club management, of specialized activities or of general problems of Citizenship and Religion. The latest

* *A Survey of Mixed Clubs*, p. 25.

National Association of Boys' Club Report records that during the past year fourteen such courses were held at Ford Castle in Durham, and we have already expressed our own conviction that some of the most impressive work being carried on by the Youth Service in Birmingham is that which is taking place at the residential conference houses belonging to the Birmingham Association of Girls' and Mixed Clubs and to the Birmingham Youth and Sunday School Union.

We were particularly interested in a visit to Crawford House, the training centre of the Liverpool Boys' Association, where courses are offered to leaders and senior members in club organization and management, adolescent psychology, handicrafts, music, discussion group technique and other subjects. A special course was recently promoted for boys who were about to be called up. This consisted of four lectures followed by a weekend camp which took the form of a 'mock entry' into the Services.

We conclude our discussion of voluntary leadership with the judgment that there is no more urgent need in the Youth Service than that of increased training for voluntary leaders and senior members. It would be an excellent contribution to the work of all organizations if a Local Education Authority could appoint a Recruitment and Training Officer whose whole time job it would be to recruit voluntary workers and to promote training courses for them. We wish, too, that more money could be made available to enable voluntary leaders and senior members to attend short residential courses. We entirely agree with Miss Margaret Allen when she says: 'One of the great needs which this Survey has impressed upon me everywhere is for a fund for the special purposes of courses concerned with Senior Members' and Voluntary Helpers' Training, and without which there will be constant frustration in efforts to meet the most vital needs in club work'.*

SPECIALIST INSTRUCTORS AND PART-TIME PAID ASSISTANTS

We have already reported that in Birmingham the Local Education Authority supplied instructors for 264 classes in clubs during the winter session 1947-48. It would appear that throughout the whole of the country the professional specialist instructor is accepted as part of the normal staff in clubs of all kinds. Instructors are usually paid by the hour, though rates of pay in different areas vary from 5s. to 15s. There is considerable variation, also, in the minimum attendance required if a class is to qualify for an instructor from the L.E.A. This figure varies from eight to sixteen, though in one place the Authority supplies an instructor for a string quartet. In some areas instructors are prepared to give the whole evening to a club and not to restrict their attendance to the hours for which they are paid.

There is no doubt, in our judgment, that the professional instructor has a valuable contribution to make to the Youth Service. On the other hand some leaders have told us that they would prefer voluntary specialist help, if it were available, because they would not then need to be so concerned about 'keeping up numbers' or tempted to 'cook the returns', and because it would not matter if a girl left the handwork group for ten minutes or so in order to get in a game of table tennis. We visited one large church youth club the leader of which refused to avail himself of the services of L.E.A. instructors because he does not want to ask young people to commit themselves to attend a particular class one or two hours a week throughout the session. His young people, he says, live on crazes. At the moment it is singing, all the evening and every evening; before that it was straight drama, and next month it may be American square dancing or plastics or 'monopoly'. Other leaders take the view that their members need help in self-discipline and concentration, and there are clubs where one night a week is 'Activity Night' when all purely recreational activities are barred or limited to the last half-hour of the evening. There are other clubs where it is a condition of membership that young people attend at least one formal class, and having joined it cannot change to another class within a period of three months.

The L.E.A. instructors we have seen in this city vary immensely, of course, in ability. Some of them are teachers who do not always find it easy to adjust themselves to the informal atmosphere of a youth club. Other instructors owe their success, not only to their knowledge of their subject,

* *A Survey of Mixed Clubs*, p. 25.

RUNNING THEIR OWN SHOW
A Committee of Club Members, under the Leader's chairmanship.

but to their understanding of young people. Few of them are like one 'dancing instructor' we saw who spent two hours leaning against a wall watching a club dance in progress and whose only positive action during the evening, so far as we could see, was the completion of the 'class' register.

We welcome, therefore, the contribution that is being made to the Youth Service by the professional specialist or instructor, but a development we regard with some concern is an increasing tendency throughout the country to appoint part-time paid leaders. Again, there is a wide variation in rates of pay, which range from £20 to £300 a year and from 7s. 6d. to 17s. 6d. an evening.

There are a few areas—and these all rural—in which L.E.A. clubs are entirely staffed by voluntary leaders and helpers. In most L.E.A. clubs all the staff are paid, as they are in Co-operative clubs. The N.A.G.C. & M.C. recently sent a questionnaire to forty-seven Associations on the subject of the effects of the payment of leaders and helpers. Replies revealed a wide divergence of opinion on the desirability of the payment of assistant leaders and helpers. It was argued by some that 'paid help is more reliable than voluntary', that 'if payment were made, we should have a better standard of work', that 'the labourer is worthy of his hire', and that 'the receipt of payment does not necessarily involve the loss of a sense of vocation'. On the other hand it was argued very strongly by others that 'the readiness of the L.E.A. to pay for help crushes voluntary effort', that 'because some helpers are paid, others who might have offered to give their services voluntarily hold back until they are sure whether payment will be forthcoming', and that 'by giving voluntary service in the club, part-time leaders are helping to keep alive in the community the spirit of voluntary service; the example of true voluntary service is a more effective lesson than all the talk in the world'. Another correspondent replied that it was increasingly difficult to find any kind of assistance either voluntary or paid.

We associate ourselves with those who deplore the tendency to offer payment to helpers and assistants in clubs. One effect of the payment of assistant leaders in Birmingham—adopted as a war-time expedient—was that some helpers who had been giving voluntary service for years applied to be put on the panel of paid assistant helpers. The Birmingham Authority was wise, we think, in its decision not to increase its present panel of paid assistant leaders. Had this not been done, it is easy to imagine how speedily the voluntary spirit of service could have been undermined. Church youth clubs and uniformed organizations of all kinds are staffed by voluntary helpers, and we decline to believe that the spirit of voluntary service in this country is so dead that men and women cannot be found to give themselves to the Service of Youth, or that senior members cannot be trained to exercise leadership among the junior members of their own organizations.

THE PROFESSIONAL YOUTH LEADER

It has been estimated that there are at the present time 2,000 full-time leaders and wardens

169

in the Youth and Community Centre services.* These, for the most part, are men and women who were originally voluntary leaders or helpers. They have found a sense of vocation in the work and have come into full-time leadership from their original trades or occupations, knowing full well that youth leadership could offer them neither security for the future nor a personal income which is comparable with that in other professions. Only a minority of them have received any adequate professional training for their present work; they are the pioneers of a new service who have graduated in the hard school of experience.

In 1942 the Ministry issued a circular *Emergency Courses of Training for those Engaged in the Youth Service* as a result of which a one-year course in Youth Leadership was established in a few Universities and University Colleges. In 1946, new and improved rates of grant were announced for approved students following any of these recognized courses.

Training Courses for full-time leaders promoted by voluntary bodies include a two-and-a-half-years course organized by the National Association of Girls' and Mixed Clubs, a two-year course provided by the Y.W.C.A., our own two-year course at Westhill Training College, and a two-year course for women members of the Church of England at St. Christopher's College, and the six months course at St. Pierre conducted by the National Association of Boys' Clubs.

The present position of professional youth leadership is far from satisfactory, and the difficulties that are being experienced in recruiting suitable persons are due to the lack of security and to the general unsatisfactory conditions of service. In July, 1947, the National Association of Youth Leaders and Organizers carried out a Survey of conditions of employment of full-time youth workers. It was found that there were considerable variations in remuneration and conditions of employment. Salaries as low as £176 were reported, and on the whole salaries paid by voluntary organizations tended to be lower than those paid by statutory authorities. The most disquieting fact which came to light as a result of this Survey was the discovery that the average length of time leaders spent in one appointment was about two-and-a-quarter years only. The reasons given for changing appointments included low salaries, long hours, and difficulties with management committees. Two leaders were given notice when the Local Education Authority withdrew or reduced grants in aid of the appointment. Conditions of service were generally found to be unsatisfactory. A number of leaders in voluntary clubs had to devote a large amount of their time to raising money for their own salaries, there was often no provision for any increments, some leaders had no agreements with their employing body, and often there was no provision for the leader to have regular free time weekly.

In view of all these facts, it is not surprising to discover that large numbers of youth leaders are leaving the profession annually. It has recently been found that of 89 men and women who have taken the one-year course in youth leadership at one University, only 27 are now fully employed in the Youth Service. There is certainly a marked tendency among full-time leaders in voluntary clubs to move to L.E.A. posts because of the higher salaries they offer and the more satisfactory provision for superannuation. This tendency may become accelerated with the opening of the County Colleges, as the Ministry of Education has expressly stated that the Youth Service will be one source of recruitment for County College staffs. 'There is thus a real danger that the Colleges may denude the club bodies of their best trained workers.†

Another matter which gives rise to considerable concern is the declining number of women who are offering themselves for training for youth leadership. We understand that very few women indeed are taking the University courses during the session 1949-50. This dearth of women candidates may not be wholly due to the unsatisfactory conditions in the Youth Service, but may be a consequence of other factors which seem to be leading to a general decline in the number of women helpers and workers in clubs generally. It has been suggested that it is easier to find men leaders for boys' clubs, which are pre-eminently sports clubs, than it is to find leaders for girls or mixed clubs where more skill is required in providing programmes. It has

* *Report of the Committee on the Recruitment, Training and Conditions of Service of Youth Leaders and Community Centre Workers, 1949, p. 1.*
† *Outlook for Youth Work*, by L. J. Barnes, 1948, p. 105.

also been suggested that a woman who takes up youth work as a profession is limiting her chances of getting married because her own social life becomes necessarily restricted.

In January, 1947, the Ministry of Education set up a Departmental Committee to consider the recruitment, training and conditions of service of Youth Leaders and Community Centre Wardens. The long awaited Report of this Committee was published in March, 1949, and it is clear that the main object of the Committee was to suggest means whereby Youth Leadership could be given a security and status which would be comparable with that in allied professions. The recommendations of the Committee were also shaped by the conviction that 'Youth Leadership in itself cannot usually offer, and should not be expected to offer, the prospect of a career for life'. The two reasons for this were that 'for most people the physical and mental demands of continuous club work are too exacting to be sustained for more than a limited period with the vitality that the service demands', and that 'by the circumstances of their work, which is mainly in the evenings and with adolescents, leaders tend to be cut off from the normal leisure interests of their contemporaries'.

The suggestion offered in the Report, therefore, is that 'Youth leadership, community centre service and teaching should be regarded as branches of one common service' and that 'full-time youth leaders should normally be recruited from the ranks of teachers after a few years' teaching service, with the prospect of returning to teaching at about the age of 30 to 35'. It is also envisaged that, while teachers should provide the main source of recruitment for the Youth Service, there might be a few entrants from other sources, e.g. university graduates, men and women who hold a diploma or degree in social science, and a 'limited number' of 'men and women without these recognized qualifications who have an undoubted sense of vocation and a flair for the work'.

We strongly welcome proposals which are designed to establish youth leadership as a recognized and properly paid profession, but we question very much whether it should be so closely identified with teaching. Very few of the youth leaders we have met in Birmingham are, in fact, teachers, and recruits to the profession have been drawn from a very wide field—from industry, commerce, trade, crafts, and from clerical occupations. We recognize that some teachers may be happy to find a temporary sphere in youth leadership and that some youth leaders may pass on into teaching—particularly into the County Colleges—but youth leadership is more unlike teaching than it sometimes seems to those who have never done it because it involves a very different kind of approach to young people.

It is, we think, undeniable that there may come a time when most men and women will feel too old to face the very strenuous physical demands which club leadership makes, though we would not wish to limit a leader's length of possible service to ten years. Still less would we agree with the suggestion that community centre wardens, like youth leaders, should only give a few years to this work. We see no reason indeed why community centre wardens, like ministers of religion, should not find a lifetime's career in their chosen vocation.

It is highly desirable, of course, that it should be possible to offer youth leaders the prospect of a career for life, but we do not think that all or even most of them will want to become teachers. Some of them could become youth organizers (some present club organizers have never been club leaders!) others could become wardens of community centres, while others might well find a congenial sphere in the Youth Employment Service. We would like to record our judgment that if youth leadership, youth organization and youth employment service were linked together, they would constitute a profession which could stand on its own feet and in its own right, and which could offer men and women a career for life. It could still be possible for interchange to take place between teaching and youth leadership or between youth leadership and other work in the field of social service.

An earlier Report declared:

We have suggested a course of training for youth leaders which, although it may have in it many elements in common with training for other related professions, is yet a specific course designed for its own purposes. We do not think that training for youth leadership should be attempted within the course designed to train teachers or other kinds of social workers, although during their training youth leaders, teachers and social workers will necessarily take some account of each other's field of service.*

The McNair Report recommended that the course of training for those without any special qualifications who are seeking to prepare themselves for full-time posts as youth leaders should extend over three years of combined full-time study and practice, and that courses of not less than one year's duration should be available for those whose previous experience and qualifications make a three-year course unnecessary.

The more recent Report recommends that teachers, men and women with university qualifications in social science and graduates who wish to enter youth leadership, should be given three months training, and that men and women without such qualifications should be required to take a course of training of one year's duration.

We cannot agree with these more recent recommendations, and would testify to the proved value of our own custom at Westhill, where we offer a two-year course of practical and academic training for men and women who come to us without any antecedent qualifications, and a one year's course for those who possess them. We believe that the length of time required for adequate training has been gravely under-estimated in this recent Report. Nor will youth leadership be given the status it should have if it is accepted that all the specific training required can be offered in a three months' supplementary course.

With all that is said in the new Report about the content of training that youth leaders should be given and about improved conditions of work in youth leadership we find ourselves in general agreement, and the only comment we wish to make is that in any course of training attention should be given to those weaknesses in leadership which we have discussed above.

Finally, the Report recommends that both types of course envisaged should be arranged under the supervision of the 'Area Training Organizations'. We presume that this phrase refers to the University Institutes of Education. If this suggestion is implemented, as it undoubtedly should be, we think it most essential that these Institutes should co-operate very closely with the voluntary organizations, making use, where possible, of the training facilities which they can provide.. The Ministry has in the past repeatedly stressed the desirability of partnership with the voluntary bodies, but if this Report were implemented as it stands it would mean, we think, that the Ministry no longer desired to encourage or help the voluntary bodies. We cannot believe that this is the intention of the Ministry. These bodies, however, will no longer be able to promote their own training unless students taking their courses receive the same measure of grant-aid and the same recognition as students who take courses conducted directly in the Universities. We suggest that courses promoted by the voluntary organizations should come in, as it were, under the umbrella of the Institutes, provided that their courses are approved and that the Institutes act as the final examining bodies.

In drawing this discussion of professional youth leadership to a conclusion, we would like to stress the importance of all forms of 'In Service' training both for professional and voluntary leaders. We have already seen that the majority of present full-time leaders have received no training. Much of the poor work that is being done is due to this lack of training and to sheer ignorance of programme planning and of problems of group relationship. We would like to see an extension of the two-year part-time courses which are promoted in a few areas by the N.A.G.C. & M.C., a great increase in the number of training officers appointed by Local Education Authorities, more specialized courses in drama, music, handcrafts and other subjects ; the provision of more mobile training wings, the appointment of more 'supply leaders' who could take charge of a club while the leader was away attending a refresher course, and above all, more liberal provision of grants to enable professional leaders, voluntary helpers and senior members to attend residential courses of any and every kind. Important as is the training of the professional leader, however, the proportion of full-time leaders will always remain small, and we repeat our conviction that there is no more urgent need in the Youth Service than the recruitment and training of additional voluntary workers of every kind.

*Teachers and Youth Leaders. The McNair Report, p. 104.

CHAPTER XII

PURPOSE IN THE YOUTH SERVICE

AFTER TWO YEARS AND OVER spent in the visitation of some hundreds of youth organizations in our city our main concern arises from the lack of purpose and direction in the Youth Service generally. 'Our aim in this club', as one leader, already quoted, told us, 'is to keep young people off the streets and to give them a good time'. Yet another leader, when invited to tell us his aim, looked completely bewildered for a moment, and then turned to one of his helpers with the question: 'What are our aims, Bill? Have we got any?'

We have made clear in an earlier chapter that we fully recognize the positive values of the recreational activities in which young people engage in most youth units, but only rarely have we met groups of young people who have been drawn into association with one another because of any common conviction or shared purpose.

The problem of course is one that concerns the community as a whole, for the lack of purpose which has become apparent in so many of the youth organizations we have visited is only a reflection of the life of the total community of which young people are a part. This fact, of course, underlines the argument of our tenth chapter, viz. that the only adequate training is that which is offered in the setting of a total community which is itself an embodiment of the values and truths which are commended to the young.

It is inevitable that one should contrast the present situation with that which obtained during the war years, when boys flocked in their thousands into the pre-Service organizations and the girls refused to be ignored and demanded similar opportunities for themselves. Both boys and girls joined Youth Service Squads and Messenger Corps, while magnificent and valuable service was rendered in many ways by Boy Scouts* and Girl Guides. The Scottish Youth Advisory Committee said, in 1945:

> The opportunities which war has brought into the lives of the young have provided a vital element which was lacking in pre-war years and may be lacking again—a sense of over-riding common purpose which has inspired them to the effort of preparing themselves for a future near enough, big enough, exciting enough, and general enough to appeal greatly to their imaginations. It is the spirit engendered by this sense of purpose which has helped to fill the ranks of the pre-Service organizations and also of the voluntary organizations which have offered suitable forms of training and service. Youth needs banners, adventures, crusades, and the war has provided them. Peace in the past has not produced any comparable stimulus.†

In England and Wales the Youth Advisory Council said:

> We are convinced that our young people will respond to the challenge of the post-war world just as courageously as they have met the challenge of war, if only they can be offered as careful and as thorough a training for citizenship as they are now given for battle.

The Council hoped that further consideration would be given above all, to 'the discovery of a post-war purpose for our young people which will evoke from them in peace time the magnificent devotion which they showed in war.'

It cannot be said that we have found that 'post-war purpose'. Did not William James say, indeed, that 'the problem of modern society is to find a moral substitute for war'?

While we would deplore any suggestion of a 'nationalized' Youth Movement under State

---

* The story of the Boy Scout movement during the war is told in *The Left Handshake*, by Hilary St. George Saunders.

† *The Needs of Youth in these Times*, page 31.

direction, we cannot fail to contrast the Youth Movement in Britain with that in some continental countries, where young people have shown themselves eager to share in the rebuilding of the nation. In 1946 a United Nations War-Damage Sub-Commission, on a tour of inspection in Jugo-Slavia, discovered in the heart of Bosnia a railway, fifty-five miles long, being built by young people of Jugo-Slavia and of neighbouring Balkan countries. This enterprise was so successful that it was followed by a larger project—the building of a railway, 150 miles long, from Samac to Sarajevo. Some of our own European students suggest that perhaps the work of these Jugo-Slav young people was not as spontaneous as has sometimes been assumed. However this may be, we in this country do not want any more railways, and the kind of service of which we are in need is much more humdrum and unromantic. We have, perhaps, often been told what is needed, but the challenge has not been put in such a way as to win the understanding and response of youth. Perhaps there was a moment, on 21st April, 1947, when H.R.H. Princess Elizabeth, in her 21st birthday broadcast from Cape Town, dedicated herself to the service of the great Imperial Family to which we all belong, and invited us all to join her. We are not aware that any attempt was then made to enlist the association of young people with the Princess in her self-dedication, or to show them practical ways in which that dedication could be made effective.

THE QUEST FOR A POST-WAR PURPOSE

It may be that some of our readers are beginning to wonder whither the argument of this chapter is leading. Are we suggesting that the State should give direction to the activities of our many and varied youth organizations? And if not the State, from where else could such direction come? Do we really wish to indoctrinate our young people with any political or religious creed? Have we not been warned against the evils of inculcation? Do we wish to force a precocious development? Is it not better that young people should spend the week-end cycling or playing football than marching in coloured shirts behind military bands? In France, we are told, young people are so politically conscious that there are no less than four political youth hostels associations, and youth hostellers are to be seen marching in political processions and shouting party slogans. Is it not better and less dangerous that young people should be more interested in the probable promotions to and relegations from the First Division than in the rival ideologies of of Sir Oswald Mosley and Mr. William Gallacher? Those young people who sometimes disturb the political peace of London's East End would be more healthily occupied were they playing football on Hackney Marshes. We do not forget that in some countries, youth movements have been used to crush independence of thought and to nurture a fanatical faith in false creeds. We wonder, however, if we are so afraid of the dangers of dictatorship that we have become distrustful of any kind of leadership at all. The fact that leadership can be abused is no condemnation of leadership itself. Is it unfair to suggest that the great need in the Youth Service in our country today is of more inspired and more inspiring leadership? There is no youth organization in this country now whose leaders have been accorded the kind of devotion that was given to Lord Baden-Powell.

We have been warned of the danger of using youth movements to inculcate young people with our own beliefs. It seems to us that there are few youth movements which stand in this danger. On the contrary, many youth leaders are so afraid of the dangers of 'indoctrination' that they even conceal from their members any religious or political beliefs of their own. Other leaders are so uncertain of their own beliefs, that they are quite unable to offer direction to their members. In some clubs it is a rule that 'religion and politics are barred'.

We cannot believe that youth is well served by this neutrality, or that it is outside the duty of the youth leader to train young people to become free and responsible citizens of a liberal democracy.

Writing just before the outbreak of the second World War Mr. T. S. Eliot said:

It is my contention that we have today a culture which is mainly negative . . . . I do not think it can remain negative, because a negative culture has ceased to be efficient in a world where

174

economic as well as spiritual forces are proving the efficiency of cultures which, even when pagan, are positive; and I believe that the choice before us is between the formation of a new Christian culture, and the acceptance of a pagan one.*

Ten years later Mass Observation conducted a survey of popular attitudes to religion, ethics and politics among young people living in a London Borough, and in the preface to the report the general conclusions suggested by the survey are summarized in these terms:

The majority of people are open to exploitation by any resolute opportunists with any ideology, because people are looking for something to believe; the explosion or disintegration of orthodox beliefs has left a vacuum which will be filled, and will be filled by worse if it is not filled by better . . . . the creation of faith in democracy is not less urgent than the creation of faith in purposive living.†

We wonder if these two phrases, 'the creation of faith in democracy' and 'the creation of faith in purposive living', may not suggest the direction in which we should look for the motif which should inform the activities of youth movements, and which we have found so often to be lacking. These phrases, of course, would need to be expressed in much more precise and concrete terms if they are to win the understanding and allegiance of young people. The Scottish Youth Advisory Council, in the 1945 Report from which we have already quoted, said:

The warfare which has encompassed the globe for the past year is, in large measure, a conflict of conceptions of society. Totalitarian philosophies are hard and clear-cut, easy to apprehend, easy to teach to the young. Our philosophy has . . . . remained vague and unstated except in catch phrases. There are strengths in this vagueness which we do not deny. But there are also grave weaknesses in it, especially with the young, and, most especially of all, at this juncture in our history.‡

We are far from suggesting that the Youth Service should be perverted to political ends, or that we should commit young people to any particular pattern of society. We do suggest, however, that whatever form the structure of our society may take in future, it should be based upon those ideals of freedom, courtesy, tolerance, justice and brotherhood which have been evident in the best moments of our history, but which even yet have been only partially embodied in the organized life of the nation, and the maintenance of which is in peril.

There cannot be as much adventure in fashioning a society inspired by such ideals as there is in meeting the stern demands of war, but the peril in which we stand, if less immediately apparent, is no less real. Writing in *The Boy* shortly after the end of the war, Mr. W. McG. Eager said:

We have just emerged from a heroic phase, in which democracy was vindicated by men who scarcely knew that they valued it. We have passed into a time of fiercer testing, in which our task is plain. It is to give boys not only training in, but love for, democracy, because it is the fairest form of society, which can only be maintained by the virtue of the men and women who compose it.

We wish that youth leaders, whatever their individual religious or political beliefs, and acting through their own various organizations, through the National Association of Youth Leaders and Organizers, or through the Standing Conference of National Voluntary Youth Organizations, could unite in setting before their members the ideal of a democratic society. The future shape of such a society is by no means pre-determined, but must be worked out by those who are now young. Is it not possible to persuade young people that we in this country are attempting something that is in every way as praiseworthy as what is being accomplished in Jugo-Slavia or anywhere else—that we are not tagging along behind other nations, backward in our industrial, economic, educational or cultural life, but still leading the world along untrodden paths towards a newer, fairer and more wholesome society? One recalls a passage from Mr. J. B. Priestley's *Linden Tree*, where the Professor says to his daughter Marion, who has married a wealthy Frenchman:

* *The Idea of a Christian Society*, page 13.
† *Puzzled People*, pages 7 and 9.
‡ *The Needs of Youth in these Times*, page 84.

Call us drab and dismal if you like, and tell us we don't know how to cook our food or wear our clothes—but for Heaven's sake, recognize that we are trying to do something that is as extraordinary and as wonderful as it is difficult—to have a revolution for once, without the terror, without looting mobs and secret police, sudden arrests, mass suicides and executions, without setting in motion that vast pendulum of violence which can decimate three generations before it comes to a standstill. We're fighting in the last ditch of civilization; if we win through, everybody wins through.

We believe that it should be possible, not only to give young people some understanding of the nature of our achievement, but also to convince them that the service of their lives—to use the phrase of the late Earl Baldwin—is as urgently needed today as ever in our history.

We have already suggested that any ideal which is to win the understanding and allegiance of young people must be put to them in terms which are precise and concrete. The lives of young people centre round home, work and leisure, and any purposeful living must involve each of these realms.

If the Youth Service is to fulfil the kind of purpose of which we are thinking in this chapter it must provide within itself an experience of democratic living, it must help young people to discover significance in their daily work, it must contribute to the strengthening and enrichment of home life, it must enlist young people in service to the community, it must offer them general training for future unspecified service, and it must provide education in citizenship.

To a discussion of these six requirements we now turn.

EXPERIENCE OF DEMOCRATIC LIVING

The most obvious way in which the Youth Service can train young people for membership of the Democratic State is by giving them experience of the working of democracy in their own youth groups.

We have discussed in Chapter VII the extent to which different organizations are, in fact, providing training in self-government. Membership of a Scout Court of Honour or of a Club Committee can be a true education in democracy. When a boy or girl has learned to listen to the views of others in debate, to accept the ruling of the chair, and above all, to carry out a majority decision with which he personally may be in disagreement, he is indeed qualifying for the larger citizenship which the years will bring. It is not only members of club committees, however, whom the club is able to help in this way. The boy who monopolizes the table tennis table or the girl who fails to turn up for the dramatic rehearsal will soon learn that contemporaries have their own way of dealing with such forms of anti-social behaviour. A club is a society in miniature, and the more mixed and varied its members the more adequately will it offer them opportunities of learning the art of living with other people.

Discussion provides one such opportunity and should have a place in the programme of every youth organization. Democracy is government by discussion. We have already referred to the comparative failure of the uniformed organizations in this connection, a failure which is illustrated by the very inadequate and almost apologetic advocacy of discussion in the newly published *Senior Scout Handbook*: 'The up-to-date idea, it is said, is that discussions should be "occasionally arranged as a part of the programme, i.e. every third or fourth week".' In fairness to the uniformed organizations, however, we would like to recall our earlier judgment that they usually succeed, where the clubs often fail, in developing such virtues as social responsibility and loyalty to accepted authority—virtues, the observance of which is absolutely essential to the smooth working of democracy.

SIGNIFICANCE IN DAILY WORK

In an ideal society it should be possible for every man to regard his work as service which he is rendering to the community, so that 'service' is not something that one offers in one's spare time, but in one's working hours. Can the Youth Service help young people to find joy and satisfaction in their daily work? The Youth Advisory Council said in 1942:

176

The need is to restore to every kind of work that sense of social significance which has largely been lost as machines have replaced men. In a modern society much of what has to be done in factory, field, shop, office or home, is dull. The remedy for this is not to draw social distinctions between one kind of employment and another, but to make all workers everywhere realize the inspiring truth that their work, whatever it is, is an essential contribution to the life and well-being of the community.★

This is well said, but how is this desirable end to be realized? In what ways can this 'inspiring truth' be seen by those thousands of boys and girls who earn their living in repetitive or semi-skilled occupations in factories or workshops? Here we touch one of the most difficult problems of our modern society. The increased industrial productivity of modern times is being bought at a very great price. Many boys and girls in Birmingham spend the whole of their working life drilling holes in brackets, putting lids on tins, or performing similar repetitive actions. These young people are not unhappy in their work, (90 per cent of Birmingham girls and 86 per cent of the boys give an affirmative answer to the question, 'Do you enjoy your present job?')† but it is not surprising if many of them do as little as they can or dare, and work with one eye on the clock. There are many whose attitude to their work is like that of one boy who, shown how he might do his job a little more efficiently, replied: 'What, and put another half-crown in the pocket of the boss? Not bloody likely!' The tragedy is, not that much of their work is monotonous —all occupations involve certain monotony, and many young people definitely prefer repetitive jobs—but that so often no attempt is made to enable young people to see the importance and social significance of the work they do. We spoke to one boy who did not know whether the screws he was turning were destined to become part of a motor car, an aeroplane, or a wireless set. By contrast, in another factory, a lad whose job it was to attach steering wheels to an endless procession of motor cars boasted to us with obvious pride of the number of dollars which had been earned that day on the assembly line on which he was at work.

We are not qualified to suggest to what extent workers should be given any increased share in industrial management and responsibility, but we do wonder if Trade Unions and Managements are doing all that might be done to associate young workers with their activities. Most of the larger firms offer new young employees some initiation training, but more important than what is said to a young employee before he begins to work is his experience of participation in the life of the firm that may be accorded to him after his work has begun.

The advent of the County College will greatly assist the transition of the adolescent from school to work, and a close association of the Youth Employment Service with the work of the County College should make it increasingly possible to offer young people more adequate vocational guidance and to follow it up with After Care observation. One wishes, however, that leaders of youth organizations would interest themselves more, not only in the leisure-time activities, but in the working lives, of their members.

One local attempt on the part of a youth organization to help young people to discover more purpose in their work was an 'Adjustment to Industry' Course which was held near Warwick in April, 1947. This course was attended by twenty boys who had just left school after receiving vocational guidance and who were selected by the Birmingham Juvenile Employment Bureau. The course was held under the auspices of the National Association of Boys' Clubs, and during the week the boys lived together lectures were given on such subjects as production, the history of industry, safety and welfare, trade unionism, broadcasting, current affairs, and the use of leisure. This course may be regarded as an interesting and valuable experiment, though far too many lectures were given (*seven sessions a day!*) and it is not surprising that inattention and fatigue became evident. Those who promoted the course admit that the subject matter was put too academically, that insufficient use was made of demonstration material and of visual aids, and that much more use might have been made of dramatization.

Young Farmers' Clubs are unique among youth organizations in that their activities centre round the occupational interests of many of their members. The Yorkshire Council for Further

★ *Youth Service after the War.*
† See Chapter III

Education suggested, in 1945, that similar clubs might perhaps be established for young people who are associated with other occupations such as mining or engineering. This is an interesting suggestion, though it is to be remembered that many young people, like their elders, will want to get away from the associations of work during their leisure hours.

THE ENRICHMENT OF HOME LIFE

The charge is sometimes made that the Youth Service, by drawing young people away from their homes, is responsible for the disintegration of home life. We do not think that this charge can be substantiated, because the number of young people who spend more than two evenings a week at a youth organization is small, as we have seen. It is true that members of youth organizations spend fewer evenings in their homes than do the unattached, but it cannot be assumed that they would necessarily be at home if they were not at the club.

So far from youth organizations being responsible for the decline of home-life it is possible indeed that the free mingling of the sexes in the modern youth club helps young people to choose their life partner more wisely than was possible in the days of the stricter segregation of the sexes. At the same time, we doubt if the Youth Service generally is giving young people all the help it might to prepare them for successful married life.

Asked 'What job in life do you aim to do?' some girls of all ages answer 'housewife', 'have a home of my own', 'get married', or 'become a mother'. Miss Pearl Jephcott, in her study of a hundred working-class girls, suggests that the thought and conduct of the adolescent working girl is completely dominated by her expectation of early marriage. The comparative lack of success of youth organizations of all kinds in retaining the adolescent girl in membership beyond her middle teens is partly due, in our judgment, to their failure to take sufficient account of this fact.

> In 1939 about a third of all women of twenty to twenty-four in England and Wales were already married; so that her marriage was indeed more imminent for the adolescent than one would suppose from the lack of attention paid to it by some of the agencies which hope to guide her leisure-time activities into profitable channels.*

Any organization which wants to hold the allegiance of girls in their later teens will need, not only to satisfy their natural desire to meet men of their own age or a little older, but also to help them to learn all they can about health and beauty, child care, home nursing, cookery and home-craft. We recall how successfully one of our own students secured the interest of a group of girls in the making of a portfolio containing a 'picture' of each room of a house made by cutting out and arranging illustrations of furniture, pictures, ornaments, etc., taken from magazines and catalogues. We would like to make the point that it is as important—or almost as important—to prepare boys for their responsibilities as home-makers as it is to offer such training to girls. The emancipation of women is leading to a change in the traditional pattern of family life, and it may well be that in future some of the domestic responsibilities which have always been regarded as falling within the province of the woman will be mutually shared by husband and wife. There are too many youth clubs where it seems to be tacitly assumed that the washing-up of the canteen crockery is the exclusive responsibility of the girls. Where leaders have succeeded in persuading boys to take their share of kitchen chores, it seems to us that both boys and girls are being put on the way to the discovery of a fuller life of shared interests as husbands and wives.

Is it possible for the Youth Service to make a contribution to the enrichment of the homes from which its members come? Mr. L. J. Barnes has said: 'There are some areas in Britain where the entire educational system, formal and informal alike, spends much of its time figuratively on its hands and knees, going round after parents to clear up the psychological mess they have made of their own children.'† Mr. Barnes adds that this is not the work that clubs and schools are equipped to do, and he speaks of 'the unrewarded fumbling of the club bodies with this problem of influencing the home.'‡

* *Rising Twenty*, page 72.
† *Outlook for Youth Work*, page 76.
‡ Ibid., page 77.

We would not ourselves take quite such a pessimistic view of the influence of home life upon young people or of the extent to which the Youth Service is bringing a direct influence to bear upon the home. It is unfortunately true that there are many broken homes and many homes which are intellectually sterile, and in such cases the Youth Service has a compensatory function to perform. It is difficult to see what a youth organization can do for the broken or loveless home from which some of its members may come, but it can certainly make a contribution to the home that knows nothing of books, hobbies, or intelligent conversation. Mother is interested in the cakes Mary made in the club cookery class or in the frock she cut out in the dress-making group; father has many questions to ask about Tom's visit to the Scout Jamboree in France, or John's visit to a coal-mine with the members of his club. Both mother and father will sometimes forego their visit to the pictures or the pub when they are invited to the annual Open Day or to the show in which both Mary and John are taking part. Both may hold the club leader, Scout Master or Brigade Captain in high exteem. He will be consulted, very often, about all kinds of domestic and family problems. He is less busy than the doctor and more familiar than the parson.

A large number of youth units in our city report the existence of Parents' Associations. In the main, however, the activities of these associations appear to be limited to occasional whist drives or dances in aid of the funds of the unit with which they are associated. Other units arrange occasional 'Open Nights' or 'Parents' Evenings', when members provide a P.T. display, a concert or an exhibition of club handicrafts.

More important, however, than any influence the Youth Service may have upon the homes from which its members come is its contribution to the quality of the homes which they themselves will establish. The extent of this contribution will depend, not so much upon classes in homecraft or cookery, or upon discussions on decoration and colour schemes, but on the nature of the personal relationships fostered in the club and on the qualities of character nurtured among its members.

SERVICE TO THE COMMUNITY

Whatever success may attend any effort to lead young people to see their daily work as a contribution they are making to the community, we fear that those whose work is unskilled, monotonous or repetitive will not easily be persuaded to accept the idea that their work is a service to other people as well as a way of earning a living. For many of them we may be compelled to the conclusion that any inspiration for purposeful activity will largely have to be found in their leisure time. We wish therefore that youth organizations made greater efforts than they commonly do to encourage their members to give service in their own neighbourhood. One Birmingham leader said: 'We are catering for a type of boy or girl who has a long way to go before he will do this'. This leader may have been right, but on the other hand it is possible that young people would give more if more were asked of them. We do not suggest, of course, that community service is entirely absent from the activities in which members of youth organizations engage. One large industrial club has a scheme whereby each weekday evening six members visit crippled children in hospital, where entertainments and film shows and given and hobbies like model aeroplane making are encouraged. The club has recently acquired a second-hand car which it proposes to use to give patients Sunday outings into the country. A 'hospital fund' has been opened to raise the £100 a year which will be required to run the car.

The following are representative of service projects which have been promoted by youth units in Birmingham:

Red Cross and St. John

> Domestic help in hospitals and nursery schools.
> Library collection for hospitals.
> Assistance to senior officers with First Aid duty in cinemas and theatres.

Girl Guides and Rangers

> Summer holiday spent preparing a camp site for physically handicapped Guides.

179

Money raised for charities by carol singing.
Church cleaning.
Shopping and gardening for old people.
Collection of rose hips.
Christmas good turns.
Blankets knitted and sent to lepers.

Scouts

Christmas breakfast to old people.
Salvage collections.
Blood transfusion service.
Harvest camps.

Boys' Brigade

Money raised for leper hospital.
Flag selling.
Handwork for church bazaar.
Distribution of harvest festival gifts.

Girls' Life Brigade

Adoption of Chinese war orphan.
Clothes and food sent to Germany.
Bibles sent to Norway.
Baby minding.

Youth Clubs

Entertainment of people from overseas.
Mending toys for nursery; entertainment of children from Cottage Homes.
Percentage of subscriptions regularly set aside for good turns to folk in need.
Boxing display to patients in hospital.
Sunday school teaching.
Breakfast to blind people.
Knitting for displaced persons.
Furniture repair for old folk.
Bombed site cleared to make children's playground.
'Tin Night' (No members allowed in without a tin of food to be sent to Germany).
Car park constructed on waste land adjoining club.

The above examples are intended to be illustrative rather than exhaustive, but less than half the leaders to whom we spoke were able to think of any community service rendered by the members of their organization. Our comparative failure to enlist the devotion of young people in service to the community is all the more regrettable when one remembers that youth is naturally idealistic and capable of great self-sacrifice. In the course of our own investigations in Birmingham we visited one Youth Service Corps whose members were loud in complaint that the only service for which they were asked was help in flag-selling. 'We would like to *do* something worth while', said one boy, and these words received general assent. We recall another experience of our own when, towards the end of the second World War, we were present at a Youth Rally when the speaker suggested that when the war was over and Europe lay stricken and bleeding, it might be possible for young people to enlist for a year to two years in a Peace Army, so that they could give themselves to works of rebuilding, reconstruction and reconciliation. At the close of the meeting the speaker was almost mobbed by young people who wished to give him their names and addresses, and for months afterwards he was receiving letters from them asking if anything had come of the suggestion. These are the young people who join our youth clubs and sometimes leave them after a few months 'because there was nothing to do' or 'because it was not interesting'.

During and since the second World War many young people have found opportunities of rendering service in connection with schemes promoted by the Youth Service Volunteers.

Twelve thousand young people between fifteen and twenty years of age joined Y.S.V. in war time and gave up their holidays from school and their leisure from industry to assist the national effort. Boys helped to prepare pit-props for the Ministry of Supply, while others were engaged in the salvage of spent ammunition components, and harvest camps for both boys and girls were conducted for the Ministry of Agriculture. Since the war there have been forestry camps in the Lake District, farming camps in many parts of the country, and several camps to help improve play-ground facilities in certain places in Scotland. Sports grounds have been laid out in the devastated towns of Normandy, while some young people have gone to Vienna (in connexion with *Jugend am Werk*, a Youth Organization sponsored by the Vienna City Council) where boys have helped to lay out public parks and children's playgrounds, and girls have given assistance in day nurseries and infant feeding centres. An older organization which offers similar opportunities is the International Voluntary Service for Peace, the members of which are sometimes popularly known as the 'Pick and Shovel Peacemakers'. During the summer of 1949 also, some 700 students and young workers of both sexes took part in reconstruction work in war-scarred countries as far afield as Japan, attending fifteen work camps sponsored by the World Council of Churches Youth Department.

The Boy Scout and Girl Guide Movements have always laid great stress on service, and while it is easy to poke cheap fun at the Boy Scouts' daily good turn, there must be few of us who have not benefited at some time or another from this excellent institution. In the Girl Guide Movement even Brownies at seven years old are taught to darn, to sew on buttons, to make tea, to clean shoes, to tie up parcels, to light fires, to fold clothes, while at the same time they may be encouraged to send some of their precious sweet ration to invalid children in a sanatorium and to save 'ship half-pennies' or 'bun pennies' with which to purchase flowers for old people. This emphasis on service runs right through the whole organization. We visited one Birmingham Ranger Company which has produced no less than forty-three Guiders during the last twenty-one years, and whose proud boast it is that every one of the twenty girls at present in the company is rendering definite service of some kind. All this, in our judgment, is magnificent, and it is just because this work is so good that we deplore all the more the failure of this movement to retain more than a small proportion of its members on into adolescence.

It is not uncommon for boys in our great public schools to be encouraged to make a contribution in manual labour to the beauty of the school's immediate surroundings. The boys of one such school took charge of a local monument, cleaning and repairing the railings surrounding it. They rebuilt drystone walling for local farmers, and even restored some broken carving on nearby historic buildings. During the war they ran a boys' club, organized salvage campaigns and did an immense amount of agricultural work. They are now building an open-air theatre.

Projects of this magnitude might be beyond the reach of any individual youth club, but not impossible for a group of organizations working together. If Youth Councils could be set up, as we have suggested, in each of Birmingham's thirty-three areas, these Councils might well be invited to carry out a survey of their own districts. Such a survey might reveal needs which could be met by personal service given by young people and it might also suggest ways in which members of youth organizations could add to the amenities of their own neighbourhood.

We suggest that it might be a major duty of the L.E.A. Youth Officer and his colleagues (working in close co-operation with the Town Planning Committee) to provide leadership and inspiration of this kind. If members of Brigades, Scout Troops and Youth Clubs are to work together in this way, leadership cannot come from any one of the voluntary organizations—it must come from some co-ordinating body. We suggest that an Authority's Youth Officer should be a man who is in the truest sense a 'Youth Leader'—one who is able to offer young people the kind of leadership for which many of them are looking in vain, and to which, when it is given, they are often eager to respond.

If, as we have suggested in Chapter VII, certain standards were asked of clubs before they became eligible for recognition and assistance from the Local Authority, this readiness to offer service to the community is one requirement that might be included.

181

ON A BOMBED SITE: *Getting into mischief and danger.*

CO-OPERATION: *Not many city clubs possess their own playing fields. The team in the photograph is playing on a pitch lent by a more fortunate club.*

TRAINING

We wish we could think that all youth organizations could be regarded as pre-Service units in which young people were being trained for all kinds of unspecified responsibilities and duties in later life. Those who plan such training could draw upon the experience of Scouts, Guides, the Youth Service Volunteers, and of the Outward Bound Sea School at Aberdovey. This school was founded in 1941 to train boys for the sea for service in the Navy and in the Merchant Navy: it continues to train youths, not merely for the sea, but through the sea. A wise man once said that every man should be able to swim, to ride a horse, to sail a boat, and to find his way by the stars; but the greatest achievements of the Outward Bound School have been not merely in the teaching of such skills or in physical education, but in the realm of character-building. We wish that the opportunities offered at Aberdovey could be made available to many more boys and girls.

Earlier in this chapter we ventured to draw attention to the inadequate treatment of Discussion in the plans of the Scout Movement for its Senior Scouts as laid down in *The Senior Scout Handbook*. It is indeed surprising that there should be little or no reference in this book to mixed activities, to the discovery of significance in daily work, to the importance of the home, to service to the community, or to citizenship generally. We would like to express our unqualified approval, however, of all that is said in this Handbook about character-training through all kinds of physical activity and adventurous expeditions. No one could offer the kind of training of which we are thinking more competently than could the Scouts and Guides. During the second World War the Chief Scout was invited by the War Office to run a school for young potential officers and to see what could be done with ten weeks of concentrated scouting, as the quality of leadership in these young men did not seem to be developing under normal military training. The invitation was accepted and at the Cairngorms in the summer and at West Ross during the winter trainees were first shown how to do things and then involved in positions from which they could only escape without grave discomfort to themselves by putting into practice the lessons they had learned. At the end of the course the President of the War Office Selection Board said: 'You may have produced 75 per cent of officers, but even more important it is that you have produced 95 per cent of men.'

CITIZENSHIP

If young people are to be helped to become good citizens, it is necessary not only to encourage them to give service to the community, but to become well informed about local conditions and local affairs.

> They may come to this study in a variety of ways, through personal experience of intolerable housing conditions, inadequate public open spaces or the shortcomings of a rural water supply. Such inquiries, if they are properly presented and carried out, do not bore young people. There is in fact a good deal of enthusiasm, latent it may be, but certainly present, ready to be called out.*

One local attempt to give young people a larger knowledge of the local world in which they live is a Young Citizens' Club, promoted in connexion with one of the city's Evening Institutes. The programme consists of discussions which either precede or follow a visit of observation or a talk from a visiting speaker. Expeditions have normally been made on a Saturday afternoon and among other places visited have been an agricultural college, a hospital, a fire station, an airport, a meteorological office, a general post office, a newspaper office, a telephone house, a gas works, a reservoir and the 'back stage' of a theatre. Among the speakers have been an economist, a member of parliament, an ex-commando officer, a local historian and an international footballer. There are some units in most types of organization in which place is found for this kind of activity, and when carried out it is usually as popular as it is useful. We regret that more such opportunities are not given to members of youth organizations.

* Purpose and Content of the Youth Service.

RELIGION IN THE YOUTH SERVICE

In all that we have hitherto said in this chapter we have tried so to write that we might reasonably hope to carry the consent of all men and women of goodwill, whatever their individual political or religious convictions. In suggesting that young people should be challenged to play a part in the creation of the free democratic society of the future we have not been unaware of all the evils of State worship and we are not unmindful of the fact that in more than one country in recent years education has been perverted to political ends. We think, nevertheless, that a middle way can be found—indeed, must be found—between State idolatry on the one hand and civic irresponsibility on the other.

At the same time we imagine that many readers will feel with us that the most challenging word remains to be said. The ideal of a free democratic society which embodies principles of freedom, courtesy, tolerance, justice and brotherhood for all, and yet which fully recognizes the worth of the individual, derives alone from Christian faith. It has grown out of faith in the Christian God, and will only be sustained as it continues to be derived from the same source. Many educationists are so afraid of tendentious teaching that they seem willing to allow people to grow up ignorant of that Christian tradition which has shaped the lives of the western democracies, and without which they can neither be understood nor rebuilt. Sir Richard Livingstone has said that we are living on character formed in the past by beliefs which are now shaken or destroyed. It is equally true, we think, that sometimes men are encouraged to 'look for a city', but are not reminded that its only Builder and Maker is God.

In this chapter we have made the plea that the Youth Service should seek to offer its members experience of democratic living, should help them to discover significance in their daily work, should contribute to the enrichment of their home-life, and should give them genuine training for future citizenship. Desirable as these ends are in themselves, however, they can only be most truly realized by those who can live in a truly Christian spirit, and without it they carry within themselves the seeds of their own destruction. Men must believe that the local and temporal pattern for which they work is part of the ultimate design of things. In our own lifetime we have seen more than one example of the dangers that threaten when any mere pattern of human society or when the State itself is allowed to become an object of worship. We do not think we are free from this danger here today. Anxious as we are that the devotion of young people should be enlisted in the service to the community, the more successfully this aim were achieved, the more would we fear its consequences, unless through it and in it young people are led to a deeper faith in God. Professor Herbert Butterfield, in a recent broadcast, has well said that the Christian religion:

> does at least save men from making gods out of sticks and stones, and offering vast human sacrifices to abstract nouns, and running amok with myths of self-righteousness, as people have so often done in the twentieth century.*

The Youth Service, we have said, suffers from the lack of any clear purpose or direction. The only adequate purpose, we maintain, is one that derives ultimately from religious belief. Any purpose which is merely man-centred will be subject to all the ills which afflict human nature.

In the light of this conviction we would like to make a few comments suggested by what we have seen in our city of

(a) Church youth organizations generally,
(b) Organizations with a religious foundation, and
(c) Other youth organizations.

(a) Church Youth Organizations

It is, of course, in the Church youth organizations that we should expect to find a regular recognition of the truth that religion is of the *esse* and not merely of the *bene esse* of Youth Service.

* *Christianity and History*, p. 130.

There are indeed many churches in our city with groups of young people who have found in religious faith the kind of purpose we have been describing in this chapter. Thay have discovered personal significance for themselves, meaning in their daily work, joy in home-life, and their relations with their fellows are governed by their recognition of them as children of God. Fewer experiences during the whole course of our Survey have afforded us as much satisfaction as have several week-ends spent at the Conference House of the Birmingham Youth and Sunday School Union, where we have shared with young people in hard thinking, healthy laughter, and honest worship. We wish, however, that there were more such groups. One of our own students—a young German doctor who had at one time been a member of *Hitler Jugend*, had fought in Hitler's armies and had been wounded on the Russian front, but who is now a convinced Christian, said to us on the eve of his return to Germany: 'The young people in your churches have everywhere received me with kindness and courtesy, but I am concerned about the casual quality of their Faith; they do not give to Christ anything like the devotion which we once gave to Hitler. They do not see the urgency of the present situation'.

We believe that churches in our city fail to offer enough teaching to those young people who are prepared to apply themselves to a study of the Faith. There is in fact, no danger of too much 'inculcation'. Birmingham churches appear to be giving young people very little systematic religious instruction.★ The popularity of the Moral Leadership courses which took place in the R.A.F. during the war, and the eager response of many young people to recent conferences sponsored by 'S.C.M. in Schools' suggest that churches have been under-estimating the readiness of some of their young people to accept training. These methods, whose success has been so well demonstrated, might be more generally adopted.

During recent years the churches have opened many youth clubs in which contact is being made with thousands of young people who are without any kind of religious background. We welcome this development, but think that there is a real danger thát time and energy devoted in these new directions may mean a diminution of the more intensive training which was given in the past in Bible classes and Study Groups of many kinds.

We have been particularly interested in the activities of the Roman Catholic Young Christian Workers—little 'cells' of half a dozen fellows or girls working in a factory or stores who meet together to discover ways in which a Christian witness can be made effective in factory, trade union, political party or local government. We do not minimize the importance of giving young people opportunities of service within the Church. There is probably no better form of Christian service for the fifteen-year-old boy or girl than to become a helper in the Primary Department of the Sunday School, provided only that this is combined with attendance at a weekly training class. At the same time churches need to recognize that it is just as important a form of 'church work' to make a Christian witness in industry, in local government, or in politics, and that some young people can find a vocation in one or other of these fields. It is just here that the Young Christian Workers are making such a significant contribution. Such young people, however, will need training. The late Archbishop Temple once suggested that every church youth club should have its 'witness team' which should be as ready to give Christian witness in other clubs as the football team was ready to meet them on the field. Both teams, he added, would need appropriate training. Many Birmingham church youth clubs give training to their footballers; very few seem to be training their members for Christian witness. We have been interested, also, in some of the 'school-leavers' services' which have been arranged in some areas, when young people have been invited to think of the jobs to which they were going, not only as a way of earning a living, or even as a way of service to the community, but also as an opportunity of Christian witness.

(b) Organizations with a Religious Basis

Under this general heading we are thinking of local units of movements like the Y.M.C.A. and the Y.W.C.A., the Stonehouse Gang group of clubs, and those uniformed units which,

★ We are thinking here of young people in their 'teens: not of children in Sunday School.

though possessing a distinctive religious inspiration, are not attached to any particular church or congregation.

The achievements of this diverse group are so varied that it is quite impossible to make any generalization which would apply to them all. What we have seen of them, however, underlines our own conviction that the two essential requirements for any successful religious education are firstly, Christian leadership, and secondly, the setting of a Christian community. If the Christian Faith is to be communicated to young people of our generation they need above all to come under the influence of Christian people. It is people all the time who are the influencing factor. It was said by the Youth Advisory Council in 1943 that the men and women we require as leaders in the Youth Service are those who are 'proud of their faith, though humble in the practice of it, and who are, besides, capable of transmitting it to others'. We have met many such men and women among the leaders of youth organizations in our city, but their work is often made much more difficult than it need be because the teaching they offer to young people in words is not embodied in the life of a community. When a boy finds that the ideals commended by him by, say, the Scoutmaster, are scorned and rejected by his mates at work, it is not surprising if he says to himself: 'This Christianity may be all right to talk about, but it does not belong to a world like this'. The only way in which to help that boy then is not to offer him moral uplift, but to anchor him in a community the whole life of which is an illustration of the truth and beauty and manifest superiority of the Christian way of life. When then the boy hears a religious talk, it will not be 'a lot of hot air about nothing, but an explanation of something he has met, and the offer of something he has seen'.* The supreme task of religious education, therefore, is not that of communicating ideas—even right ideas—to the minds of young people, but rather of introducing them to Christian communities in which they can grow up. In this way Christian truth is communicated, not only or chiefly through the spoken word, but through the shared life. An occasional hour of religious teaching is very slender equipment for Christian living in a world like this, and young people need to be much more deeply involved in the life of a Christian community. One of the most illuminating remarks in Miss Pearl Jephcott's study of a hundred girls was her comment on one girl—almost the only one of the hundred who seemed to evidence any degree of social responsibility, when she said: 'Phyllis leads the kind of energetic and socially responsible life that her home and Methodist upbringing make so normal as to be entirely un-selfconscious'.† Unfortunately, tens of thousands of young people today are growing up in homes in which for two or three generations there has been no profession of religion. Their religious needs will not be met by a monthly church parade, or even a weekly Bible class : they need what can only be given by their association with the total life of a worshipping community of young and old.

In stressing as we do, however, the importance of social influences in religious education, we would not forget that it is only too easily possible for young people to grow up in a Christian home and under the influence of a Christian community, and yet never to become self-committed to Christian values and to the Christian way of life. It is particularly possible for those who belong to the type of organization of which we are thinking in this section to give a nominal allegiance which is not implemented in life. In the last resort the final decision is a personal choice which every man must make for himself. We are concerned that legitimate ways should be found of putting to young people a challenge and appeal to which each must be left free to make his own response.

(c) Other Youth Organizations

We would not wish anything we say in this chapter to seem to suggest that it is only men and women of religious faith who have a contribution to make in the Youth Service, and we would dissociate ourselves most strongly from any attempt to impose a religious test upon youth leaders, but we are concerned that in about forty per cent of the clubs in our city religious activities of any

* Rev. Douglas Griffiths.
† *Rising Twenty*, page 14.

186

kind are deliberately excluded. This is sometimes because such clubs number among their members Roman Catholics who would not be allowed to share in any non-Roman religious exercise. It is sometimes because 'our members wouldn't stand for it'—a reason given by many leaders for the absence from their programmes of any educational activity at all (in spite of the fact that many of their members lapse because 'there was nothing to do'). It is sometimes because leaders themselves are indifferent or even hostile to religion. It is very often because leaders who would like to introduce religious education do not know how to set about it.

We believe, however, that it is never permanently possible to evade the religious issue. There are few subjects indeed which, when carried to a logical conclusion, do not involve fundamental questions of faith and morals. It may be, of course, that the leader who is anxious to help his members at this point must come to the religious issue indirectly. With many young people religious education, as we have already said (Chapter XI) must be occasional, opportunist and spontaneous. A great deal of religious education fails because it assumes both the knowledge of a vocabulary and the possession of an experience that young people are without. It does not proceed from the known to the unknown. Our Lord did not make this mistake:

> He spoke of grass and wind and rain,
>   And fig trees and fair weather;
> And made it His delight to bring
>   Heaven and earth together.
> And yeast and bread, and flax and cloth,
>   And eggs and fish and candles—
> See how the whole familiar world
>   He most divinely handles.*

If the religious educator knows what he is doing, any and every activity can be a method of evangelism and a means of religious education, because whether he is playing table tennis or discussing the latest film at the local Odeon, he is introducing young people to Christian ways of thinking, talking and living together. The Birmingham club leader who led the thinking of some girls from the art of make-up to personal health, from health to hygiene, from hygiene to sex, from sex to standards of conduct and behaviour, and from standards of conduct and behaviour to belief in God, knew how to do her job.

We invite the churches to consider that our survey has revealed the fact that three-quarters of the youth population of our city is completely out of touch with any form of organized religion. We are convinced that few people in the churches appreciate just how far away from them in thought and outlook these young people are. One group of Birmingham boys went to church one Sunday evening—for the first time in their lives—when a Birmingham footballer was billed to read the Lessons. The Lessons read, they went out—and they did not know that they were behaving in any unusual way. Many of these young people are religiously almost illiterate. In some cases they do not know, for instance, that Christmas or Easter have any religious significance; they may know nothing of Christ except that His Name is a swear-word. To many of them religion is a harmless and irrelevant hobby, like ballet or stamp-collecting, in which certain people indulge; but as for them, they 'couldn't care less'.

But the Churches must care more. The fact must be faced that existing methods have failed to convince these young people that there is either relevance or importance in what the Churches have to say. If the Church is to save its life, it must be prepared to lose it. Some Church groups are far too introverted. They need to go out into the world to meet people where they are to be found. We have visited open clubs in our city whose leaders would eagerly welcome the presence and help of men and women of Christian conviction.

CONCLUSION

We hope that we have said enough to persuade Christian leaders to consider what re-examination of any particular traditional technique, or organization, or time-table or vocabulary is called for if the relevance of what they have to say is to be brought home to young people of

* T. T. Lynch.

187

our generation. We hope, too, that we have said something that may lead those youth leaders who have not yet found it possible to accept the Christian Faith to examine the implications of their own neutrality. In the present moment of history something much more sure and dynamic than idealism is required. It is possible, with the best intentions in the world, to do a disservice to young people by offering them the good instead of the best.

We reaffirm as we close this Report that unless a sense of purpose can be found, the Youth Service as we see it today may disguise from young people themselves as well as from the community as a whole the great need in which young people stand. We have only a short span of years in which to train a generation of young people who know what they think and why they think it, and who can withstand the pressures of propaganda. What this country can contribute to the world at this time cannot be given save out of the quality of the individual citizens. Democracy can only be maintained 'by the virtue of the men and women who compose it'. We wish that the Standing Research Committee recently set up by King George's Jubilee Trust, or the Ministry of Education itself, which is happily seeking to establish material conditions of Youth Leadership, would now call together the leaders of responsible youth organizations, to seek how this common democratic task may best be achieved.

THE DIRT TRACK

Cycle-racing on tracks improvised on bombed sites and other derelict open spaces is a favourite leisure-time occupation today.

For Product Safety Concerns and Information please contact our EU
representative GPSR@taylorandfrancis.com
Taylor & Francis Verlag GmbH, Kaufingerstraße 24, 80331 München, Germany

9 781032 398204